SMUGGLING

SMUGGLING

Seven Centuries of Contraband

Simon Harvey

REAKTION BOOKS

For Audrey and Louis

Published by Reaktion Books Ltd
Unit 32, Waterside
44–48 Wharf Road
London N1 7UX, UK

www.reaktionbooks.co.uk

First published 2016
Copyright © Simon Harvey 2016

Printed and bound in Great Britain
by TJ International, Padstow, Cornwall

A catalogue record for this book is available from the British Library

ISBN 978 1 78023 595 0

CONTENTS

INTRODUCTION

Romance, Rebellion and Power

W hat do we see of smuggling in the world today? Most likely we will know something of it from the newspapers or from television. Perhaps we build up an image of it through reading historical novels with smuggling at their heart. Is smuggling actually anywhere near us or in any way important? It seems usually to be beyond our compass, over the horizon. What relevance does it have to the world that we live in?

There is of course contraband that we can't ignore – heroin, cocaine, guns and sex slaves spring to mind. These are often in the news. We treat them seriously – they are threatening or worrying – but still, generally speaking, they are elsewhere. They seem to circulate in larger worlds, not in our own.

Notwithstanding this apparent absence of smuggling from our lives, there is increasing anthropological, sociological and political-science research into flows of contraband of all types, not just the dangerous ones.[1] Growing interest is being shown in smuggling's entanglement in cultures and communities in borderland regions of the developing world, and in its contribution to society as a whole in the developed world, particularly regarding illicit economies of undocumented work and the semi-licit supply of goods. Running against the grain of our minimal awareness of smuggling, special attention is being given to its ability to make and transform the world that we live in, for better or for worse. This all helps to bring smuggling into focus beside concepts like globalization and geopolitics. These reports generally tend to indicate that smuggling does affect us, even if we don't see it beneath our window.

If we are asking these questions of trafficking today, then why not ask them regarding smuggling in the past? After all, the terms 'globalization' and 'geopolitics', which are considered especially relevant to international smuggling, might be new to us but they are hardly new phenomena. What, then, are the historical counterparts of the guns, cocaine, heroin and sex slaves that are so important, and so menacing, in today's international relations?

Well, guns, drugs and slaves for starters, but we might also consider a number of other kinds of contraband over the past six centuries. Some have been hugely influential in shaping our world, such as silk, spice and silver in the Age of Exploration, or gold guineas, opium, tea and rubber as empires were expanding. Other commodities, like the afore-mentioned dangerous or exploited contraband items, have featured in all ages: diamonds, art and artefacts have been smuggled for thousands of years. Technology is another example, alongside the priceless contraband of illicit ideas.

Each of these has brought about major shifts in the distribution of power around the world. Smuggling, as this book will argue, has always been political – and, because of its extent and interconnectedness, geo-political. In other words, it has been a key factor in international relations, conflict and globalization.

The Silken Path of Smuggling

Smuggling is not the world's oldest profession, although it is certainly one of its earliest. What is surprising is that over seven centuries of the modern era since the time of Columbus, smuggling has been persistently perceived as romantic and rebellious, to the exclusion of most other images of it, other than as an occasionally violent activity. Little, by contrast, is said of smuggling's politics. In this book I am attempting to broaden and deepen the history of smuggling without dissipating the energy that circulates around its local dramas.

Is a history that combines the political and romantic sides of smuggling possible? On the one hand we might concede that they are incompatible, and romanticization can only be a problem in a serious history of contraband. On the other, one could look back to see if, how and where the two have interacted at key moments in the past, even co-mingled, and use these as a starting point for mapping out their synergy more extensively and over longer periods. Choosing to take the second path, I am encouraged by the fact that some of the great narratives of illicit trading do indeed weave together each of these apparently disparate threads of romance, rebellion and geopolitics.

The Silk Road provides the scene of one of the most remarkable of these stories. In ancient times trading conditions were tight: China under the Han Dynasty had an extensive customs organization, initially reaping taxes on salt. Silk was an altogether more exotic product. It was traded lucratively along the famous routes that were brought together in the popular imagination as a single road to which this fabulous material gave its name. But silk's profitability was also tied closely to the imperial purse: it was strictly forbidden to export either mulberry seeds or silkworms, and techniques of production were a jealously guarded secret. Nevertheless silk technology slipped out, at first through the kidnapping of Chinese weavers to work the thread that, along with the refined cloth, found its way in abundance down the trail. Later, in a momentous coup for China's rivals some time during the first quarter of the fifth century CE, seeds and silkworms were smuggled out in the headdress of a Chinese princess betrothed to the king of Khotan (now in southwest China), who was determined to escape the ruinous price of importing the cloth.

This myth, whatever its basis in fact, tells us at least three things about smuggling: that it can change the history of the world; that it is often rebellious (even sometimes instrumental in revolution); and that narratives around it usually have an air of romance around them. The order has perhaps shifted a little in this story, with the political effects of this particular smuggling event standing out from the legend even more than its romance. But whichever way we approach the problem of the historical romanticization of smuggling in relation to territorial competition (without actually eliminating the former) – romance and rebellion illuminating geopolitics, or geopolitics dressed up in romance – it seems that we cannot easily untangle these threads.

My emphasis in this book is on the involvement in smuggling of powerful political and economic interests, in particular nation-states and their agents, and how it has affected the history and geography of the world. This is not, however, to the exclusion of the concepts of rebellion and romance that run alongside it. The eastern princess is something of a rebel; this points to the idea that smuggling can also be about resistance, that this counter-trajectory can change the status quo and that it might, in a slightly more abstract way (for instance through the circulation of contraband ideas), alter our views of the world and the fortunes of our countries. And then, of course, as the Silk Road story demonstrates, we can never entirely disentangle the romantic projection of smuggling from its motivations of economic or political profit. Romance distorts our perception of smuggling but we must allow some of it to filter through because it has such a presence in smuggling's discourse.

To begin this history, then, I would like to elaborate a little on three propositions: first, my main hypothesis, that smuggling has so often had influential forces behind it that it must be thought of, alongside its local importance, as part of a global politics; second, that it has sometimes gone hand-in-hand with change through rebellion; and third, that the act of smuggling will often be interwoven with romance and that this provides an extra lustre to its profit motive. In this smuggling dialectic, rebellion and romance might even be thought of as geopolitical acts.

Smuggling and Geopolitics

The idea that there might have been, at certain crucial periods in history, powerful and cohesive forces behind smuggling – for instance, nation-states or large financial corporations, or agencies of the state such as intelligence services and scientific organizations – is not the only or even the most commonly held view of smuggling across the ages. For some commentators it has been a much more atomized affair.

As an individual-orientated free-trade response to protectionism, albeit an underground one,[2] smuggling has often been seen as a threat to the state. It has been analysed as an extreme form of transnational trading and was considered by protectionists, in their debates with free-trade advocates during the first half of the nineteenth century, to have eroded sovereignty, challenged the authority of the nation-state, threatened community and taken the wind out of the sails of patriotism.[3] According to the enemies of free trade, this threat from smugglers, quite apart from entailing the loss of customs revenue, was associated with a range of moral deficiencies, particularly character flaws and dubious lifestyle choices related to their rebellious, individualistic, alien and sometimes even 'vacuous' natures.[4] On the negative side, smugglers were depicted as disloyal (to homeland, companions, even to customers) and detached, while, a little more positively, they were also seen as adventurous and free. They were antisocial in the sense of being unable to form bonds to national or even local communities, and in having almost no family values. This portrait of nineteenth-century smugglers hardly considers them capable of concerted action in the name of a larger power. Smugglers are not contributors, they are takers; irresponsible, even promiscuous, and interested only in profit. How, then, do we arrive at the proposition that smugglers can be informal agents of the state or of great merchant companies, key participants in geopolitical power games, even occasionally acting as patriots?

A curious kind of smuggler loyalty emerges in some literature. We see this, for example, towards the end of Walter Scott's novels *Guy Mannering* (1815) and *Redgauntlet* (1824), both originally published as simply 'by the author of *Waverley*'. In the former a Dutch smuggler, Dirk Hatteraick, while in all other respects portrayed as a self-centred and cruel man, remains loyal to his shipowners, to the business and to his cargo. In the latter book Nanty Ewart, another smuggler, loses his life protecting his contraband (the Stuart prince and a Jacobite rebel).[5] They are professional in a crooked sort of way but in working loyally for their investors and backers, they enter a line of more distinguished adherents to a kind of business ethic of smuggling, which perhaps began with the Englishmen Sir Francis Drake and Sir John Hawkins during the sixteenth century.

Analyses of eighteenth- and nineteenth-century British smugglers in relation to free-trade thinking might emphasize their emotional detachment and individualism but there is a more romanticized projection of these bands of smugglers that is surely much more sociable and agreeable than the one that has been suggested in either literature or academic commentary upon it. Oral histories have handed down to us the narrative that, even if for the most part they remain impervious to patriotism, smugglers have thrived in and among local communities. One of the most prominent examples of this is the Carter family of Cornwall who, according to the chronicle of one of their number, Harry, enjoyed great loyalty from their local constituency around their base at Prussia Cove during and after the Napoleonic Wars. Privateer Jean Lafitte's smuggling community just outside New Orleans at more or less the same time was also held together by familial and business ties, as was the contraband culture of Buenos Aires at the beginning of the seventeenth century. This involvement in community enabled smugglers occasionally to gain influence over officials of the state, in particular legislators and bureaucrats.

If we follow up on this more nuanced image of smugglers, it is no great step to imagine that at the same time as working for individual profit, they might, in addition to maintaining attachments to community, operate loyally within larger business networks and even on occasion work in the national interest. And as their involvement deepens, nor is it a quantum leap forward to imagine them swept up in geopolitical events, even acting at the vanguard of them.

Smuggling and Rebellion

Covert trade, while often in compliance with state ambition, has always contained a concealed hazard for the state in that ultimately it can be uncontrollable and has often allied itself to rebellion and revolution. This potential attack on the status quo from smuggling will, then, be a secondary, counter side to this story.

There have been a number of high-profile instances in which smuggling has been crucial to the origins, perpetuation or outcome of rebellions and revolutions. José Gervasio Artigas Arnal, cattle smuggler, was the hero of the Uruguayan wars of independence during the early part of the nineteenth century, while the reformist army of the mid-century Carlist Wars was actually a mobilized and enlarged band of smugglers. The American War of Independence began through an act of smuggling when the patriot John Hancock's ship *Liberty* was seized on refusing to pay excessive duties. It was also in part fuelled by demands for free trade, and ultimate victory for the Americans owed much to the supply of contraband of war.

As smuggling is by its very nature a rebellious act, and transcends individualism when it becomes allied to a cause, it easily lends itself to revolution. Clandestine skills come in handy here, and the type of contraband carried can, with little modification in means of conveyance or much extra difficulty, become something more subversive, particularly if it comes in the form of agents of change carrying revolutionary tracts and looking to spread dangerous new ideas.

From another perspective, the work of smuggling, and in more recent times the broader industry of other illicit economies with which it is associated, for instance the black market, might be viewed within an alternative history of labour in which it effects necessary social resistance and readjustment. Reaction to punitive taxes, often socially disastrous impositions, has been a common catalyst towards taking up smuggling, and subsequently revolution. Even on an individual level, smuggling has performed a rebellious role when, for instance, the only way to hold onto a proscribed identity, such as being a Catholic in Reformation England, was to see it through, covertly, until more liberal times arrived.

However, it is smuggling as collective resistance bringing about change that implicates it in broader contexts.

Does this focus on the bigger picture instrumentalize smuggling's innately rebellious nature? What profit is there in framing it in this way, or for that matter in removing the romance from smuggling? It is doubtful that one could ever actually achieve this anyway. Romanticism blows around smuggling like a whirlwind; we cannot simply eradicate it by using words like 'geopolitics'. The question is, should we even attempt it?

Romance and Profit in Smuggling

The complex relationship, or contradiction, between the geopolitical or economic forces of smuggling and its romanticized projection should not be lightly or indiscriminately brushed aside because the two are often so intricately bound up. Political intrigue goes hand in hand with the trappings of romance.

This book might well be about the involvement of powerful interests in smuggling, in particular nation-states and their agents, but there is also in it, I hope, something of the excitement conveyed in Rudyard Kipling's poem 'A Smuggler's Song' (1906):

> If you wake at midnight, and hear a horse's feet,
> Don't go drawing back the blind, or looking in the street,
> Them that asks no questions isn't told a lie.
> Watch the wall, my darling, while the Gentlemen go by!
>
> Five-and-twenty ponies
> Trotting through the dark –
> Brandy for the Parson.
> 'Baccy for the Clerk;
> Laces for a lady, letters for a spy,
> And watch the wall, my darling, while the Gentlemen go by!

We could get carried away here. Through the rhythm of this verse we become agitated; it dares us to be curious. It is of course easy to be seduced by the romance of smuggling, although in its favour it might be said that we will be missing something if we limit our approach to the subject to something as dry as an economic or political analysis. The poem is certainly more than just about the stirring of mercenary greed.

Somebody is about in the dead of night; it's none of our business, but how it gallops through our imaginations.

This shimmering image of smuggling seems inexhaustible and its appearance in fiction has almost certainly, if only occasionally, been informed by experience. It is known, for instance, that the outbuildings of Thomas Hardy's house in Higher Bockhampton in Dorset, lying on a smuggler route, were sometimes used as a contraband store. Did this perhaps feed into his smuggler story *The Distracted Preacher*? Smuggling often conjures romance for us: a secluded cove or a hidden airstrip briefly alive with the industry of an illicit shipment, the taste of a brandy all the richer for being contraband. It often seems sexy or at the very least hedonistic: laces next to letters for spies; bounteous tobacco and spirits.

On second thought, let's not get too carried away; mightn't this image be a little too rich? We could approach smuggling in a very different way. Is it not instead simply a sordid business, more to do with opaque forces behind the scenes, far removed from the excitement on the surface? There is a rationale to smuggling that is resolutely unsentimental, even quite mundane. Its logic is very simple: wherever a line is drawn and a heavy duty demanded, smuggling will take place across the border. Is it not more logical simply to look for a motive of pure profit?

Well, not exactly. Profit can be thought of as producing other effects in smuggling. If we reason that anything that can be smuggled will be smuggled (in other words, that anything that can turn a profit significantly higher than normal trade just by being carried across a border is a potential contraband), it follows that there will always be a great variety of goods carried and that this diversity of contraband will attract a broad spectrum of smugglers. Some of these informal traders will be colourful characters; cultures around smuggling develop.

Profit, one way or another, seems to be at the bottom of it all. To paraphrase Thomas Jefferson, no contraband that can lead to national advantage should be overlooked. Even here, though, profit comes in several guises because some of this contraband will amount to cultural capital or, even as a commodity, evoke a fascinating culture. There is no shortage of examples of smuggling that are business-like at the same time that they are politically sinister, romantic and overblown: guineas, spies and ladies' laces each turn a profit!

If the inverse proportion of weight to value is the golden formula of smuggling, then those damaging substances cocaine and heroin are its ideal material contraband. Nevertheless, even at its most practical, smuggling often retains an aura that continues to fascinate. Perhaps this is something that one must always recognize when one approaches the subject of smuggling: we can't seem to make up our mind about it. Smuggling is always going to be complex and, to reiterate, it doesn't make sense to entirely separate its political or material rationale from its romantic allure.

I appreciate that this approach lays me open to the criticism that I am myself romanticizing smuggling, or at least perpetuating its mythology. But this book doesn't set out to be an academic critique of the ethics behind smuggling and how it has been misrepresented historically, important though this is. In another context I have followed that path,[6] but here I am attempting something different; I am presenting a simpler, more straightforward relational history, albeit one tinged with a small amount of romance and rebellious spirit.

Before I move back onto the geopolitics of smuggling, there is one more side to it that we must consider regarding its romanticized projection. We might imagine that customs provides the dull backdrop for smuggling's romantic adventure, but here too that is not the whole story.

Distinguishing Customs

There has always been a blurring of hue in illicit trading. The pirate, sometime explorer, navigator and occasional smuggler William Dampier financed his adventures abroad by working at home in the slightly more dour occupation of customs official. Otherwise dutiful Royal Navy personnel often ran profitable sidelines in contraband during the eighteenth and nineteenth centuries. Despite the occasional appearance of pirates on the staff, the deepest shade of grey in smuggling, then as now, seems to be reserved for the preventive force. Customs cannot seem to shake off its reputation of being a spoiler and irritant to more colourful characters. When Louis Bleriot landed in England after the first flight across the English Channel, customs inspected his aeroplane. In the opening chapter, 'The Custom House', of Nathaniel Hawthorne's novel *The Scarlet Letter*, customs officers are even deemed to suffer 'moral detriment'.[7] The customs house, always so forbidding and prominent in most ports, is here somehow damned, or as Hawthorne puts it: 'Neither the front nor the back entrance of the Custom-House opens on the road to Paradise.'[8] Customs men are always seemingly one step behind smugglers, who are often more sympathetically portrayed in adventure films such as Fritz Lang's *Moonfleet* (1955) or another classic 'owling' tale, *Dr Syn, Alias the Scarecrow* (1963).

This judgement is somewhat harsh. Indeed, the supposedly strait-laced and officious profession of customs officer can boast some famous men among its ranks. Sir Richard Whittington, Dick Whittington of the fable, held customs responsibilities (although he exempted himself from paying duty on wool exports) before making it big as Mayor of London. Thomas Paine, radical author of *The Rights of Man*, was an excise man, as was another brilliant social commentator before him, Geoffrey Chaucer. Other brilliant minds had the occupation as their bread and butter. Robbie Burns, for instance, worked for the preventive force, although of course he is somewhat better known as a Romantic poet, while the nineteenth-century French painter Henri 'Le Douanier' Rousseau, celebrated for his deceptively simple exotic tropical fantasies, was never simply an artist. Captain Frederick Marryat, author of a series of nautical novels that dealt with smuggling in a romanticized if unsympathetic way, had been a Royal Navy officer and spent much of his career chasing smugglers on the high seas.

One begins to respond imaginatively to this thawing of the customs image and to gain an appreciation of its complex relationship with smuggling. However, in popular imagination, it is only ever the smuggler who becomes the folk hero. In the end, Burns and Paine were somewhat ambivalent about their bread and butter occupation, the former denigrating the corrupting nature of the work in no uncertain terms in his song 'The Deil's Awa' Wi' the Exciseman'. It seems that smuggling will always be the greater draw.

THIS BOOK IS ORDERED, more or less chronologically, into three formal or structural parts, each of which represents a shift in focus.

Part One covers the interweaving of smuggling and exploration by emergent colonial powers in the fifteenth and sixteenth centuries, and the growth of broad cultures of smuggling during the following two centuries. Part Two is about smuggling and empire-building in the nineteenth century. In Part Three I examine differing scales of smuggling while continuing to focus on its deployment as an arm of political and economic power and reach. On a large scale this has meant looking at how smuggler networks are used as a means of achieving global foreign policy ends. On a smaller scale we see the spread of all-pervasive micro-economies of smuggling of everyday goods, precious objects and people. In bringing these two together we can begin to talk about the smuggling world in which we live.

Although there will of course be omissions in this history, I hope to have brought some of the larger smuggling stories into relation with one another, and placed them in a context with other lesser-known but nevertheless globally important smuggling narratives. As well as being a history, then, this is also a kind of geography, bringing together a broad range of globally dispersed smuggling narratives.

After all this and despite the near omnipresence of contraband in a lot of parts of the world at times,, we don't actually see much of smuggling. But if we were to be woken by something equivalent to Kipling's five-and-twenty ponies that shouldn't be out quite this late, would we ask no questions and hence avoid the lie, or might we, against all better judgement, pull back the blinds and risk the consequences? But then, what would our glimpse tell us? Perhaps little more than that smuggling is going on – neither who is behind it nor why. *Smuggling: Seven Centuries of Contraband* is, in a sense, about looking over and beyond what occasionally clatters beneath our window in order to piece together what can be seen and heard of smuggling in world history and geopolitics, and the relationship between them.

PART ONE

SMUGGLING EXPLORATIONS

ONE

GREAT AMBITIONS

Smuggling in the Age of Discovery

In the spring of 1568 Francis Drake, then a young and unknown sea captain, lieutenant to and cousin of the privateer and slave trader John Hawkins, sailed towards the South American colonial town of Riohacha at the neck of New Granada's desolate Guajira Peninsula. As he neared the town at the helm of his small warship *Judith*, accompanied by another, *Angel*, he pondered his mission: a 'contrabanding' one to circumvent the monopoly on Spanish goods.[1]

Riohacha today is a sleepy place in Colombia, the last substantial town at the edge of an expanse of desert known primarily over the centuries as smuggler territory. Then as now, smuggling was the main form of trade in the area, and as recently as ten years ago renegade ports dealt almost entirely in the illicit import of untaxed wares, particularly hi-fis and other electronic goods, as well as brand-name fashions and alcohol. It is still an important zone for smuggling cocaine, which transits either by sea from remote coves or by air out of the numerous hidden airstrips.[2]

The Guajira is an area that I will come back to repeatedly in this part of the book because it offers continuity. It is a corner of the old Spanish Main that has had a very particular relationship with smuggling from the time of the early New World Empire through the Bourbon period and to the present day. The petty contraband trading of the Elizabethan English with Spanish colonists and Wayuu indigenous people in this part of the Caribbean bears comparison with what has been going on in the peninsula in more recent times. For instance, we find (or more likely don't detect) arms shipments beside more everyday contraband. We can't necessarily read into this any kind of state involvement, although of course in the case of Drake and his compatriot Hawkins – privateers and contracted traders backed by noblemen and merchants back home, even by the queen – we might discern aspects of smuggling as a directed project. A lot of modern smuggling on the peninsula is petty and everyday but questions about broader influence still arise here: what, in aggregate, is the importance of extensive petty trading? Does it become a counter-state project if it infiltrates significantly into society? If smuggling has become a new norm, shouldn't more formal entities such as nation-states be paying more heed to this trend that, in the Guajira, has evolved over six centuries? I am surely getting ahead of myself here: we are after all only talking, in the case of Drake and Hawkins, about precarious probing of as yet unformed markets.

Drake's cargo, like shipments in and out of today's Guajiran informal ports, was a mixture of the abject and the ordinary – slaves on the one hand, iron and linens among other commodities on the other – and he assumed that the town's citizenry would comply with his 'strong-arm' trading overtures as they had done during Hawkins's 1564 contrabanding voyage along this coastline.3 However, this time the town treasurer Miguel de Castellanos refused to comply and the future pirate and national hero was welcomed with a hail of gunfire, to which he responded with his own bombardment, blowing up the governor's house in the process. He sacked the town with the loss of just one man, Thomas Surgeon, before carrying out his smuggling mission, threatening further pillage and hostage-taking should the settlement not acquiesce. Drake, of course, was to go on to bigger things – the circumnavigation of the globe, to national adulation, opening up new possibilities for trade. But for this trip, and many others that have since gone down in history as voyages of discovery, contrabanding was the bread and butter.

Geopolitical Smuggling

The Age of Exploration was by now well under way and offered exciting opportunities for men like Drake who were interested not so much in finding new lands as in filling their ships' holds with new 'species' – rapaciously sought-after commodities like gold, silver and spices. This was not just a time of exploratory circumnavigations, of rounding land masses and crossing oceans, but of other new circulations, of free and forced migrations of people and goods, both licensed and contraband, although often it was difficult to tell which was which. Although in his smuggling efforts Drake might have been thinking mostly about imme-diate profit, perhaps on occasion giving momentary thought to his backers at home in England, he was nevertheless a man of his times. When acting as an illicit trader, he was pioneering a new geopolitics.

Expansive exploration began in the 1440s when the Portuguese prince Henry the Navigator and his associates tentatively explored the western coastline of Africa. It surged further afield with the expeditions of Christopher Columbus, Vasco da Gama and Ferdinand Magellan, which coloured in the map, from a Western perspective, over a period of 200 years or so. Exploration diminished in the early part of the eighteenth century, after which most of the world's coastlines were deemed to have been discovered. This was a period of intense mercantile rivalry between the Spanish, Portuguese, Dutch, Venetians, Genoese and English, and it opened up new trade routes, particularly for spices. However, whoever declared a monopoly on a particular route faced a challenge from each of the other powers, both as a way of obtaining a measure of the spoils and as a strategy to usurp the position of top dog.

Was Christopher Columbus a trafficker? He hardly fits the profile of the crafty smuggler habitually crossing leaky borders with bags full of salt or cloth. Nevertheless with the onset of European exploration we might imagine a much larger theatre for smuggling. One must go back to Columbus's predecessors in world exploration in order to speculate about this possible defamation of the reputed discoverer of the Americas. When the Portuguese captain Bartolomeu Dias became the first European to round the Cape of Good Hope in 1488, reaching as far as the Great Fish River, or Rio do Infante, a few hundred miles up this eastern African *Contra Costa*, his motive was related to smuggling: it was to undermine the Gujarati, Malabari (western coast of India), Arab (particularly Mamluk Egyptian) and Venetian stranglehold on the spice trade. Spices came to Europe in a relay of land and sea transports from the east, often via the Arabian Gulf or the Red Sea. But if a maritime route could be established all the way to India and beyond, then, paradoxically for a free trader, a new Portuguese monopoly was a possibility.

It might be argued, then, that the first smugglers on a global scale were the Portuguese. Vasco da Gama rounded the Cape in 1497 and made it to India, although on this first trip he came back empty-handed. His second trip, spanning 1502–3, proved more fruitful but in June 1501 a fleet led by Pedro Alvarez Cabral had already arrived back in Lisbon laden with spices, which at that time were a fabulously precious commodity.

Of course, this is a distorted reading of some of the early heroes of the Age of Exploration. Nevertheless when Columbus pitched his venture to Queen Isabella of Castile to discover a western passage to the East Indies, five years earlier than da Gama's flanking manoeuvre, he had had a similar motivation, although at that time his intention was not only to undermine the Venetians but to pre-empt the Portuguese. There is a less mercenary way of looking at this overlap of smuggling and exploration: one thing smuggling had and has in common with exploration is a desire to discover and try out new things.

The cloak-and-dagger nature of the spice trade cannot be denied. The Portuguese were great seafarers rivalling the Vikings and the Basques, and even better navigators. Piecemeal experience and rough chartings of distant seas were worked over in the royal repositories of knowledge to produce magnificent but classified maps. One such map became known as Cantino's world chart after an Italian agent, Alberto Cantino, managed to smuggle a copy out of Lisbon in 1502, delivering it to his paymaster, the Duke of Ferrara. It showed Brazil and the Caribbean but the southern part of the Americas was a bit vague, perhaps encouraging others to keep probing for that elusive western route to the Spice Islands. The Americas, a great barrier, got in the way of this passage and a route was not to be sailed until Ferdinand Magellan found a way, later named the Straits of Magellan, between mainland South America and the island of Tierra del Fuego. On reaching a calm sea that he called, descriptively, the Pacific, he set a course for the Spice Islands. His voyage handed the Spanish an interest in the spice race but the Portuguese had already gained an advantage on the eastern route by this time.

This game of smuggling by exploration continued with the rounding of Cape Horn at the tip of South America by Isaac Le Maire and Willem Shouten from Hoorn in Holland in their ship *Eendracht* in January 1616. Thus the intermittent colonial thrust, throughout early modern history, in the trafficking of new commodities played out simplistically across a bare map. It opened up oceans and new worlds, offering possibilities both for the control of trade routes and commodities and also, at least at first, for state-sponsored smuggling of spices.

Quite how simplistically initial colonial exploration was mapped out can be seen in the Treaty of Tordesillas of 1494, which carved up the world for Spain and Portugal. An imaginary meridian line was drawn some 370 leagues west of the Cape Verde Islands. Spain would own all the lands to the west of it and Portugal those to the east. It gave the Americas, minus the South American bulge of Brazil, to Spain, while Asia, including the spice lands, was to go to Portugal.

How did this potentially hugely profitable world look to the smugglers and proto-free traders of the early sixteenth century? The partially regulated marine mercantile worlds of India, Indonesia and beyond were now of as much interest as the ancient terrains of the Silk Route. Insular, inland territories like China, Mesopotamia, Arabia, the Levant and Anatolia were bypassed as Europeans rounded new peninsulas and surfed into the lagoons of exotic islands that they had heard were the source of spices. They quickly began to think of establishing trading factories along the new maritime corridors – repositories of pepper, cinnamon, nutmeg, mace and cloves in what would become the great entrepôts of East Asia.

How far can we go with this logic of considering smuggling a part of exploration, a contributor to the early geopolitics of colonialism? On the one hand it seems to be an important factor to take into account. Although many of these early smuggling projects were uncoordinated, speculative and haphazard, they did have some backing from the state and sovereign. Smuggling did play a part on the ground, and its effects indicate just how important it could potentially be, as a counterpart to monopoly building, in the reordering of the world. It was just the beginning of an ongoing covert redistribution of economically crucial contraband that would include not only spices but silver, opium, tea, rubber and diamonds, as well as art and technology, and it would change the geopolitical configuration of the world. Smuggling's relationship to statecraft, economic development and scientific advancement would become particularly complicated and entangled during the nineteenth and twentieth centuries.

On the other hand, perhaps exploration as smuggling sounds a little speculative, a bit too abstract. Maybe smuggling during the early modern period should not be thought of as quite such a strategic activity. In this vein, one only has to look at the Spanish Main to survey, on a smaller scale, something much more grounded that was a part of everyday life. The question here becomes: what importance did this bottom–up informal trading have on the larger geopolitical picture? Did it simply create alternative contraband-fed communities that survived apart from the broader context?

Contrabandista Caribbean

Peru and Mexico were now under the yoke of the *conquistadores*. But all along the Spanish Main, outside of the massively fortified towns of Veracruz in northern New Spain (a territory bounded by what is now California in the north and Costa Rica in the south), Portobelo in *Tierra Firme* (what is now the Panama isthmus) and Cartagena (Colombia, then part of New Granada), there were vast swathes of nominally Spanish coastline that were either unconquered or had Spanish outposts that were happy to buy into the alternative, *contrabandista* Caribbean. The desperate or defiant inhabitants of often neglected communities like Caraballeda, Coro and Burburata in what is now Venezuela, La Yaguana and Santo Domingo in Hispaniola (modern-day Haiti and the Dominican Republic), or Manzanillo in Cuba, looked not so much to the viceroys for their vital commercial supply as to small, barely colonized islands with exotic names like Margarita and Tortuga (off New Granada) and tiny islets such as Mona and Saona (which on the map look like flies buzzing off Hispaniola). These unruly islands fed the crews and careened the ships of the smuggling marauders coming in increasing numbers from England, Holland, Portugal and France. Even if these small settlements practised contrabanding out of necessity, for the sake of their own internal communities, taken together they do paint a picture of extensive informal trading patterns that in sum were a significant irritant to the Spanish colonial authorities.

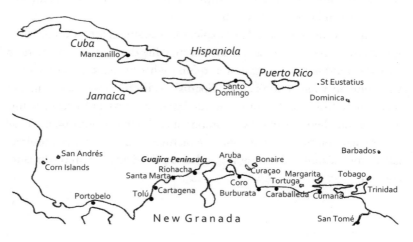

The Spanish Main and Caribbean.

Portuguese Attempts at Monopolizing the Spice Trade

It is hardly credible to suggest that nascent imperial powers might fully control vast and diverse territories and seas around the world: countless archipelagos of island potentates and unassailable regional fiefdoms had traded together for thousands of years. Nevertheless, with its superior ships, Portugal made the early running in the spice race from a European point of view. Under the stewardship of Manuel, whom the French called the 'Grocer King', Portugal had moved quickly to fill its sacks with spices, and soon he was also known as the 'Pepper Potentate'. But a cursory look at the second phase of exploration towards the spice lands shows us how insecure this dominion was.

A series of adventurers took up Vasco da Gama's flame, often quite literally as they burned and bullied their way across southern Asia from the Straits of Hormuz, over the Arabian Sea, all down the Malabar coast of India and as far as Melaka in southern Malaya. This port commanded the Malacca Straits, a fearsome channel on the spice route that then as now was plagued by piracy. It was situated halfway between India and the Moluccas and Bandas (which together make up the Spice Islands). The Portuguese strategy was to attempt to control the oceans and ports, and so when in 1505 Francisco d'Almeida was named Viceroy of *Estado da India* his vicereality was largely an expanse of water.

The key moments in this Portuguese phase of the spice race were the taming of the Malabari ports of Cochin, Cannanore and Quilon (although another local power, Calicut, successfully resisted), the establishment of a colony at Goa that was to be a dominion for another 450 years, and the storming of Melaka in 1511 by Affonso d'Albuquerque. Later that year a mission heading eastwards under Antonio d'Abreu set out from this important port. It was comprised of three ships and a supply junk and rounded Borneo and the Celebes (Sulawesi) before planting the grocer's flag in the fragrant and semi-mythical lands of spice.

The race was won, so it seemed, and in 1522 a formal Portuguese monopoly was declared on cloves from the northern Moluccas, on nutmeg and mace from the southern islands (Bandas), and on all cinnamon from India and Sri Lanka and further to the east. Was this the end of the spice race, a foreclosure of the possibility of smuggling/exploration by other powers muscling their way around the region?

The monopoly lasted just seventeen years, until 1539, and was porous from the outset. One of the reasons why the Portuguese were able to make some initial headway, ahead of their close rivals the Spanish, was because at this time little of the silver or gold from the Americas that would make Spain such a powerful force was arriving in Seville. However there were always too many other interests in the region for a distant potentate like Portugal to hold sway. Gujarati, Malabari and Chinese merchants, among others, had traded out of Melaka, but on the arrival of the Portuguese they simply decamped for smaller ports like Aceh at the western tip of Sumatra, and Bantam on the northwest coast of Java. Regional leaders such as the Malay Sultans and the Zamorins of Calicut in India at the head of a powerful Mappila merchant community were equally unimpressed. They were used to the freedom of the seas (the principle, incidentally, that most of the European explorers also espoused unless they were in a position to create a monopoly), and to conducting trade efficiently on the same maritime entrepôt model as the Western interlopers. They therefore simply and silently turned over the coin and continued with their own effective spice trade, even if the Portuguese might now call it smuggling.

As later in the Americas, it can be argued that the effect of the monopoly was not to squeeze out unofficial trade but rather to stimulate all activity, including smuggling. According to this argument, regulation not only boosts smuggling (because it is what smuggling, in getting around it, relies upon for generating its profit) but helps to magnify trade in general. Of course free traders would contest this, and might instead suggest that it holds back the potential for growth. The paradox is that while smuggling needs high duty on goods in order to circumvent them, its trajectory is actually towards free trade and so it eventually consumes itself. This is perhaps why the Enlightenment free-trade thinker Adam Smith, in *The Wealth of Nations*, was so interested in smugglers.

On the ground, regardless of the reason, prices were pushed up generally, making smuggling all the more profitable, particularly out of Java during the sixteenth century. It was all a bit loose, though. Take for instance Calicut and pepper. Manuel might have been known as the pepper king, but it was actually the Zamorin who traded the best-quality pepper. The Portuguese had no control over where it was grown and so were reliant upon local channels of supply, and the Zamorin, knowing the source, could control and offload it to whomsoever he desired. The Portuguese attempted to bring spice plants closer to their ports and *feitorias* (forts), trying, in vain as it turned out, to transplant nutmeg to Timor, for instance. But if smuggling always had the upper hand in this early part of the sixteenth century it was not simply because cultivation of spices was beyond the net of any monopoly. The Portuguese themselves, officially monopolists, were up to their necks in contraband.

Portuguese Smuggling

One of the claims of this book is that the projection of national power has often been facilitated by and is bound up with smuggling at its edges and as its vanguard, but this wasn't the case for the Portuguese. The monopoly seems to have fallen apart not just because other powers smuggled around it but to a large extent because of its own informal trading habits – smuggling within its own monopoly.

The Portuguese were something of a paradox: they loved monopolies but were pretty good at smuggling too. Engrossment – the practice of amassing profits for oneself, disregarding others – was common and there were great opportunities for self-enrichment among the new mercantile class. And yet merchants, in Catholic Portugal just as in Confucian China, had little social standing. Smuggling was much more widespread than just the occasional sailor secreting a few peppercorns about his person as his ship neared Lisbon. Colonial officials, on the pulse of trade both geographically and administratively, were poorly paid, and many from the lowliest scribe to the governor carried on this double trade. It was generally tolerated so long as private gain did not eclipse the Crown's profit or visibly compromise the appearance of a working monopoly conducted through official factors and customs.

Colonial governors and other senior officials were silent partners or creditors in many 'private' ventures. Smuggling was even made semi-official through the system of privileges (*liberdades*) or grants (*foros*), although the other side to this parallel living was that these engorged officials were expected to contribute to the national purse in times of emergency. Francisco Barreto, for example, ex-governor of India, made a fortune as captain of Baçaim from 1549 onwards but still patriotically contributed most of it to sovereign matters.[4]

This quasi-unofficial recognition of smuggling prevailed well into the seventeenth century. Even the Church was involved, exploiting its tax-exemption status to the full in a manner that could only really be called licit smuggling: during the 1630s the Bahian plantation of Sergipe do Conde, part of a Jesuit mission, would ship its tax-free sugar to Portugal if the price was low in Brazil.[5] In some areas smuggling was quite formal: galliots (small seagoing vessels) trading between Macao and Goa during the 1620s carried two sets of cargo books – one of them set aside for customs.[6] The contraband trade was quite ingrained, although if ever it caused an international incident so-called 'New Christians' (Jews) were scapegoated, just as they were in the Americas, particularly around the River Plate between present-day Argentina, Brazil and Uruguay.

Smuggling is important geopolitically not just as a tool for empire-building from above, or from the centre, but in the creation of significant other worlds, built upon a ready supply of contraband and producing their own hierarchies of governance. It might be seen as constructing worlds not just outwards and extensively but internally as well – a con-solidation. (One example is the smuggling world of privateer Jean Lafitte, as discussed in Chapter Seven, which involved digging in and embedding the trade on islands off New Orleans and the Texas coast.) So, too, the effect of this early modern Portuguese smuggling was to create an internal structure of informal trading; an alternative to monopolizing ambition that was also bound up with it. Smuggling, for some of these Portuguese, was what held society together, though perhaps not quite as much as for the citizens of Buenos Aires.

So should we consider smuggling as Portuguese trade's most entre-preneurial activity rather than a disease at its heart? For the health of the monopoly, perhaps too many Portuguese were enthusiastic about smuggling and this distracted them from the declared state project. However all this must be put in context: at its best the monopoly barely warranted the name anyway. Cinnamon was the most effectively monop-olized of all the spices and yet during the first half of the sixteenth century only one-third of its value accrued to the royal coffers in Lisbon. The rest was siphoned off by smugglers and officials acting on their own rather than on the king's behalf.[7] After 1539 the futility of enforcing an unworkable system was recognized and the trade was opened up to all, provided that one-third of all cargoes were offered to the crown at cost price. Portuguese efforts were, then, a false start in the spice race.

Smuggling through the Spanish Caribbean Monopoly

There was a similar modus vivendi of smuggling – a kind of publicly known but unspoken secret – in the Americas throughout much of the sixteenth century. The Spanish were always stretched: uncolonized parts of their domain offered good launch pads for contrabanding missions like the ones that Hawkins made during the 1560s. During that decade he swept along the north coast of South America from east to west, selling slaves along with French and Dutch linens. He would end up off the Mexican part of the empire before making the journey home on the westerly winds to face his backers, for better or for worse, depending upon his haul.

The Caribbean monopoly was as riddled with holes as the Portuguese one in the east. If the towns and cities of the Spanish Main were like a

Sir John Hawkins,
18th-century
engraving.

variable set of teeth – some strong and gleaming, others rotten and
neglected – then the islands were like a pearl necklace, a mixture of
white and black. Some, like Dominica, lay in between. This Lesser
Antillean jewel is familiar to many as the setting for the second and third
Pirates of the Caribbean films, and in reality the Indian River on the west
side of the island was a popular careening place for adventurers like
Drake and Hawkins.

Smuggling in the Caribbean was both an opportunity and a necessity.
New World settlers needed contraband goods because the Carrera de
las Indias, the Spanish transatlantic trade monopoly that gave just a few
asientos (licences) to foreign traders, was never adequate to provide the
new lands with either enough staples or luxuries. The *flota*, or merchant
convoy from Seville, was infrequent; supply was often held back in a
bid to keep prices high in the colonies. We might discern in this an early
rehearsal for today's black-market economies that shadow and intertwine
with formal ones and which also involve illicit supply from distant places.
Then as now, certain parts of the world could not function without some
smuggling activity. Perhaps this is also why peripheral places like the
Guajira Peninsula continue to trade in this way.

Those who took the opportunity actively to smuggle practised what
was called *rescate*. The Portuguese term *resgate*, literally meaning ransom,
always had a trafficking connotation because in the Mediterranean sub-
Saharan African captives, supposedly repatriated on the Barbary coast
upon receipt of a ransom, were often actually transacted in an earlier
version of the slave trade.[8] In the Caribbean the Spanish word *rescate*
meant barter, which was usually contrabanding, and so it came to mean
smuggling.

There was always ambiguity in contraband trading relationships.
Smuggling on the locals' side was at times willing, at others coerced.
Alcaldes ordinarios, local functionaries sent to investigate *rescate* ports,
were frequently involved in the trade as well, and this is a pattern that
continued right up until independence. Often there was discrepant attribution of criminality according to the nationality involved: for instance,
for similar transgressions the Portuguese were considered smugglers
whereas the English and French were pirates. Hawkins once claimed
that he did the Spanish a favour by policing the Caribbean but in reality
this was probably just a carrot and stick tactic to try and persuade the
Spanish to trade. He traded at Riohacha in 1564 but in 1568 Drake was
met with fire as a pirate. In that same year a French contraband ship

out of Le Havre, captained by an opportunist trader named Borgoing, put in at Isla Margarita to trade for pearls and was attacked by the Spanish, but only after ten or twelve days of tolerating its business.[9]

The background to this period of smuggling in the Caribbean during the late 1550s and '60s is one of expanding trade, both official and unofficial. In fact the period from the 1540s to the late 1560s was a mini golden age of smuggling. One of the earliest recorded encounters was in October 1544, when the French were contrabanding in Rouen cloth and laces at the pearling post of Santa Maria de los Remedios near Cabo la Vela in Guajira.[10] As well as linens and soap, wax and quicksilver were smuggled in. The preferred return at this stage was gold and pearls but tobacco was an interesting contraband novelty. Gold dazzled somewhat, despite the fact that neglected contraband like hides was far more likely to turn a quick profit than this scarce precious metal.

The French, seasoned seafarers and smuggling associates of the English in the wool and cloth trade over the Channel out of ports like La Rochelle and St Malo, were becoming increasingly active. Initially they preferred operating off Curaçao but later also Burburata and Mona and Saona. On encountering Spanish interceptors they sometimes used the excuse of bad weather to explain their trespassing. However, until the Dutch arrived with their light boats, small Portuguese caravels were the most frequent and preferred visitors.

Menéndez and Hawkins

The Caribbean is often associated with daring defiance against the 'dastardly' Spanish because of the myth-making of popular Hollywood films such as *The Sea Hawk* (1940). In this adventure Errol Flynn plays a pirate during the Elizabethan era, one of confrontation with the Spanish Armada and privateering off the Americas. His fictional character is an amalgam of Drake and Hawkins, who were involved in both. It is all part of English maritime mythology and its importance in creating its nation-state. Two things are missing from all of the pirate films set over the several hundred years of smuggling's heyday in the region. The first is smuggling itself, although many of the privateers practised it when not actively engaged in piratical activities, and the second is the appearance of bold and effective Spanish adversaries to the romanticized and righteous English, Dutch and French seafarers. The parallel careers of John Hawkins and Pedro Menéndez de Avilés tell another story.

Francisco de
Paola Marti, *Pedro
Menéndez de Avilés*,
1791, engraving.

Both the formal and informal economies of the Atlantic were now highly energized. Silver and gold were flowing out of the mines and over to Seville via either Portobelo or Veracruz. Menéndez de Avilés, appointed Captain General of the *Armada de la Carrera* in 1554 at the age of just 35, commanded the fleet from Veracruz in 1561. Just one year later, in 1562, and in defiance of the Spanish monopoly, John Hawkins became active in the so-called triangular trade that saw slaves traded for contraband goods in the New World, generating wealth on sale in Europe, which was then reinvested in expeditions to seize more slaves in West Africa for export to the Americas.

The Portuguese, as ever, were also on the pulse of smuggling. The slave trade was meant to be rubber-stamped by the merchant guild of Seville, the Consulado, but many Portuguese actually bypassed it. From early on, despite this being an era of envy of Spanish wealth in the

Americas by other European powers, the Portuguese were at the forefront of making money out of trafficking slaves into Hispaniola, Puerto Rico, Cuba and *Tierra Firme*.

Although Menéndez's career later became entangled with the French as each vied for control of Florida, his role in massively fortifying the main towns of the Spanish Main had a direct effect on the smuggling activity of opportunists like Hawkins. This show of power from the Spanish in response to piracy and contrabanding was not entirely successful. The smugglers not only headed for the weaker, increasingly freelance ports like Puerto Real de Manpatare on Margarita island, Riohacha in Colombia, Burburata in Venezuela and Santo Domingo in Hispaniola, but were pulled there by their citizens. These small havens resisted Menéndez's overtures, preferring to remain weak in order to avoid being sacked, and they really needed the goods that the *rescatadores* brought with them. Perhaps, though, this is the balance that suited both sides best; there was no wholesale escalation into privateering and piracy of the type that occurred periodically from the 1570s onwards.

Had they encountered each other directly, Hawkins and Menéndez would each have recognized many of their own characteristics in the other. Both were born to wealthy families and were men of business who were fiercely loyal to their respective sovereigns. They were also patrons of their kinsmen to the extent of nepotism: Menéndez made his brothers Bartolomé Mendez and Alvaro Sanchez Mendez admirals in the Carrera, while Hawkins, through his contrabanding expeditions, launched the careers of his cousins John Lovell and Francis Drake. Each was ruthless and ambitious, both tactically and strategically. They were born sea dogs and relished raiding. But beyond this close-quarter manoeuvring, on a broader stage, they were each architects of their respective countries' foreign policy, and ship and fleet builders in rival navies in which they rose to high office. Menéndez became governor of Cuba in 1568 and Hawkins treasurer and later admiral of the English Navy. The former designed a lighter galleon that was low-built and less beamy, with both oars and sail. It enabled his fleet to become hunter rather than lumbering prey. The counter-tactic of seizing laden corsair ships became a strategy that financed his ambitious fortification programme. In the case of Hawkins, in 1588 in the English Channel, the use of light and manoeuvrable ships against the armada would prove very effective (although by this time Menéndez had long since died). They were an enforcer and a pirate-smuggler, but one wonders whether given altered circumstances their roles might have been reversed.

Hawkins's Smuggling Expeditions

Hawkins's first two contrabanding expeditions were a success if measured in profit alone. The first made £3,000, although one must take into account lost ships, and the second about the same amount, although overall profitability was lower as more money had been invested in it.[11] However you cannot hide the brutality of trading in *piezas de negros* (units of black capital).[12] Indeed Hawkins is discredited as the entrepreneur who began the English slave trade.

He had the occasional setback: on the first of his expeditions Hawkins took the extraordinary step of 'colouring' (disguising) a seized vessel to make it look like a *suelto* – a licensed freelance vessel that sails apart from the main Spanish fleet – and sending the contraband to Seville to be laundered by an English factor, Hugh Tipton. The plan failed and the merchandise was confiscated.[13]

The earlier expeditions succeeded in large part for the same reason why later ones failed: because they were heavily armed and coerced, rather than persuaded, the marginalized Spanish settlers to trade. Hawkins's ships were powerful, although some were a little unwieldy. At least one, the 700-ton *Jesus of Lubeck*, was too big. They were captained by fighters like Drake, Martin Frobisher and Thomas Wyndham, who all at first succeeded in strong-arming contraband trade, but the maxim 'once bitten, twice shy' could not be more appropriate here and compliance became rarer. Hawkins's third expedition took place by proxy and the commander, his cousin John Lovell, met with muted response or outright aggression as he trawled up the coast of South America, succeeding a little at Margarita but being rebuffed at Burburata and Riohacha, even though he augmented his strength by allying with the French smuggler and pirate Jean Bontemps.

The expeditions were quasi-state ventures – Queen Elizabeth had donated *Jesus of Lubeck* and Hawkins was also backed by Benjamin Gonson and William Winter, respectively treasurer and surveyor of the Queen's Navy. At this stage, though, this was not foreign policy; rather these noble sponsors were mainly concerned with making money and they pressured Hawkins hard to succeed. Large, expensively armed fleets like the one that Hawkins took on his fourth voyage, which included the

Lubeck and the smaller ships *Minion, William and John, Swallow, Judith* and *Angel*, could not idle in the Caribbean without maximizing trading activity. Indeed this ill-fated expedition ended in disaster when he tangled with a Spanish armada at San Juan de Ulúa near Veracruz, Mexico, losing *Swallow, Angel, Lubeck* and three-quarters of his men by the time he made it back to England.

In the main Hawkins skirted around his adversary during each of his three contrabanding trips during the 1560s while still dealing with the Spanish at the margins of their empire to a greater or lesser extent. For instance in 1562, on his first trip, he found himself off the Banda del Norte, the wild north coast of Hispaniola, filling his ships with hides, ginger, sugar and pearls. He was helped in his smuggling activity by Lorenzo Bernáldez, the man sent to stop him. Bernáldez allowed limited trade in order to avoid attack while at the same time publicly stating that trade with Hawkins was illegal.[14]

Menéndez's Response and its Effect

The Caribbean was far from being a secure fiefdom for the Spanish, and some pragmatism was always going to be likely; that is, until Menéndez decided to put his foot down. The final straw for him came in Hispaniola. First there was the devil-may-care raid on the Banda del Norte coastline by Jean Bontemps in 1565. That year had been a lucrative one for the French, Portuguese and English traders who garnered small fortunes in silver and gold out of smuggling and piracy. It was a time when things were hotting up, when resistance to smuggling in some places led to its increase in others and also to the beginnings of the pirate era. Juan del Buen Tiempo, as Bontemps was known to the Spanish, had the audacity to attack Puerto de Plata, partly because Menéndez had left only 50 men in its defence.[15] Other ports along the Banda refused to be reinforced with such a small garrison. Justifiably, they feared that it would simply incite the interlopers and, perhaps more to the point, would interrupt their own contraband business. Bontemps brazenly contrabanded in Monte Cristi and Puerto Real along this north coast as well as at La Yaguana on the west coast but it was the sacking of Puerto de Plata, the port of silver, that incensed Menéndez. In reprisal he caught up with the smuggler-pirates at Manzanillo in Cuba, seizing five rich cargoes. This and other aggressions along the Florida channel earned him the epithet 'pirate hunter'.

The Spanish strategy of reprisal had some success. After Hawkins's debacle at San Juan de Ulúa the English refrained from slave trading for twenty years and didn't return to more varied smuggling for another ten years after that. However, smuggling continued throughout the rest of the sixteenth century and by 1600 it dominated trade in Hispaniola.

Outlaw activity in the Caribbean periodically changed its character: as the screw was turned, smugglers resorted to piracy. There was a vicious cycle. The English might have called it privateering – legitimate confrontation with a national enemy – but piracy, as in reality it was, impoverished marginal settlements, especially on the eastern Main (parts of present-day Venezuela and the Guianas). Contrabanding again became a necessity, with a renewed demand for goods that the Spanish could not supply.

Smuggling out of necessity was a fact of everyday life in both the Americas and the Spice Islands: during shortages, staples like rice and cotton clothes in the Moluccas could only be obtained in sufficient quantity through smuggling, and this was the bane of monopolists trying to control commercial flows. The islanders, like the impoverished settlers outside of the glittering colonial cities in the Caribbean and the oppressed natives beside them, were always open, out of dire need, to trading in contraband in exchange for this everyday fare, and generally with whomever other than the monopolist sailed over the horizon.

IN THE CONTEXT of geopolitics it is easy to overlook the importance of petty smuggling in the early period of colonial expansion and rivalry. It is a greater omission when one considers that it seems to foreshadow today's informal black- and grey-market economies, which have become such an important underbelly of globalization. If this early micro trading is important, then what of the macro, of the idea that exploration can have a smuggling logic? I've made a case for this, but it is not that these expeditions were great smuggling projects per se; rather they indicate that smuggling is not out of place at the scale and in the frame of geopolitics.

History might play out simplistically in Technicolor dramas of smuggling and piracy but there is obvious asymmetry and complexity missing in this romanticized, geopolitically blind illusion. In a broader framing this asymmetry is exemplified in the Dutch smugglers and expansionists: while in the Americas they joined the English, French and Portuguese in the share-alike theatre of smuggling, in the east they were ruthless engrossers. The romantic smuggling and piratical activities of Drake and Hawkins, and even their own admiral, Piet Heyn, could have no place in the new Dutch Empire of the east. There was never to be a loose smuggling domain like that in the Caribbean beyond the massively fortified primary Spanish ports; instead there had to be a measured monopoly. On one sea the Dutch were laissez-faire freebooters and on another intolerant monopolists.

One wonders, then, what the settlers and islanders in both the Caribbean and the Banda Sea (the waters of the Spice Islands) might have thought as this new orange sun arose over their struggling lands at the turn of the sixteenth century. For the Caribbean it meant relief but for the Spice Islanders things were about to go from bad to worse. The Dutch had arrived.

TWO

MONOPOLY!

The Spice Islands and the
South China Sea

The Moluccan spice islands, officially known as Maluku since 1999, provide few spices for today's world markets. They have a multi-cultural populace – such has been the effect of repeated colonizations and population manipulations, both European and Indonesian. At the beginning of the new millennium the islands were in the news regarding flare-ups of sectarian religious violence between Christians and Muslims, but before the arrival of Europeans the original Melanesian islanders, later decimated as a population during the seventeenth century, had little to worry about other than the occasional erupting volcano. The islands are beautiful and lush, and back then supported an Eden-like existence so uninvested in the ways of capital that the *orang-kaya*, the presiding councils of 'rich men', didn't even particularly value their precious nutmeg, cloves and mace.

The islands are surrounded by coral reefs and deep ocean, but these were insufficient defences to keep away the rapacious European invaders. Before this, Muslim and Indian traders were welcomed. They came and went with holds full of spices, turning a good profit. Most significantly, at least from the Moluccans' point of view, they went away. The Portuguese and Spanish played with the islanders but the Dutch were there for serious business – paradise over!

It was all very different from the games of smuggling and interdiction being played out among the West Indian islands and along the Main, although here too business prevailed over adventure. The English were said to practice 'strong-arm' trading in the Americas, the contrabanding equivalent of gunboat diplomacy. The Dutch on the other hand were *Vrijbuiters*, 'freebooters', in the Caribbean. It sounds like a much more romantically rebellious activity, which is probably why it is a term still in use today in broader contexts, but there was a steeliness behind the Dutch smugglers as well. The term actually means 'free plunder', and like the other northern European interlopers they did plenty of that, most famously when the freebooter admiral Piet Heyn captured the Mexican treasure fleet at Matanzas Bay in Cuba in 1628. Heyn worked for the shareholders of the Dutch West India Company but an altogether more ruthless and efficient trading organization was operating in the east: Vereenigde Oost-Indische Compagnie (VOC), the United Dutch East India Company.

The VOC and Jan Coen

Heyn is admired in the Netherlands in the same sort of way that Drake is revered in England: through rose-tinted spectacles. His equivalent in the east, in terms of profile at least (he was actually the enemy of smugglers), was Jan Pieterszoon Coen, the VOC's governor-general of the East Indies from 1617, and he too is admired to this day. But it is difficult to sense love here given Coen's ruthless approach to securing the spice trade for his country and advancing his personal fortunes. The lordly and dark Heren XVII (the seventeen major shareholders and leaders of the company) seem to us formidable in their pursuit of profit but even they were shocked by some of Coen's acerbic words and violent deeds. He was an efficient man, an excellent mathematician and a learned book-keeper but he had a cruel streak of ambition and a missionary zeal for the cause. In some ways, paradoxically, he fits the archetype of the smuggler at the service of the state – opportunistic, daring and always just beyond reach – but he was also an officer of the company and genuinely patriotic. While in the Caribbean theatre of operations one can imagine the monopoly enforcer Pedro Menéndez de Avilés in the role of his counterpart John Hawkins, one cannot quite imagine Coen, ultimately, as anything but the gamekeeper. Coen's directors knew his zealous drive and managed him accordingly.

On the face of it there were many similarities between what was going on in the East and West Indies: both seemed to be about empire haves and empire want-to-haves. On a personal level, bravura, ambition and ego drove exploration and trade. There were plenty of colourful characters jostling for position in both east and west. At times the confrontation was peripheral, or misaligned in the case of Hawkins and Menéndez; at other times it was head on.

Jakob van de Schley and Pieter de Hondt, *Jan Pieterszoon Coen*, 1763, etching.

However, relations in the east between the rude and violent protag-onists of empire-building were even more edgy and personal than those in the west. For instance, the English trader John Jourdain managed to get under the skin of Jan Coen as the latter set his mind to merciless monopolizing. When they encountered each other in 1613 on Ceram, one of the Spice Islands, Coen challenged Jourdain about the legitimacy of his trading mission only to be mocked sarcastically for the impertinence of one with such a 'long beard' (he had only a short one). Nevertheless at the age of 31 he became the VOC's governor-general of the East Indies. Despite such corporate responsibility he carried his earlier personal resentments with both the English and, occasionally, his own employers into his vicious but effective genocidal campaigns in the hitherto idyllic Spice Islands.

The VOC was itself a determined organization. The Heren XVII re-invested profits into the company, much to the annoyance of investors out for short-term profit. From the start there were plenty of backers – 1,800 at the outset – and so the company was able to consistently outgun its new rivals, the English and occasionally the French, and put to flight the old powers, the Spanish and Portuguese. There were setbacks but, as later on in India for the British East India Company, such was its commitment and investment that these were overcome. Each of these respective East India Companies had similarities to a state, including a large private military force and the will and licence to wage war with each other in Asia while favouring a peaceful status quo at home. This led to bizarre contradictions: in the year 1609 the English and Dutch were allied at home against the Catholics at the same time that they were at loggerheads in the East Indies. There was certainly inconsistency in foreign policy and perhaps, from the English point of view, the feeling of a right to smuggle in the context of the Age of Exploration was just such a kink in the line.

The Dutch in the Spice Islands

The first exploratory expedition had left Amsterdam in April 1595. Early on an alliance was made with the Sultan of the island of Ternate in the northern Moluccas, posing a threat to the Spanish and Portuguese who had a joint garrison on nearby Tidore. Ternate was strong locally because it had many *kora koras* (large canoes) and so, in these duplicitous early encounters at least, the Dutch made the right friends.

Things moved pretty quickly from here. By the turn of the sixteenth century the Moors and the Indians had faded from the scene and cloves had been transplanted from the northern Moluccas to the southern islands – to Ambon and a peninsula on the southwestern tip of the nearby larger island of Ceram. Geographically Ceram is like a big brother wrapping its right arm around Ambon facing on to the Banda sea, and the Dutch soon identified this as a key node in their planned monopoly. The VOC had a strong foothold within three years of its foundation in 1602 and a Portuguese fort, Victoria on Ambon, was taken in 1605. They transplanted more spices into the incipient colonial hinterland – nutmeg/mace trees were taken from the Banda islands, which hitherto had been their only habitat.

Ceram, Ambon and the Bandas were to be the strategic kernel of the spice monopoly. It was a strategy of restricting the flow of spices, first through transplantation – drawing cultivation into the tight arc of these islands – and then further restricting trade through exporting them only via the tightly controlled Dutch factory system in the entrepôts of Makassar (on Sulawesi), Malacca (Melaka, Malaysia), Bantam (Java) and Batavia (present-day Jakarta). Batavia, from 1619, became the main Dutch base in Asia after they took control of the city.

The Bandas were brought into the arc with brutal rapid-fire campaigns across each of the islands. Neira, the main nutmeg island, became the headquarters. There were reversals, if only temporary ones. On Neira Peter Verhoef and 42 of his men were massacred but his deputy,

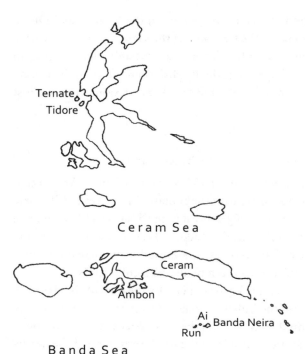

The Spice Islands
(Moluccas, Maluku)
in the 17th century.

Ternate
Tidore

Ceram Sea

Ceram

Ambon

Ai
Banda Neira
Run

Banda Sea

Simon Hoen, backed by more than 900 men, secured Dutch control. On 10 August 1609 the Bandas joined Ceram and Ambon, and Ternate and Tidore in the north, as subservient territories of the VOC. All foreign ships were to anchor off the new Dutch fort, Nassau, on Neira, and inter-island trade was prohibited. The monopoly was in place, at least in theory. It wasn't long before smuggling once again proved itself a significant irritant.

Smuggling in the East Indies

This was neither the beginning of smuggling in the region nor exclusively a case of European rivalry: during the late sixteenth century Siamese and Bornean ships had brought cloves, nutmeg, sandalwood and pepper to Malacca that could only have come from one place: the Moluccas. Smuggling had always gone on throughout the east and always would, but now it became a key part of the trade of the Spice Islands as well.

One should not forget that the Portuguese had a declared if ineffective monopoly before the Spanish, English and Dutch eyed an opportunity, and so, in a sense, all non-Portuguese spice trading was smuggling. The foreign invasion turned the islands into 'spice islands' because spices, formerly wild and uncultivated, suddenly became cash crops. Staples like rice were no longer grown. The Dutch took spices for a pittance and bumped up the prices on what little rice they brought, leaving the door open for English and Asian traders to make up the shortfall of money in exchange for spices that to Dutch eyes were contraband.

The English aim over the years was to dominate the spice race but they almost always played the role of semi-licit trader, although often in open defiance, initially of the Portuguese and later of the Dutch. Francis Drake was in just such a position when he anchored off Tidore during his circumnavigation in 1579. Before he could land he was intercepted in the lagoon by an emissary from Sultan Baab of nearby Ternate. This hospitable and independent-minded potentate lavished Drake with largesse and a hold so full of spices that his ship stuck fast on the seabed. It was only refloated after he ordered the upending of eight cannon into the water, along with much of the food ration and three tons of the contraband cloves that he had so fortunately secured.[1] It could be argued that the Dutch were forced to play their hand at the beginning of the seventeenth century and try to set up a monopoly, beginning in the northern Moluccas, because the English had played theirs in citing Drake's early contact as a licence for trading rights. In other words the English were insisting that they were not smugglers, and the Dutch wanted to designate them as such. But for the Sultan of Ternate nothing was set in stone and he continued to deal in cloves with English, Portuguese, Javanese and Malay merchants.

The English continued their troublemaking. Sir Henry Middleton, on his 1604–6 expedition, visited Ternate in his ship *Red Dragon* and his lieutenant, Captain Colthurst, successfully filled the hold of his vessel *Ascension* with nutmeg and mace after a speculative diversion to the Bandas. But eventually on this same expedition they were pushed aside by the Dutch, who had sent a sizeable fleet of nine warships along with sundry pinnaces and sloops. The battle of Amboyna (the main town on Ambon island) and the seizure of Tidore were the first steps towards Dutch hegemony.

Were the English incursions only brief and opportunistic? They were certainly the latter but they were also drawing on earlier experience. English smuggling had reached the Bandas several years before the Dutch began to turn the screw. In 1601 James Lancaster had sailed to the region and sent out a probing reconnaissance in a small pinnace led by his subordinate, Master Keche. They reached the Bandas and brought nutmeg back from one of the islands, Run, to the newly formed East India Company's small outpost in Bantam. Later, Henry Middleton's brother David flouted the Dutch monopoly and on his second voyage in 1609 was profitably trading with Banda merchants, even as the Dutch were declaring the monopoly in place following the invasion of Neira. Rather than risking his large ship *Expedition* in the treacherous waters off Ai and Run, he based himself in Ceram and shuttled his small pinnace *Hopewell* to and fro picking up large quantities of nutmeg.

On another expedition, departing from England in 1610, the smuggler Sir Henry Middleton found himself smuggled. While making a trading excursion into the Red Sea, he was imprisoned at the port of Mocha. He daringly had a bottle of *aqua vitae* smuggled into the prison, got the guards drunk, hid himself in a barrel and was rolled down to the beach, making his escape back to his ship, the *Darling*.[2] Another interloper in these latter years of the spice race was William Keeling, who was a smuggler at heart. On a later voyage, against company policy, he smuggled his wife onto the ship. While David Middleton traded surreptitiously by night at Tidore, Keeling, sailing in Sir Henry's former flagship *Red Dragon*, was trading openly and defiantly by day with Ai. They were all taking full advantage of the instability in the Moluccas created by the ousting of the Portuguese and Spanish by the Dutch.

The Story of Run

The English managed to hold on to some territory, much to the annoyance of Jan Coen. For much of the middle part of the seventeenth century the English and Dutch were at loggerheads in Europe, mainly over trading rivalries, and so the smuggling activities of the English in the Spice Islands poured fuel onto the flames of intense rivalry at home. The island of Run was the last piece of territory that the English could lay claim to in the Moluccas and, although it was a ragged little trading colony, its symbolism for the Dutch as the face of the illicit trade was an affront. Eventually they overran the island in 1620 and its heroic defender, Nathaniel Courthope, was lost at sea during the struggle. His name doesn't resound in the popular imagination like that of Drake or Hawkins but he continued the tradition of smuggling as an informal tenet of foreign policy.

It was another island swallowed up by the orange tide but this wasn't the end of the story for little Run. This erstwhile contraband outpost was to play a large part in one of the most momentous colonial acquisitions in history. In 1664 the English overran the Dutch trading port of New Amsterdam on Manhattan Island. As this particular English–Dutch conflict turned towards peace, teams of negotiators put their counters on the diplomatic table, at the forefront of which were the English demand for the return of Run and the return of Manhattan for the Dutch. Neither side would shift and so eventually, at the treaty of Breda in 1667, Run was officially ceded to the Dutch and New Amsterdam, now New York, became English. It was not of course a straight swap – what was to become the wealthiest city in the world was not exactly handed over in exchange for a tiny tropical island with a few windblown nutmeg trees on it – but nevertheless, the loss of a little smuggling outpost registered as a painful sting on the Dutch hide and was a symbolic moment in the monumental history of capitalism.

The Monopoly in Context

Much of this English adventuring and illicit trading points to a porous monopoly, rather like the Portuguese one before it. But despite the patchiness of their project, in many ways the Dutch, unlike their colonial forebears, changed trading patterns throughout East Asia.

Jan Coen acted decisively time after time. After taking Batavia in 1619, he followed this up by sailing for the Bandas in 1621 in response to an uprising. He brutally suppressed the Bandanese of Neira and then changed things there forever by deporting thousands of its people to Batavia, where they were sold into slavery, replacing them with Dutch settlers. Told this way, the story looks decidedly Eurocentric. What else had been going on outside, beneath and despite the Dutch invasion?

Before the arrival of the Dutch in the East Indies the map of mercantile commerce relates a narrative of local zones of influence and clear channels between traditional trading partners. For instance, the Ming-era Chinese would largely trade with familiar partners like the Srivijaya merchants in Melaka. Many ports had a system called stapling in which privileges were given to just a few, so there was little incentive to become a new trader. It kept most markets small, local and predictable. But there were larger ambitions blowing up and down the straits. The Malay Sultanates were able to challenge the Dutch on a strategic level, and continued to do so even after Melaka fell, because their predominantly maritime trading patterns were so similar to the effective Dutch model. The Srivijaya, a Sumatra-based regional power, had long employed warships patrolling the Straits of Malacca, making all vessels call in at their capital, Palembang. If Aden was the key to Arabia, and the Straits of Hormuz to facilitating Gujarati and Deccan trading to and from the west, then Melaka (and Palembang) dominated these straits. Of course such taxing presences led to much smuggling activity but not in terms of vast fleets of informal traders.

The Srivijaya, famous throughout Asia as merchants, had already opened up Melaka to extensive trading even before the Dutch came along. But the latter shook up wholesale, and in many ways overturned, the old entrepôts that dictated the formal slow-moving trading patterns of the Indian Ocean and beyond, re-orientating them towards global mercantile competition that had a distinctive orange hue. First they seized Melaka in 1641, then Makassar in 1667, and Bantam fell in 1682. Rice, cotton, cloth and other everyday items that had a world currency came under the domain of these ports, which subsequently became, in a geopolitical perspective, the seeds of empires and important recipients of the large amounts of commercial credit that were starting to be injected into what was becoming a global trading system. However, there certainly wasn't a Dutch monopoly across Southeast Asia: for instance, the English were gaining a foothold alongside the Gujaratis in Aceh (Sumatra).

Ironically the more intercontinental trading espoused by the Dutch went beyond the scope of their own beloved monopoly system. Even as they tried to shut down the spiceries for all but their own vessels, they depended upon, and wanted, an expanding market (which of course, unlike smuggling, can survive with more relaxed regulation).

Does this mean that the Dutch transcended their own monopoly? The Dutch in the east, unlike in the Caribbean, were never free traders but still harboured ever larger trading ambitions and, because they brought more firepower and fully rigged ships, to a large extent they could do whatever they liked. For some time they continued to capitalize on European advances in boat design although later, becoming complacent, they were outmanoeuvred or circumvented by the swift fleets of adaptable and opportunistic rivals.

The Spice Islands made the VOC but the monopoly never approached totality. Makassar, from the beginning of the seventeenth century until it was besieged and taken by the Dutch between 1667 and 1669, was a key transit point for contraband spices, especially cloves and mace. Junks traded between Makassar and Banda, exchanging gold and rice for cloves, nutmeg, mace and sandalwood. Even after the British retreated from the Moluccas, they were still smugglers of spices in that Asian smugglers offloaded their contraband to English merchants in Makassar and Borneo.

A little later the British, no longer harbouring great ambitions in the East Indies, incorporated their dabbling in contraband spice into a broader, self-perpetuating and escalating trading system. Exports of woollens, lead, iron and tin from Britain could be converted into the desirable Indian cottons and calicoes that the Spice Islanders preferred to wear, and these in turn could be traded for spices. This meant that Britain's exports, instead of its precious gold and silver reserves, paid for the spices, thus maximizing foreign trade surplus – the guiding logic of mercantilism. Two centuries later something similar happened, on a larger scale, with the East India Company's devastating trade of Indian opium in exchange for Chinese tea that fortified the empire into such a behemoth. Gradually the English turned away from the Moluccas but always kept their fingers in the pie of the flourishing informal trade.

The contraband trade was big business throughout much of East Asia during the seventeenth century and was not confined to the Malaya–Indonesia–Spice Islands axis. Despite our bias towards this particular story of European powers creating monopolies and other European powers breaking them, there was also another great theatre of smuggling in the east at this time: the South China Sea.

Smuggling in the South China Sea

Though the Dutch lorded it over the Ceram and Banda seas during the early part of the seventeenth century, they were small players in the South China Sea, although not for want of trying to make a larger impact. It was not so much that they feared China on the high seas (Japanese pirates could be much more terrifying), but rather that the Ming Chinese would not allow foreigners a foothold on the coast other than the Portuguese at Macao. All trade with China was strictly regulated and under the later Ming slowed to a trickle. They were only really interested in coastal, not overseas, trade: no Chinese vessel was permitted to carry more than two days' supply of fresh water and most vessels were hardly ocean-going. However the coastline was not as sacrosanct as the Ming would have it.

Fujian lies on the central Chinese coast, just to the northwest of Taiwan. The Fujianese were the Chinese equivalent of the Cornish of the eighteenth and early nineteenth centuries in Britain. They were proud, independent-minded and had considerable skills in seafaring, and their coastline was rugged and enveloped many inlets and secluded harbours: the geography was providential and they were habitual smugglers. Under the cover of moving goods to local ports or of coastal fishing, the Fujianese began to cast their nets further afield by converting their fishing boats for other purposes once they were over the horizon. They fixed shields of split bamboo around the sides of their vessels to repel waves, lowered a giant secondary keel to stabilize them, and made sail across the fearsome 'black ditch', the deep waters, to Taiwan (which, then as now, escaped the governance, both fiscal and political, of China). These daring sailors, ostensibly local fishermen, were now at the first staging post in a smuggling chain that ran northeast from here along the line of the Ryukuku islands that provided shelter from stormy weather on the way to Hirado and Nagasaki on Kyushu, the southernmost of Japan's larger islands.

The main contraband to Japan was silk, which fetched ten times the amount there that it did in China, and to a lesser extent other precious cargoes like wood and musk, along with more mundane merchandise such as sugar and iron pots and pans, which might also turn a good profit.[3] As these boats arrived home they unloaded not silvery fish but precious metal of the same hue.

Chinese smugglers also made it down the coast as far as the Gulf of Tonkin and Annam (Vietnam) and, more daringly and productively, as far as the Philippines, where the Spanish link to the Americas provided luxury contraband of chillies and tobacco and, more importantly, the new staple of sweet potatoes, which proved vital during famine years.

There were two main figures, both Fujianese, in the smuggling business in the South China Sea during the early and middle part of the seventeenth century: Li-Dan, known to the English in Japan as 'Captain China', and his protégé and successor Nicholas Iquan.

Captain China had prospered from legitimate trade in the Philippines but his career had taken a turn for the worse when he was enslaved to a Spanish galley for nine years. However, he escaped and found his true calling in a different type of chain gang, as leader of the Taiwan-Riyukuku-Hirado smugglers. He ran a clan operation, or brotherhood of traders. Although he spent more and more of his time in Japan his associates also resurrected his fortunes in Manila and Macao.

It was in Japan, though, that he really prospered. After an epoch of civil war the new shogunate of the victorious general Tokugawa Ieyasu attempted to close Japan to all foreigners – a challenge and motivation for would-be smugglers. However, the Matsuura family from the Nagasaki region, once pirates but now respectable landowners and traders, managed to keep the supply lines open and Li-Dan became the smuggling godfather of Hirado and Nagasaki, where all the foreigners now congregated. He circulated in formal society and was a frequent guest of Matsuura Takanobu, also doing business with the governor of Nagasaki. This schmoozing enabled his operation to function in a partially overt fashion, although he was not averse to deception: for instance, he duped the British by offering them potential trading opportunities in China, securing investment sums from them that would never go much farther than himself or that he knew would never yield any return. Li-Dan also teased the Dutch with the hope of trade privileges. But when they lost patience and blockaded Amoy, one of the main ports of Fujian, and flirted with the idea of strong-arm trading, he pretended to be an imperial government representative who was open to negotiation.

In fact Li-Dan was always a renegade and was treated as such by the Chinese themselves. Even the Japanese shogun, who had granted his organization trading rights in silks from Annam and the Gulf of Tonkin, was not dealt with in an entirely above-board manner. In a wider trading venture, instead of bothering to bring promised fine silks from the exotic lands in the west of China, Li-Dan simply loaded up with cheaper cloth in Fujian.

If Li-Dan was largely based in Kyushu, what was happening at the Chinese end of this now quite well-established smuggling run? One man continued the Fujian smuggling tide. The de facto rulers of coastal Fujian were the Zheng clan and the rising star among them was Zheng Zhilong, aka 'Lord of the Straits'. He also went by the name of Nicholas Iquan after he was baptized in Macao, expediently it seems, into the Catholic faith, giving him access to Western trading circles there.[4] He was Chinese by birth but Fujianese by culture and circulated among foreigners as much as with the bureaucrats of imperial China. Frequently abroad, Iquan was a sailor at heart and a natural smuggler who cultivated the kind of floating identity that works so well in the illicit trade. For instance, he was also known as a tailor, although perhaps this was just a nickname referring to his trafficking in lengths of silk.[5] Iquan had been one of Li-Dan's most trusted captains and an emissary and interpreter in dealings with the Dutch. He got on particularly well with the Dutch East India Company's representative in Hirado, Jack Specx, who would later become governor-general of the Dutch East Indies.

The straits that Iquan lorded it over were the stretch of water between the Zheng stronghold at Amoy on the mainland and Taiwan. He made a vast fortune, not least by emulating Li-Dan in playing one party off against another. But eventually events got too big for him, not in his dealings with the Dutch but through his misreading of the seismic changes that were pulling greater China apart and bringing the Ming dynasty to an end.

The grave threat to the Ming 'Emperor of Lofty Omens' was coming from two directions. The Manchu threatened to pour over the Great Wall and descend upon Beijing, although they were beaten to it by a rebellion from within. Imperial China had always been a heavily taxed domain. During the 1630s and '40s Li Zicheng, a one-eyed former postal rider, led an uprising of a 100,000 disaffected soldiers and peasants and proclaimed a tax-free future, eventually marching on and briefly taking Beijing and overthrowing the emperor, who committed suicide. Li declared himself the founder of a new dynasty. It lasted about a month before he was ousted by the rampant Manchu hordes.

The Lord of the Straits played a typical double game as master of the Chinese coastal seas, blurring his roles as appointed admiral and pirate chaser as well as pirate and smuggler himself. It worked well for him offshore but inland it led to his downfall. His identity-shifting meant that the last Ming heir made a fatal miscalculation: he put his trust in Iquan as his ultimate hope for survival as the Manchu hordes raced across China from the north. With this emperor deposed, it was not long before Iquan defected to the Manchu. He lived in Beijing as their 'guest' for several more years before they decided to use him as a hostage to secure the surrender of his famous son, the rebel and Ming loyalist Zheng Chenggong, known to all around the South China Sea as Coxinga. However this illustrious and proud rebel, who got the better of the Dutch on several occasions but struggled against the new regime, would have none of it and ignored his father's predicament: Nicholas Iquan was sentenced to death by a thousand cuts. Sometimes smugglers, like pirates, lived and died by the sword.

Smuggling of course continued in the region, more often than not without dominant or illustrious figureheads. Two thousand miles to the southeast, in the Spice Islands, things had not gone the way of the

English. They retreated from the islands and this, in the long run, was hugely significant because the English (not yet British) Honourable East India Company instead turned its attention to India, trading spices out of Surat, its new Asian headquarters on the northwest coast near to Gujarat, superseding its commercial station at Bantam in Java. Britain shifted its focus from spices to silk and saltpetre, the latter of which was important in the manufacture of gunpowder. Its ambitious rising men of empire were thinking of the struggle ahead and what might make it the dominant power in Asia.

The seventeenth century was the Dutch century so far as trade goes. Why then do we not think of the Dutch as master colonialists in the same way as we do the British and French? Why did Dutch mercantilism fail to endure? The answer is relatively straightforward: during the eighteenth century spices became less important and the Dutch spice estates were mismanaged, neglected and fell into decline. In a more general and perhaps unavoidable way their monopoly was doomed from the start: the historian James Mill and the economist David Ricardo both argued later on that, because of smuggling, protectionism was bound to fail.

In the 1790s the Dutch finally gave up their monopoly.

THREE

SEA OF CONTRABAND

The Caribbean and the
'River of Silver'

The Spanish Caribbean could be every bit as brutal as the Dutch Banda. In 1603 the English contrabanding ship *Mary* was taken into the port of Manzanillo in Cuba, whereupon its master was stripped bare and tied to a tree before being dismembered – nose first, ears next, then decapitation. His body was thrown into the river and his head was impaled upon a pole in nearby Bayamo. Three years later Sancho de Alquiza, governor of Caracas, made an example of the captain and eleven crew of a Dutch contrabander that had put ashore and repeated the deterrent in 1608, executing the captain and mate of that smuggling vessel in full view of its cowering crew.[1]

Smuggling was a dangerous business and the Spanish were heartless persecutors of the daring English, Dutch and French contrabanders – so the story goes. And yet many Latin Americans loved and relied upon the contraband trade. In other times smugglers were able to beach their ships in Manzanillo. They played bowls, set up shops and even had a guard house. The general pattern was of a gentle tide of smuggling that ebbed and flowed for some years before gently surging into a sea of contraband. How then, given the enthusiasm for reprisal coming out of Seville, did the Caribbean slowly become such a pleasure pond for the informal trade?

The story runs from salt through tobacco to silver; from smuggling on a regional scale to a massive infusion of contraband silver that for the first time, although not the last, made smuggling a global phenomenon. Salt brought the Dutch to the north coast of South America and they lingered there, becoming the first to establish smuggling in that region as something other than a quasi-raiding operation. Tobacco was the main cash crop of small renegade Spanish communities on the edge of the New World Empire, and it primarily fed into the illicit trade. Smuggled silver changed the world.

Dutch Salt Smugglers

We now consider salt one of the least precious foodstuffs but in the seventeenth century it was still vital not only for improving the taste of food but for preserving meat and fish. The Dutch came in large numbers to the Caribbean out of desperation at the loss of their salt supplies in Europe. The Spanish had seized salt-laden shipping in 1595 and 1598 in order to hurt the Protestant north, which could no longer preserve herring, a staple of its diet. In this latter year some 500 Dutch ships were arrested plying the salt trade to Castile and Portugal, especially to and from Setúbal. Out of necessity the Dutch sought other supplies. First they went to the Cape Verde Islands but by 1600 they had found a more abundant supply of salt on the Araya Peninsula in what is now eastern Venezuela. Here there were many small Spanish and indigenous settlements (*rancherias*) offering not just water but contraband pearls, tobacco, sugar and hides. The activity grew from about fourteen vessels in 1595 to 50 in 1600, and then over 100 per annum until 1605, when the Spanish cracked down on it.[2]

It endured for this long partly because the shallow waters of the peninsula were perfectly suited to Dutch craft, and less so to the heavy gun-laden Spanish ships that were supposed to enforce the commercial monopoly. The shallow-bottomed *vlie* boats used in the Zuider Zee had been taken to the Caribbean and there fed hulks (*urcas*) of up to 400 tons that raised the scale of salt export from small opportunism into an industry. Later the Dutch used the *fluyt*, a longer but still shallow-draught vessel. These were the *Vrijbuiters* – freebooters.

Although the Dutch were enforcers in East Asia, in and around the Americas they were enthusiastic smugglers. Out of necessity – the dearth of salt – came profitable trading opportunities and new territories. They set up bases on the islands of Curaçao and St Eustatius. Curaçao became particularly important because slaves were brought from here to New Granada in exchange for hides, tobacco, cacao and timber.

Behind all contrabanding operations at this time were private investors at home. These were wealthy individuals who were often linked to the state through patronage or the court. For the Dutch, in addition, there was a corporate mentality: trading profits were not simply squandered by individuals upon the return of an expedition but were frequently reinvested. This economy was often both licit and illicit: the wealth created through the licit trading of the Dutch between the Baltic and the Iberian Peninsula fed into the illicit trade at Spain's expense in the Americas.

The Dutch contrabanding mission soon shifted substantially beyond salt: 30,000 pounds of tobacco came out of Cumaná in 1603, and in 1606 some twenty Dutch ships took 200 tons of hides out of Cuba and Hispaniola valued at 800,000 florins.[3] Nor was it all one way; there was a crackdown by the Spanish between 1605 and 1611. In 1606 they engaged with a fleet of 31 smuggling vessels off Cuba that included 24 Dutch ships.[4] Generally, however, the tide was in favour of the transgressors.

Were the Dutch salt traders alone in almost literally rubbing salt into the wound of Spanish ineffectiveness at the edge of the empire? The answer is of course no: French and English contrabanding ships were also very active at this time.

Contrebandiers

For the French the licit–illicit trajectory was turned on its head: they needed raw contraband commodities from the Americas to supply their licit industries at home (although these too were initiated by illicit trade – Portuguese smugglers were bringing hides into French ports, which gave a shot in the arm to the Norman leather industry). With expansion, they required more hides which could only be supplied from South America, particularly Peru. In return they traded *ruanes*, fine linen from Rouen that could not be found in the uninspiring cargoes of the *flota* – the Spanish monopoly fleets supplying the mercantile and administrative elites of New Granada.

The French began in the same way as John Hawkins: the capital for exchange was slaves wrenched out of Africa by ruthless traders working for shipowning merchants with exotic names like Jehan le Caron, Sieur de Maupas and Guillaume le Héricy. They gravitated to Hispaniola quite early on and had similar levels of success and disappointment to the English. For instance, in 1593 a ship out of Caen captained by the seasoned campaigner De la Barbotière came to Mona, an islet just off Hispaniola, which it used as a stepping stone for trading for hides at Guanahibes and La Yaguana on the main island. But the vessel was wrecked off Bermuda on the way home. The smugglers persisted; later

Hispaniola in the late 16th century.

that year two ships from Dieppe traded off the Banda del Norte of Hispaniola for two months, and in 1594 two ships out of Le Havre, *Espérance* and *Princesse*, traded at Mona. They even collaborated with the old enemy, the English, at Manzanillo in 1604; such was the pragmatism associated with smuggling.[5]

The later French colonization of the western side of Hispaniola (now Haiti but then named Saint-Domingue) gave an added spur to the contraband trade because even at government level there was sympathy for the smugglers, and expedient measures were taken to safeguard the trade. A clemency for former smugglers was sanctioned because vigorous countermeasures would have harmed the fledgling local French economy. Also, Saint-Domingue unofficially competed with British Jamaica and Dutch Curaçao for pre-eminence in the smuggling stakes; if there was to be a black economy, better that French America keep it in-house. It was all becoming quite businesslike: on one expedition the ships *Triomphant*, *Gaspard* and *Duc de la Force* had already sold their contraband cargo to merchants in Veracruz in Mexico even before they had set sail.

Does this mean that smuggling in the Caribbean had become as much of a company enterprise as the illicit trade in spices? Not exactly. While in East Asia there were huge profits to be made by transporting moderate or even small cargoes of spices, in the Caribbean there was a different economy going on, one of scale. Profit could only be made through bulk trading, particularly as so much capital had to be laid out in advance on guns. Sometimes it was a choice of either piracy or whole-sale smuggling. In this equation, just as with the everyday informal trading today of alcohol, cigarettes, clothes and electrical goods on the Guajira Peninsula (described in more detail in the next chapter), the

golden rule of profitable smuggling of high value/low weight is con-
founded. But still, just as they do today, these operations took place
beside more violent economies.

English Contraband Business

Regarding English contrabanding around this time, there was a marked
difference to the sixteenth-century smugglers. While Drake and Hawkins
were minor aristocracy – ambitious courtier-explorers whose smuggling
operations were never wholly successful – the new breed in the seventeenth century were pragmatic merchants, more like the Dutch traders
of the VOC than the Elizabethans. They made their initial trading decisions
strategically, and only then had an eye for the off chance. For instance,
when the semi-licit trade in Europe to and from Spain became difficult
they cast their eye over the ocean to Spain's back door, South America.
Some exotic southern European products were only obtainable, by non-
Spanish people, in the Americas and, even after the great distances
covered and shipping costs incurred, when they came to the markets in
England they were still cheaper than in Spain itself.

Typical of these hard-nosed traders were the merchants John Eldred
and Richard Hall, who had watched enviously as the Genoese merchant
and smuggler Pompileo Cataneo, working with the English factor John
Williams, made his fortune from the Caribbean contraband trade. These
latter two operated officially out of London but unofficially out of
Hispaniola. One of Eldred's and Hall's expeditions saw the ships
Mayflower and *Neptune* along with the pinnaces *Richard* and *Dispatch*
in contrabanding action, with mixed success. The *Richard* was seized
off Monte Cristi on the Banda del Norte coast of Hispaniola in 1603
but the others were not deterred. The *Neptune* took two Spanish ships
heading for Havana and traded their goods for hides at Guanahibes.
This is a good example of the interaction of smuggling and piracy.
However, even if they could get away with it in this contraband milieu,
it wasn't always plain sailing at home, as it had been under Queen
Elizabeth: the goods were subsequently impounded in London at the
request of the Spanish ambassador, despite the investment in the expedition of Charles Howard, Earl of Nottingham and Lord High Admiral
of England between 1585 and 1619. Generally, though, the state turned
a blind eye and might even have used the smugglers to practise a kind
of gunboat diplomacy in the Caribbean in order to bring about greater

dialogue with Spain in Europe, perhaps also aiming to secure legitimate trading rights in the Americas.

As with the Dutch salt trade, some of the English contrabanders had an initial connection with Mediterranean trading, and with its intrigue. Robert Savage was a smuggler and business/political agent (spy) based in Lisbon who then graduated to the Caribbean. It was all about connections: Sir Robert Cecil was Savage's patron, proving that the Elizabethan connection was not entirely dead. His associate was a factor, William Resould, who sailed on a 1602 'trading' venture to the Caribbean. They were thinking big and profits meant everything; hence associations crossed class boundaries. A prominent member of the gang was Roger Myddelton who, with Resould, organized the transfer of hides onto his ship *Vineyard* in exchange for English goods.

In all some 40,000 contraband hides were shipped out of the Americas each year, equal to the amount allowed under the entire licensed quota for the 1580s.[6] This statistic is a little misleading, though, because the trade by now was almost entirely illicit. Even if many smugglers banked on the hide trade, they still often opportunistically sought the more profitable illicit tobacco trade out of eastern Venezuela active until 1605.

Romancing the Figures

So much for the numbers, but when we think of smuggling, don't we more often romanticize these dry statistics into a more colourful world of smuggling mythology? All of this pragmatism didn't hinder the mythologizing of the Main smugglers alongside the romance of piracy. No less a figure than Captain Kidd appears here. Of course the legend of his hidden treasure is his most abiding trace, but at least some of his plunder entered the informal economy when in 1699 he traded his ill-gotten gains with the smuggler Henry Bolton in Hispaniola, who in turn sold on the cloth obtained to merchants in Curaçao and St Thomas.

Two decades before this the romantic narrative of piracy – with a subtext of smuggling – had entered the popular imagination with the publication of Alexandre Olivier Exquemelin's fictional *De Americaensche Zee-roovers*, published in Amsterdam in 1678. When it was translated into English in 1684 its title could have left no one in doubt about its romantic import: *The Buccaneers and Marooners of America: Being an Account of the Famous and Daring Deeds of Certain Notorious Freebooters of the Spanish Main*. In the 1920s Rafael Sabatini used Exquemelin's book as a source for his Captain Blood books and *The Black Swan*, both made into films starring Errol Flynn and Tyrone Power respectively. The overlap of smuggling and piracy in Exquemelin's title is a theme that recurred right up until the nineteenth century. As Goethe put it: 'War, trade and piracy are one/Inseparable combination'.[7]

Nevertheless, for all the seaborne posturing of the English and French contrabanders/pirates, it was the shore-based smugglers who were most instrumental in feeding the growing Spanish need and appetite for both basic and luxury goods. The trade relied on the activities of two particular groups of people: desperate or greedy Spanish officials and, particularly around the Rio de la Plata, the enterprise of the so-called 'New Christians' – Jews – perceived by the Spanish authorities as inveterate smugglers. There was little room for romance when there were large profits to be made through the distribution of contraband silver – it had to be a commercial venture rather than an adventure.

Illicit Tobacco

If some smugglers were cast in a romantic light, while others appeared more businesslike, then the tobacco smugglers of the eastern Main were simply desperate, and needed to trade in this contraband to survive. It was a commodity which, for all its exoticism in those early years, often came out of settlements that were marginalized and quite abject. Local officials were often sympathetic to illicit economies beside their outposts on the fringes of the empire. The small-scale growing of tobacco for the contraband trade is a case in point, and it shifted ever further to the margins as the *Audiencia*, the high court of a particular region, applied pressure to stop smuggling.

Growing tobacco was banned in eastern Venezuela and on the island of Margarita. The regional governor, Pedro Suarez Coronel, ordered the depopulation of Cumaná on the mainland, but the problem simply shifted sideways and tobacco smuggling took root around the Orinoco river delta, particularly around San Tomé. It was a less sensitive problem here because the *rescates* were small enough to be tolerated, and the more profitable pearls and hides were no longer so readily available. *Cabildos*, town councils, were often complicit because *alcaldes* (mayors) were sometimes the biggest smugglers in the community.

Tobacco growing also migrated to the 'wild coast,' Guiana, where *gente perdida*, lost people (more officially known as *rescatadores*), continued its cultivation. But it was the transfer of cultivation to Trinidad that is more significant, particularly in the context of smuggling at the forefront of larger political and economic developments. Smuggling of tobacco was that intermediate moment between protectionism and plantation cultivation for a free-market economy. The renegade communities in Venezuela, Guiana, Isla Margarita and Trinidad resisted plantation organization because it would have meant the end of smuggling. Nevertheless, through its survival as a cash crop in the face of imperial eradication policies, it did prepare the ground for the plantation economy when it eventually shifted to St Kitts and Barbados, and that move would change the Caribbean forever.

Illicit tobacco cultivation in Trinidad provided a precarious bridge in this transplantation trajectory. Don Fernando Berrio, a veteran of numerous searches for El Dorado, eventually settled on tobacco as his gold. He ran the island trade using cultivators from banned areas. The English took 100,000 pounds as contraband to satisfy their new taste.[8] The boom years of this smuggling community ran parallel to the Dutch salt enterprise, 1605–12, and peaked in the final two years. Berrio was ordered to stamp out the trade but, as he was so heavily involved, he executed a callous policy of attacking a few smugglers while continuing to trade with many others. He was eventually removed in 1612.

The sacking of Berrio came at the end of a concerted campaign to control smuggling. In 1603 a *cédula* decreed that the Hispaniola towns of Puerto de Plata, Bayahá and La Yaguana be depopulated. In 1605 the brutal captain general of Santo Domingo, Osorio, in response to the presence of Dutch warships offshore, burned down Guanahibes. But other smuggling interests were defended, for instance when the *oidor* (*Audiencia* judge) Manso de Contreras in Bayamo (Cuba) took the side of some of the renegade communities who had resettled here from Hispaniola. He was a *criollo* (colonist born in South America), unlike Osorio, a pure-bred Spaniard, and he had covert investments in Santo Domingo (eastern Hispaniola), Margarita, Riohacha and Santa Marta. Manso pretended to toe the line but when Suarez de Poaga, envoy of Pedro de Valdés, Captain General of Cuba, arrived in Bayamo and sentenced 80 people to death for involvement in contrabanding they simply didn't show up for the appointment with the noose.

In Hispaniola the depopulation policy was counter-productive because such heavy-handedness simply radicalized the remaining die-hard smugglers into buccaneers a few years down the line. The slow tidal surge of smuggling activity in the Caribbean as the seventeenth century wore on did not persuade the Spanish to relax their restrictive mercantile strategy: in 1631, for instance, all intercolonial trade in the Caribbean was banned. Later, by no coincidence and almost concurrently with Exquemelin's *De Americaensche Zee-roovers*, José Veitia Linaje published *The Spanish Rule of Trade to the West Indies Containing an Account of the Casa de Contratacion, or India House* (1672, translated into English in 1688), described as a fearsome 'monopolite bible'. This handbook, the antithesis of the romantic narrative, detailed the definitive *almojarifazgo* – customs duties.

Silver

If illicit tobacco was a small but significant factor in the move towards a free market in the Caribbean, then the flood of contraband silver that escaped the monopolist's treasury changed the world.

Silver became significant as a global commodity after Bartolomeo de Medina discovered that mercury could separate silver from its ore through a process of amalgamation (it dissolves into the quicksilver, which runs off and then evaporates on heating, leaving the precious metal). It was put into industrial production around 1571. Productivity multiplied by a factor of ten. The massive silver mountain at Potosí in Bolivia became the fabled source of the kind of wealth previously only ever imagined in the form of an El Dorado. It seemed that the Spanish Empire was secured. But, as with the Dutch spice monopoly in the East Indies, contraband seepage began almost immediately.

Demand for silver around the world had been growing apace. The Dutch, English, French and Portuguese needed it to finance their East Asian imperial ambitions, and it was a universal currency. It was still important during the nineteenth century: the Spanish dollar, or 'piece of eight' (called such because it was worth eight *reales*), became the most reliable currency during the time of the Napoleonic Wars, as it did in Canton, the centre for smuggled opium during the late eighteenth century and the nineteenth.

It was a network of Portuguese, Dutch and acquiescent Jewish merchants who really stimulated circulation. As early as 1558 the Portuguese, who were officially outside the monopoly, were bringing silver from the Americas. Mexican silver from Venezuela began to line Dutch pockets. But it actually wasn't the Caribbean route that was most significant.

The official route was from Potosí down the mountains to the Pacific, up to Panama and across the isthmus, and then by treasure fleet back to Spain. The main illicit flow was from Potosí to Brazil along the Rio de la Plata, the river of silver. Argentina, co-guardian of the river opposite Uruguay, takes its name from the Latin word *argentum* meaning silver. The Portuguese generally traded with Potosí via Brazil, often exchanging the tools and other operating merchandise that they got from the Dutch along the way.

The English share in the silver bonanza was more of a Caribbean than a southern New World venture. They traded slaves and manufactured goods in return for silver to lubricate budding colonial enterprises. At the end of the seventeenth century £200,000 came through Jamaica, much of it handled by the East India Company which, through all its sources, managed to send £400,000 annually to East Asia.[9] The Dutch East India Company did the same.

France was also instrumental in the dispersal of silver wealth. One of the best ways to get silver into the French economy, under the table, was via the French Caribbean Islands. But France also obtained it in Europe: Spain, although protectionist and insular by nature, had to trade with France for wheat and sail canvas. Paris and Rouen became repositories of officially and illicitly leaked coin. Spain could not prevent its silver from becoming world capital – it needed imports and could only pay in coin.

So what was the global significance of smuggled silver and what overall quantities are we talking about? Up to a quarter of all Potosí silver seeped out of official channels during the seventeenth century,[10] but the situation was actually even worse. Even before the seventeenth century, taking into account all manner of leaks of official silver, economic catastrophe was knocking at Spain's gilded door. In 1597 more than 660,000 pounds of contraband silver headed for India and China, out of Acapulco via Manila.[11] It surpassed by some margin the amount of legal silver entering Seville. During the sixteenth century perhaps three-quarters of all American silver was distributed beyond Spain, around Europe and to Asia, devastating its balance of payments but creating the world's first global economy. Although economic decline was slowed by the influx of silver, both licit and illicit, into the Pacific Spanish Empire from the Tokugawa shogunate of Japan (easing pressure on its American silver supply), it is not going too far to suggest that smuggled silver, even as early as the sixteenth century, was the beginning of the descent of the Empire.

Spanish Smuggling

Spanish colonists themselves were rarely victims of contrabanding but rather intricately bound up in it. Spanish–Dutch hostilities after 1621 were a fillip for the trade. War tended to accelerate local trade, raising prices of scarce goods, and this is where island entrepôts really came into their own because they were the intersection for locally organized small-boat smuggling and larger illicit shipments back to Europe. There was also a shift in demand. As the empire frayed at the edges and eventually pulled apart there was a baroque penchant for luxury – not just Churrigueresque churches but contraband fashions and furnishings.

How had smuggling that had grown out of scarcity and demand at the peripheries spread to the heart of the empire? Well, it had always been there to some degree. As exemplified in tobacco, small illicit trade on the Brazilian, Caribbean and North American coasts brought into being entirely new renegade societies, a bit like the Fujian coast of China that was so profitable for Nicholas Iquan and Captain China in defiance of the Ming. But there was already something going on more centrally that was not entirely compliant with the Casa de Contratación in Seville. Strong towns often had a weak, informal counterpart nearby such as Baru near Cartagena de las Indias (Colombia) and El Garote near Portobelo (Panama). Even these great fortified centres of the empire were not entirely isolated from the wildness around them. They must have felt some trepidation as the secondary cities of the Main were assailed by privateers and pirates. One only has to look at the Colombian coast between 1655 and 1667 to sense the foreboding: Riohacha was plundered five times, Santa Marta three and Tolú eight.[12] There were, then, peripheral wild stretches of coastline but in another sense the entire Spanish Main was a savage shore.

Why were Spanish colonists at the peripheries so defiant towards their superiors at the centre? Perhaps it was because although officials were indicted for smuggling, and sometimes lost their jobs, they rarely went to jail. There was neither the will nor the means to prevent illicit circulations given that these turbulent events produced not just scarcity but opportunity. Contraband even entered official carriers: *rescatadores* in Havana and Santo Domingo sold contraband to freelance Spanish merchants who mixed it with the official cargoes of the *flota* for redistribution around the Main. The trade into and out of entrepôts such as St Eustatius and Curaçao involved big ships linking up with smaller shuttling schooners to relay the contraband towards the official heart of the Spanish Empire. But it wasn't simply a capillary influx: the aorta of the empire, the *flota*, had been infiltrated through the short-sighted policy of the Casa de Contratación. *Flota* merchants had to bear the costs of convoys, and the costs of any contraband seepage from these convoys had to be picked up by these merchants. To make up for their loss they turned to smuggling themselves, which in turn raised the costs of the official goods, leading to more smuggling – a vicious cycle.

The permeability of the monopoly can also be seen in the toleration of foreign go-betweens. The Portuguese were active in a semi-approved capacity at the heart of the Spanish Empire, out of Cartagena, Mexico City, Lima, Potosí and Buenos Aires. From the late sixteenth century onwards the Dutch began to take over from the Portuguese as the preferred go-betweens in the shipping of illicit goods in and out of the Spanish Americas, as did the British later on in Brazil. These Dutch *metedores*, or runners, operated openly and, though looked down upon as outsiders, they had a presence at Cádiz, the new operating headquarters of empire, and were showy participants in society circles there.

The Trade in Illicit Luxury

It was the bountiful display of contraband, something counter-intuitive to smuggling logic, that now appeared at the heart of the Spanish Empire, and it largely came from the east.

Perhaps it was a statement of independence from Seville, or a sign of softening lifestyles in some strata of society after the hard years of conquest, but whatever the reason, homes and bodies began to take on an Orientalist look. In 1573 came the first imports of Chinese silks, satins, porcelain and spices into Acapulco from the Philippines. There were limitations: twenty years later Chinese goods were still only legally allowed to arrive at New Spain (Mexico and Central America excepting Panama) and this on only two ships of 300 tons. But this was a King Canute moment: as the Viceroy of Peru, the Marqués de Cañete (1590–96), had warned, no ban on Chinese goods would work. In 1593, in what seemed to be a recent trend, Spanish goods were not popular and, although there was no *flota* that year, there were still many unsellable Spanish goods in the shops. Peruvian merchants were soon taking Chinese cloth for resale to Lima, where it was ten times cheaper than the Spanish equivalent. The monopoly had little chance given that everybody seemed to want their slice of the pie. Port officials, the *Audiencia* of Mexico, even viceroys, were complicit in smuggling goods between Mexico and Lima, often via Nicaragua. Sometimes covert exchanges were made at sea. At other times it wasn't necessary: inquisition cargoes were, for instance, immune from searches. The clergy presented a particular problem and although in 1615 they were urged to desist from smuggling, what went on behind their holy aura was much more profane. The Portuguese Jesuits led the way and Spanish clergy were not far behind: Fray Alonso de Guzmán, for instance, was a prominent *contrabandista* in Baracoa (western Cuba).

A SURGE IN SMUGGLING in the Caribbean had come partly out of necessity: it drove the tobacco trade on the Wild Coast and launched Dutch contrabanding with their need for salt. This was a need not just for Dutch freelancers but for the Dutch state: a link between smuggling and state activity is therefore in evidence here. Furthermore, commodity acquisition, even if illicit, translated into power and influence, sometimes through its conspicuous consumption. Smuggling was beginning to become big business. Illicit silver dispersal is an even bigger story: it created the makings of a global economic system.

So to what extent did the Caribbean eventually become a sea of contraband? The figures are pretty straightforward. Between 1599 and 1606 there had been an acceleration in smuggling.[13] By 1619 contraband exceeded the official America trade in volume.[14] Towards the end of Philip IV's reign, by the 1660s, contrabanding had become the rule rather than the exception.[15] More contraband circulated around the Caribbean than official goods right up until the middle of the eighteenth century. By this time the sea of contraband was framed by another smuggling phenomenon: the territory of Bourbon America was hopelessly infiltrated at all levels and society looked both westwards and eastwards for its contraband fix.

A taste for contraband was sweeping across the world.

FOUR

A Smuggling Desert

The Spanish Main Today

In December 1686 William Dampier, explorer, naturalist, writer and pirate, found himself wallowing in Mindanao, one of the islands of the Philippines, doubting the resolve of his captain, the pirate Swan, and many of the crew. Their ship, *Cygnet*, careened and refreshed, just couldn't quite get away, such was the exotic hospitality of Raja Laut. Dampier was impatient. He had stories to tell aplenty but little in the way of material fortune to show for his years of part-time piracy and occasional smuggling. His thoughts sailed into traditional channels: perhaps his captain was lingering here in the hope of loading up with a cargo from the Spice Islands to finally make them all men of worth back in the Old World. It never happened. Mindanao itself was ideal for nutmeg cultivation but they feared Dutch reprisals if they began trading. Instead Dampier pondered over the possibilities of smuggling cheap goods to the Spanish Philippines islands. It might have been the Caribbean 100 years before.

A weary Dampier eyed up petty smuggling possibilities on a journey of escape and promise. It is a familiar story. Drake and Hawkins seek their fortune through piracy, dreaming of Spanish gold, but must make do with the steady but much smaller profits of contrabanding. The romance of smuggling for them, and us perhaps, shimmers elusively like a barely discernible ship on the horizon. It is not so much that the reality of smuggling is much more everyday, which often it is, but rather that what makes it fascinating to us is often illusory and complex: it is at once incredible and ordinary. Take the example of contemporary smuggling on the Guajira Peninsula in Colombia that Drake and Hawkins sighted during the 1560s and identified as potential contrabanding lands. Its smuggling activities have gone on for centuries, at certain times highly visible, at others invisible and, bizarrely, sometimes both together. The illicit trade here is often mundane and conducted in a low-key, businesslike way but it also has a carnivalesque, excessive quality to it. One wouldn't quite call this contradiction magical-realist but it is certainly strange.

Literary Landings on the Guajira Peninsula

In his short story 'Death Constant Beyond Love', the Colombian novelist Gabriel García Márquez describes the sea off the 'illusory' Guajira village of Rosa del Virrey, a smuggler port, as 'arid and without direction'.[1] Puerto Lopez, on this same coast, is real but no less illusory. It is a little washed-out and a natural response is listlessness: shouldn't the sea here be *the* Caribbean, the sea of Drake and Hawkins, Menéndez, or even, in fiction, of Captain Jack Sparrow; the romantic Caribbean that draws us for winter holidays? As one stands on the jetty searching for that image, one can't help but feel a sense of abandonment.

Puerto Lopez, also called Tucacas, is one of a string of tiny ports that must have seen better days on the northeastern shore of this semi-desert peninsula. It is a desolate place, largely ceded back to the desert after its waters sedimented up, rendering it commercially unviable. There is a similar story in the nearby ports of Inglés and Estrella. It is a little puzzling that this shoreline seems so abject: the peninsula is famously where Henri Charrière, 'Papillon', found a beach paradise, a sanctuary among the virgin pearl-diving nymphs of the Wayuu tribe, as he fled from the hell of incarceration in a French penal colony.

Puerto Lopez also, strangely, makes its mark far away up in the mountains in the capital, Bogotá, where in a commercial district a few miles west of the centre a warehouse proudly displays the sign 'Comercio Puerto Lopez'. This reference, on a faceless building, doesn't exactly shout out 'smuggling' but it surely cannot be a coincidence that the building is part of a San Andrésito, one of the smuggler markets that are to be found in all the main cities of Colombia.

Here though, on the northeastern shore of the peninsula, there is little commerce, informal or otherwise, and none at Tucacas. In vainly looking for smuggling activity in these little settlements it is easy to wilt into the kind of ennui that weighs heavily on Rosa del Virrey, about which, García Márquez goes on to say: 'no one would have suspected that someone capable of changing the destiny of anyone lived there.'[2] But Puerto Estrella, Lopez's neighbour, did leave its mark on one stranger.

The Guajira Peninsula.

In 1962 a somewhat melancholy Hunter S. Thompson landed quietly here on a smuggler boat from Aruba and wrote home about his first impressions, recounted in *The Fear and Loathing Letters* and in an article, 'A Footloose American in a Smugglers' Den'. He is to the point: 'Usually they are talking about smuggling . . . there are no immigration officials and no customs. There is no law at all, in fact, which is precisely why Puerto Estrella is such an important port.'[3] He has immediate experience of the contraband, mainly whisky, tobacco and jewellery, and for a while it detains him because his Wayuu hosts, whom he fears at first, introduce him to South America by way of a three-day-long drinking binge.

Thompson lands in the midst of smuggling, by way of it, but it doesn't seem to be any kind of a big deal. However, this low-key appearance of smuggling is in itself illusory because smuggling in the Guajira, although today idiosyncratic in character and appearance, is also extensive and steeped in history. Smuggling has taken place on the peninsula for nearly 500 years. Just over the horizon are the free ports of the Dutch Antilles, which provide contraband goods of all manner and description, and further still are the more luxurious Caribbean islands that are the staging posts in the travels of cocaine to the American market.

Drift and Opportunity

Let me give two examples of this seaward gaze and its telescoping extent. The first is a personal encounter and the second an extraordinary true story of disaster at sea that García Márquez recounts in one of his earliest writings, a piece of journalism retelling what he called 'The Story of a Shipwrecked Sailor'.

When I was staying at Punta Gallinas, the northernmost point of South America, in December 2002, the eldest daughter of the large family that were hosting me at their isolated, fortified homestead (fortified against the wind as much as intruders), a young girl of about fourteen years old, related the following. A few years back, an American sailing yacht was shipwrecked and abandoned just down the coast from the point. Guajiros salvaged what they could of the contents. The girl's father had worked in Aruba some years back and had told her about its luxury and allure. Her dream was one day to go to Aruba but for now she lived it out through a battered copy of *Reader's Digest* that, as she showed me, had pictures – mainly advertisements for tourist resorts – of the island. The magazine had come from the shipwrecked yacht. Contraband has similarly washed up in this fashion, and affected virtually everybody's lives on the peninsula.

'The Story of a Shipwrecked Sailor' is a true story about a Colombian Navy warship that sets out from Mobile in the United States to sail home to Cartagena on the north coast of Colombia. En route eight men are lost, supposedly swept overboard in a storm two hours before arrival. After an epic battle for survival in an open raft the sole survivor, Luis Alejandro Velasco, makes landfall and his testimony is told, first to the authorities and then to Gabriel García Márquez (at that time, in 1955, a young journalist at the national newspaper *El Espectador*). Fifteen years later a book is published – the story retold by García Márquez. The scandal of the tale lies in Velasco revealing that the ship was carrying contraband goods on its deck – radios, refrigerators, washing machines and stoves – and that the men are lost only because the cargo, piled openly on the deck, becomes loose in a squall and they are despatched to the deck to secure it.

The Guajira is a smuggler territory that ships in and transfers out those most dangerous of contrabands, guns and drugs, but it is also the site where, so to speak, those loose radios, washing machines and refrigerators wash up on shore. We know all about the cocaine, taken up to

Florida and the Eastern Seaboard of the United States via various cays, the Bahamas and other islands. But what of the pots and pans, clothes, tobacco and electrical goods that came out of free ports at Colón as well as the old Dutch colonies of Curaçao, Bonaire and Aruba and come *into* Colombia? It is in the smuggling of these items, alongside dangerous contraband, that the Caribbean can still be imagined as a smugglers' sea, as it was in the days of the Spanish Main.

Mapping out New Contraband Flows

At the Atlantic end of the Panama Canal sits the town of Colón, named after Columbus (Cristóbal Colón is the Spanish spelling of his name). But if the canal is Panama's great contribution to formal trade, then Colón is the sugar daddy of informal trade, because situated here is one of Latin America's largest free markets pouring goods of all description into what, in the previous chapter, I called a 'sea of contraband' (referring to the gradual growth of smuggling in the Caribbean during the seventeenth century and after). From its inception, the Colón market, along with those on the Dutch islands, has provided untaxed goods for the Guajira Peninsula.

The more recent contrabanding ports to the west of Puertos Inglés, Estrella and Lopez are called Puerto Portete and Puerto Nuevo, and were built to accommodate the arrival of more and bigger ships. Gangs of hired labour, mainly indigenous Wayuu, unloaded cargoes onto purpose-built quays – *muelle artesanal* – on this desert shore and loaded up trucks. The contraband was mostly cigarettes, liquor, clothes and electronic goods that were then driven some 100 kilometres across the desert to the contraband capital of Colombia, the regional town of Maicao. Here the goods were 'legalized' – given documentation – and some of it was taxed at a minimum rate found nowhere else in Colombia. At that moment this 'public secret' of contrabanding on the peninsula was given an official stamp.

Some of the goods were distributed locally, particularly to the Department capital Riohacha, and the rest went to the aforementioned semi-official but very established modern mall-like markets in the big cities around Colombia called 'San Andrésitos' (named after the old pirate island San Andrés that during the 1980s and '90s was a favourite cocaine staging post and money-laundering spot). The warehouse in Bogotá that bears the name 'Comercio Puerto Lopez' is probably called

'Unloading contraband, Puerto Portete, Guajira Peninsula, Colombia', from the author's film *Contraband Desert* (2005).

that because for many years Lopez was an 'important', to use Hunter S. Thompson's adjective, landing point. We begin to see here the makings of an imaginative geography of the contemporary smuggling Main, and the Guajira Peninsula is at the heart of it.

The Topography of a Smuggling Territory

Guajira is *the* contraband state in a land stereotyped as being a smuggler country and little else. One might be forgiven for thinking that contraband has been the only industry of the Guajira Peninsula but in recent times it has steadily churned away beside the region's other big industry, coal. This has also relied on its proximity to the Caribbean, whose currents sweep past the Main, up to North America and around towards Europe. The coal is still mined relatively cheaply and is mainly for export. The peninsula's port, Puerto Bolívar, is actually not far from the *contrabandista* ports out of which much cocaine goes, a decade ago often on those very ships that brought in the hi-fis and cigarettes. The cocaine would go out alongside substantial sums of dollars to be laundered through the purchase of more tax-free goods. Import-export, black- and white-market,

'Smuggling ships at anchor, Puerto Portete, Guajira Peninsula, Colombia', from the author's film *Contraband Desert* (2005).

industries *oficial* and *extra-oficial*. It was a bit like the board game 'Risk' with its mobilizations of resources, infrastructure and competing forces.

The board game might look something like this: the state is inscribed on the landscape through coal and salt extractions. El Cerrejón is a huge opencast coalmine in southern, or Baja (lower), Guajira. It is linked to a large deepwater port in northwestern, or Media (middle), Guajira by a dead straight railway line. To the west of the railway, some 20 kilometres distant at its nearest point, still in Media Guajira and on a coastline where the waters are *seco* (shallow: literally 'dry' in Spanish) and smuggling has diminished as the draught of boats has become deeper and as loads have got bigger, is the port of Manaure and its centuries-old *salinas* or salt-extraction reservoirs. A great 'S' at the gate marks the warehouses and offices of the state concession. Largely publicly owned, the operation stretches for miles to the south but is most striking near the town, where the salt is gathered and poured onto permanent 50-foot-high white mountains that are visible for miles around, and replenished from a giant conveyor-belt crane as fast as workers bag it up and load it onto trucks.

Salt is now no longer contraband. Most smuggling takes place to the east of the railway line and the coal port Bolívar, just along the north coast (named after Colombia and South America's independence-era hero Simón Bolívar). We are now in Alta (upper) Guajira, where the waters are *profundo* and where the bays have names like 'Bahia Honda', also meaning deep, and 'Bahia Hondita'. The state presence is notional and there are no officially sanctioned industries with their machineries and piles of mined produce serving as markers of legitimate presence. Smuggling too has often been open-cast, nothing hidden.

Running into the twenty-first century, the modus vivendi between interests on either side of the law seemed to be quite comfortable. Then in 2004 the kind of violence that surrounds modern smuggling ruptured this calm. On 18 April right-wing paramilitaries carried out a massacre in villages around Bahía Portete, killing twelve people and 'disappearing' another 35. This was in revenge for the theft of a large amount of cocaine that was being stored near the port awaiting shipment out by a gang, Cono Conitos, linked to Wayuu clans. As a consequence the area, including the port of Portete, was entirely abandoned by the Wayuu labourers. The paramilitaries have now officially disbanded but in reality they have morphed into more cast-iron criminal groups who are mainly interested in high-end contraband such as drugs and weapons.

Is this the end of the story for smugglers of household goods, lifestyle accessories and luxury consumables?

No Such Thing as Smuggling Here

Smuggling, having been a part of so many people's everyday lives for so long, won't just go away. It is unlikely, after 500 years of activity, that this is the end of low-end smuggling in Guajira. In any case it is difficult to dissociate it from more violent trading in narcotics and guns. For some years now there has also been a boom in the illegal importation of petrol from Venezuela: smuggling of everyday goods remains deeply ingrained in the public consciousness.

But can there be any remaining illusion about smuggling in such a violent and apparently culturally arid place? Surprisingly a sort of romanticism and pragmatism have always gone hand in hand in Guajira. A certain enchantment has always persisted despite the violence. Smuggling has led a charmed as well as abject life and so probably this will be just another temporary lull.

If we go back to García Márquez we can see something of this translucent image beside opaque reality. The paradoxically strange and everyday smuggler peninsula has more than once attracted his eye. He wrote about the mirage-like trade in several of his short stories, including 'The Incredible and Sad Tale of Innocent Eréndira and her Heartless

Grandmother' (later made into a film in 1983); 'Blacamán the Good, Vendor of Miracles'; 'Death Constant Beyond Love'; and 'The Last Voyage of the Ghost Ship'.

One of the first contradictions that he presents is an oscillating visibility. Smuggling was so evident at Puertos Portete and Nuevo that it was reported on Colombian (RCN) television. García Márquez, on the other hand, in *Innocent Eréndira* dramatizes its absence through the voice of a truck driver giving the girl Eréndira and her grandmother a lift: 'There's no such thing as smugglers . . . Everybody talks about them, but no one's ever seen one.'[4] On cue, the real extent of smuggling is dramatically exposed as Eréndira finds a contraband pearl necklace in a rice sack and pulls it out even as the driver is speaking.

Smuggling is everywhere in these García Márquez stories, if not on the roads then always nearby. Oranges grow on trees from diamond seeds and are transported across the peninsula by Dutch immigrants from Aruba to an unspecified border, doubly hidden in a lorry of caged birds. In the story 'The Last Voyage of the Ghost Ship' we encounter schooners of smugglers from the Guyanas loading up with cargoes of parrots, their claws beaded with diamonds.

In another exchange smuggling's visibility is deplored. It comes in an encounter between a policeman (seeking information on another matter) and a passing *contrabandista* in his laden truck who asserts that they are smugglers, not 'stool pigeons', to which the former replies: 'At least . . . you could have the decency not to go around in broad daylight.'[5]

I myself encountered this ambiguous relationship with smuggling when talking with an old salt worker in Manaure who claimed that 'there is no smuggling.' It is not that he was denying the existence of the contraband ports, the convoys of goods across the desert, or the smuggler markets, but rather he was indicating that it has been such a way of life, and so visible, that it has become legitimatized. This is reinforced by the 'legalization' of the goods in small market kiosks in Maicao, the regional entrepôt, where false papers are issued for a small sum – a tax.

Larger-than-life Smugglers

It is perhaps not so surprising, then, given this self-deception, that García Márquez can take an inherently strange situation one step further into the realm of magical realism. But in assessing smuggling's profile in

Guajira, need we even bother with magical realism when confronted with its colourful profiles in collective consciousness, a very real presence? Smuggling certainly adds some spice to everyday life here, and in certain people and places it looms pretty large.

Take the case of the man dubbed by the Colombian press 'the Marlboro Man'. Samuel Santander Lopesierra dealt in huge shipments of contraband cigarettes to Guajira, which he purchased duty-free through business associates in the Dutch Antilles from markets where, allegedly, the tobacco companies Philip Morris, manufacturers of Marlboro, and British American Tobacco were dumping cheap cigarettes (knowing full well, it was implied, that they would be smuggled to South America). He was featured smiling on the cover of the Colombian magazine *Cambio* in May 2003 as he was extradited to the United States on a DEA plane wearing a red-and-white tracksuit and baseball cap, both emblazoned with the name and brand 'Marlboro'. Lopesierra's public face was as an elected senator to the Colombian congress but according to *Cambio* he had a much darker side and was implicated in the narco financing of the successful presidential campaign of Ernesto Samper in 1994 (through his associates the Aruba-based Manzur clan, who supplied his cigarettes both there and in Curaçao, and paid $550,000 to the campaign to protect their business). He was also linked to the assassination of rival politician and lawyer Álvaro Gómez Hurtado as part of the cover-up for that act of bribery.

Other figures shimmer in the haze like ghosts. Several American dope smugglers slipped in and out of Guajira when Santa Marta Gold was considered among the best marijuana on the planet and fetched a high price stateside during the 1970s. One of these adventurers, Allen Long, as described in Robert Sabbag's book *Smokescreen*, crashed his plane in Guajira after loading up too many bales and failing to clear the trees. In front of the terminal at the small airport in Riohacha, the capital of Guajira, there is a line of twisted light aircraft looking like an alternative art installation (or a sick joke on those fearful of flying), effectively a warning to smugglers. People living in the small village of Camarones some 10 kilometres or so to the west of Riohacha still talk about a plane crashing into the flamingo lagoon there and the pilot disappearing. Nobody will say whether he died or not but these coastal lowlands of Guajira are not so different from the drifting sands of García Márquez's 'Blacamán the Good', the milieu for listless characters who sold 'escape suppositories that turned smugglers transparent'.[6]

Wrecked aircraft at Riohacha Airport.

Cultures of Smuggling

Marijuana made fortunes for some foreigners, and it also created a veneer
of prosperity along the Caribbean coast of Colombia. The *bonanza
marimbera*, or marijuana-smuggling boom, which ran from 1974 until
the early 1980s, generated a new socio-economic class, mainly from
cachacos (émigrés from the interior of Colombia). The big money men
remained invisible but the middle-ranking organizers of shipments were
highly visible in coastal towns such as Baranquilla, Santa Marta and
Riohacha. The last, actually on the peninsula (although not in the Alta,
upper, more remote part), features as a scenario for machination in the
1990s telenovela *La Guajira*. In this soap opera it is *marimberos* who,
from their marble mansion on the beachfront, fulfil the role of mediators
between the exaggeratedly foreign *civilizados* from the capital Bogotá
and the Wayuu. This new entrepreneurial group, barely 35 years in existence, has quickly come to represent the local mythology of smuggling
on the peninsula, and it is quite visible.

In the drama, mules have been replaced by SUVs that are almost
always driven at speed, and automatic weapons are carried by young
gangsters guarding mansion compounds. Is this true to life? Colombian
journalist José Cervantes Angulo thought so in his book *La noche de las
luciérnagas* (The Night of the Fireflies). He has written not just about
the *pistas clandestinas* (secret tracks) and *embarcaderas piratas* (pirate

coastal landings) but about the social lifestyles of the *marimberos* and even their domestic consumer preferences, factors predictably overlooked by Hollywood but not by the Colombian telenovela. Soap operas inevitably reflect everyday life to some degree, and the smuggling of spirits, clothes and hi-fis, not to mention washing machines and radios, is sometimes obliquely connected to the smuggling of drugs. Sublimated into a popular soap opera, in Colombia it all becomes *alimento cotidiano* – everyday fare.

Contrabandista chic tends to be middle-class rather than super opulent, quite different from the tastes of the big cocaine kingpins of the 1980s and '90s, such as Pablo Escobar and Carlos Lehder of the Medellín Cartel and the Rodríguez Orejuela brothers of the Cali Cartel. For instance, in Barranquilla (outside of Guajira but the largest city on the coast) there is a street, Calle 72, that became popular with people benefiting from the bonanza. Many furniture shops sprang up here on the back of the influx of nouveau riche Guajiros. Marble was the most popular material. The Hotel Royal in Baranquilla was bought and renovated to rival the 1920s-built Prado (a national monument) and to poach a beauty queen contest – not a trivial thing in Colombia – from the latter where it had been traditionally held.

There isn't a single community of contrabanding in Guajira: Angulo identifies the wholesale business of contraband in Maicao as being in the hands of not only *cachacos* but also Arabs, Syrians, Lebanese and Turks. Such are their numbers that there is a thriving Muslim community here and a large mosque.

It is also somewhat carnivalesque. In song Rafael Escalona, the celebrated composer of *Vallenato* (music originating in César Department around Valledupar, the state capital, but popular all over the country) and friend of García Márquez, has penned several works about the *contrabandistas* of the Guajira and has written specifically for telenovelas. *Vallenato* is similar to *corrido*, a north Mexican folk genre linked to storytelling, reportage and protest against maladministration in government, which is very popular on both sides of the Mexico–U.S. border. *Corrido* has a subgenre called *narcocorrido* whose songs mythologize stories of cocaine smuggling to the United States. A narco-cinema industry has flourished in conjunction with this mythologizing in song. *Vallenato* did not develop the same subgenre, a *narco-vallenato*, because the *marimbero* style to which it is linked was created out of the now largely defunct marijuana-based traffic. However, not to be outdone, a (sub-) subgenre to the Mexican *narcocorrido* surfaced in Colombia in the form of the *corrida peligrosa*, the most 'dangerous' version of the genre – that is until the emergence of *corridos enfermos* (literally 'sick' ballads) to reflect the blood and gore of Mexico's recent drug wars.

In Guajira one doesn't see much of this dangerous energy. The ennui that I encountered in Alta Guajira is more a languid way of life in 'Baja', the southern part of the state. In Riohacha, where the customs office is located, there are murals revelling in the contraband way of life although, instead of depicting champagne on ice at the beach, it is Scotch whisky.

PAPILLON WAS DETAINED in Riohacha. I looked for the prison but was told that it had been demolished and replaced by another at the other end of town. Many doubt the veracity of the Colombian part of Charrière's story, and as one stands in the arid desert at Punta Gallinas staring out towards Aruba over the horizon there is certainly little sign of the lush tropical paradise that detained Steve McQueen in the film version of 1973. But the story of smuggling on Guajira isn't a shrivelled bud: it might have seemed like an arid sea for Gabriel García Márquez's narrator in 'Death Constant Beyond Love', but the Caribbean has always been profitable.

The Guajira opens out onto a sea *and* an ocean. The smuggling outlook of the peninsula could never have been envisioned and realized without tapping into oceanic currents and encountering the Dutch, English, French and Portuguese contraband traders swept to and from Europe on the *Volta del Mar* wind giro. I have just related an American story but currents in smuggling were becoming much more global.

FIVE

A TASTE FOR CONTRABAND

Smuggling Blows Across the World

Rivers and seas of contraband, regional theatres of smuggling – the Caribbean, the River Plate, the Banda and the South China Sea – had by the nineteenth century become much more integrated. There were now oceans of possibility for smuggling. But how did we reach this state of affairs in which smuggling has become globally geopolitical? As is so often the case with smuggling, the story unfolds with romantic and stylish overtones but, as ever, it is actually all about power and influence. It is the logic of competition and incentive of profit-making, informed by the new laissez-faire doctrine, that really drove smuggling beyond the local. Before dealing with this reality, let's begin with the romantic angle.

In Alessandro Baricco's novella *Silk*, Hervé Joncour, a French adventurer (heir to Marco Polo who first unfolded the Silk Road into Western imagination, and the princess who smuggled silkworms out of China), makes the arduous journey overland to Japan, now at the heart of the silk myth. The West has still not mastered its production and Joncour's mission is to steal eggs and smuggle them back to southern France where, should they survive, the fledgling silk production industry, blighted by epidemics, might just take wing again. While in Japan he is distracted from his economic purpose and falls for the beautiful and mysterious concubine of a powerful warlord, Hara Kei.

Not for the first time a lust for finery, combined with a vision of romance, creates a kind of Orientalist fantasy, and a motivation for smuggling. Baricco's story is set in the 1860s but it was during the previous century that Orientalism became a consuming passion. Columbus had dreamt of a western route to the Spice Islands to supply Europe's luxury markets, and when he encountered the Americas he at first refused to believe that such an obstacle existed. This obstinate continent was now very much on the map, and its increasingly wilful centres of population, in particular Lima, Buenos Aires, Mexico City and Quito, had, at least in some parts, accrued such fabulous wealth that they were ready for their own Oriental experience. Dandyish and metropolitan, Bourbon Pacific America was only one ocean, not two, away from the 'Far East', and, familiar as it was with the ways of smuggling, supply was not a problem. By 1750 an envious lawyer for the guild of merchants in Buenos Aires was writing to Ferdinand VI that it seemed as though the Peking Fair were being held in Lima.[1]

Conspicuous Consumption in Bourbon Peru

Mexico City's governing *consulado* was the dynamo behind the illicit Pacific trade. Fine cloth and garments, furniture and jewellery as well as scarce household goods flooded into Acapulco, all largely forbidden by the Casa de Contratación and especially so when they were shipped on to Lima, Piura and Guayaquil in the Peru vicereality. During the 1730s Paita, Piura's port in northern Peru, became one of the main smuggling centres for the region, along with Guayaquil. The Peru vice-reality's elites, *Los Señores peruleros* – Orientalists and Francophiles – had a weakness for Chinese silk and ribbon as well as Carcassone finery and lacework from Flanders. Crimson stockings from La Laguna in the Canary Islands made the drab streets of Lima a good deal more colourful. Guayaquil, now in Ecuador, contributed towards Quito, high in the mountains, becoming not just a destination for contraband but an entrepôt, a transit point. From here some of it would be transported along overland routes northwards into New Granada, particularly down the Rio Magdalena to the Caribbean and Cartagena de Las Indias. This eastern contraband even made it as far as Portobelo and Nombre de Dios in present-day Panama, which had been the original monopoly ports for Spanish official trade.

Smuggling was now a mix of exhibitionism and refined performance. While on the one hand there was flamboyance, on the other contraband display was cannily understated. For example, in an early instance of 'shabby chic', fashionable silver lacework was worn as a way of avoiding paying the royal 'fifth' (*quinto*, tax) because it could be battered, burned and generally made to look worn out (*de chafalonía*): in other words not to look like silver at all. Inlaying precious metal made it almost impossible to weigh it. Silver was even passed off as gold to avoid the silver tax. In some ways, then, smuggler style drew on Spanish conservatism but in others opulence knew no bounds: mixed-race and black women could be seen on the streets wearing diamonds and pearls.

The Bourbon colonies represented a decadent phase of the Spanish Empire and contrabanding, much more so than during the sixteenth or seventeenth centuries, seemed to emanate from the top. The history of eighteenth-century smuggling in Peru is characterized by a succession of pompous decrees against smuggling but also by the fact that so many of the great and the good of the land were implicated in it.

Attempts to Control Smuggling in Eighteenth-century South America

During the early years of the century only lip service was paid to a succession of decrees against smuggling, even at the highest level. Sometimes there was blatant disregard of them. In 1705 the High Court in Lima issued a decree against smuggling gold and silver on pain of losing all of the cargo and equipment, and yet still the Viceroy of Peru between 1707 and 1710, Manuel de Oms, was known as the *Ladrón de Tesoro Real* (thief of the royal treasury). Ships bound for New Spain sometimes stopped over in Puerto Callao, Lima's port, to undercut the local merchants. The viceroy had a nice little contraband sideline in unlawfully licensing French ships to trade (*registros*) during the years of disruption caused by the War of the Spanish Succession (1700–1713).

There were attempts to fight smuggling but they lacked will and the only serious ones tended to come from Spain rather than the men in situ. Manuel de Oms's successor, Diego Ladrón de Guevara, sometime bishop of Quito, carried on this covert trading. After the war the first Spanish Bourbon, Philip V, tried to crack down, and Guevara was duly dismissed for embezzlement in 1716. In 1720, and again in 1723, Philip issued a penalty of death and confiscation of all property on those caught trading with the smuggler ships. Scrutiny was particularly directed towards the Chilean ports of Valdivia, Concepción and Valparaíso.

Anti-smuggling decrees sometimes denounced its immorality. Viceroy José de Amendáriz y Perurena, in his *Relación de Gobierno* of 1736, lectured citizens against this decadence and censured its exposure in risqué fashion plates.[2] He might have been something of a killjoy but his actions in fortifying coastal towns and restructuring the navy to combat smuggling were not simply cosmetic. However his anti-smuggling leadership was an anomaly: on the other side of the coin were men like Fernando Álvarez de Castro, who was appointed in 1744 to police smuggling and was himself indicted for it in 1745. Things were no cleaner up in the mountains. The president of the high court in Quito, José de Araújo y Río, defended himself vigorously in 1743 and 1744 against charges of corruption and involvement in the contraband trade even though his guilt seems obvious: when he arrived in Paita he had so many trunks of contraband from Asia and Spain that muleteers could not carry it all. In the crates were cloth, spirits and 130 *planchas* (sheets of silver), and he had another 66 boxes waiting in Riobamba.[3]

Very occasionally there was more focus in the anti-smuggling laws as they targeted specific transgressions on both sea and land. At sea the problem of infiltration of the *flota* system with contraband and the threat from tenacious foreign companies such as the British and Dutch West India Companies and the British South Sea Company, smugglers in all but name, led to the founding of new Spanish-linked trading companies intended to be more efficient and innovative. They included the Honduras Co. (1714), the Caracas Co. (1728) and the Havana Co. (1740). Naval patrols more closely regulated the postal ships, *avisos*, that arrived from Spain because they were often bolstered with contraband. But these regulators' relative success merely boosted the profits of the Dutch and French smugglers in the Pacific arriving from the other direction.

On land the royal postal routes also came under scrutiny. These *caminos reales*, royal roads, were the paths travelled by *caminantes*, traders, and here smugglers saw their opportunity.[4] Precious metals were secreted within cases of tobacco to the extent that 'king's tobacco' became a euphemism for gold. Many of these mule trains 'fell down ravines', their goods entering the black market in the same way that merchandise 'falls off the back of a lorry' today. Some smugglers among the *caminantes* were targeted through a reward system for informants who if indigenous would gain lifetime tax exemption, or if *mestizo* – Latin American of mixed indigenous and Spanish descent – would receive one-third of the confiscated goods, usually much more than the exemption. Even slaves might be freed and receive a small financial reward. But it was a cutthroat world and one scam led to another; one example is the practice of selling contraband and then denouncing the recipient before buying the goods back with the reward money, now legitimated, at a cheap price.

Another decree, this time in 1773 from Viceroy Marmel de Amat y Junient, further dented merchant impunity because cargo bundles could now be inspected at the time of often false declaration of goods.

Most countermeasures, as today with cocaine production in the Andes, could not significantly reduce the supply of contraband at source. If much precious metal only became contraband somewhere down the line, other material seeped into the informal economy straight from the mines: *kajchas* or *calcas* were indigenous labourers who put in a bit of unofficial overtime and sold off the gold and silver on the side. These were micro contributors but collectively significant, and any number of high and mighty decrees were not going to affect this seepage into the contraband world. Connected to the east by these networks of trading roads and the great rivers Paraná and Uruguay that flowed into the Rio de la Plata estuary, vast amounts of unminted silver, *piña*, now went out of Buenos Aires. In addition, mercury for silver extraction was smuggled into the mines, for instance in Huancavelica in Peru. There were other ruses: a mystery surrounded the 'cathedral of silver' at Charcas, near Potosí, where silver torches – prestige objects – seemed so weightless that the suspicion was that the church had cut the metal into a cheap alloy, selling off much of the pure metal.

The Spanish generally fared better in counter-smuggling operations at sea and a fully laden smuggler ship was a fat prize. But overall they were unsuccessful: only one peso was recovered for every six or seven spent on enforcement.[5]

The Treaty of Utrecht (1713) brought with it a peace that changed the character of illicit operations in the Caribbean and Pacific. Official trade soared with the issue of new licences but so too did smuggling and piracy. Times of peace often led smugglers to piracy (not to privateering, which was a wartime justification for piratical activity) because the policing state was now focused on the illicit trade. Smugglers sometimes switched to high-seas robbery in response to sustained low-key aggression. Weakened states tended to tolerate smuggling. Nevertheless between 1714 and 1750 there was frequent overlap and blurring of smuggling and piracy.

Contraband Rivalries

On one of the stores in the market at Maicao, Colombia, the entrepôt for contraband goods on the Guajira Peninsula, there is a sign: *Deposito El*

Pirata. Two doors down, another reads *Comercializadora River Plate*, alluding to the *Río de la Plata* at the other end of the continent between Argentina and Uruguay, another area notorious for smuggling. The interconnectedness of smuggling worlds today is apparent but this is not a new phenomenon. Silver flowed like blood through veins all around the continent and the extensive postal routes helped its transit. But as among all pirate bands there was much rivalry and this in particular is the story in the Bourbon Americas between Lima, Buenos Aires and Mexico City.

Lima sometimes waxed indignant at Mexico City and Acapulco's enthusiastic embrace of new Asian trading possibilities, and was envious of the River Plate region's energetic illicit economies. Lima merchants felt put out that smugglers heading for New Spain from Asia docked at Puerto Callao and offloaded some of their illicit goods. However it was frequently a case of the pot calling the kettle black: for all their transgressions the merchant classes cried like babies to the sovereign if their own smuggling operations were undercut by those of others.

So how did Buenos Aires and the River Plate become such a smuggling heartland? There was a different contrabanding structure here to that in Lima. Smuggling was perhaps more broad-based in Buenos Aires. In Lima the mixed-race *criollo* elite sat at the top of the contraband pile, while in Buenos Aires merchants, descendants of *hidalgos*, wealthy Spanish, fed them with illicit luxuries. From the Seville viewpoint in the middle years of empire, Lima was supposed to be the big brother: goods were to be unloaded at Lima and then to proceed overland to Buenos Aires. Smugglers reversed the trajectory: now they came to Lima from Buenos Aires. Latterly imports were allowed directly into Buenos Aires and this simply augmented the flows of contraband. Reducing the risks, the trick now was to unload in Buenos Aires legally but then to re-export illegally. The British South Sea Company was typical in this regard. It traded illicitly with Peru from here and through Brazil. It set up a legal slave-holding operation in Buenos Aires but this soon became a smuggling one. By 1728 a third of all illicit circulations in the Vicereality of Peru were conducted by the South Sea Company.[6]

Sometimes there was a crackdown in the River Plate area. One such incident spiralled spectacularly out of control. In 1731 Spanish officials boarded a British merchant ship captained by Robert Jenkins, accusing him of smuggling, and cut off his ear. After protracted protests – at one stage Jenkins displayed his severed ear to Parliament in London – the British engaged the Spanish in what came to be known as the War of

Jenkins's Ear (1739–48), leading to the dissolution of the South Sea Company's slaving operations in 1750. Contraband of war was rife, particularly after Portobelo, one of the other main east coast Spanish ports, was closed when it was briefly captured in the early stages of the conflict. War didn't eradicate smuggling; it simply changed its character.

Rivers of Contraband

The River Plate, like the Guajira, is an area where smuggling has seemingly gone on forever. During the late 1980s and early '90s, if one travelled upriver on the Rio Paraná as far as the Paraguayan Ciudad del Este (City of the East) on the Brazil border, one could get a flavour of what the informal economy of backwater South America might have been like. As in many smaller towns dedicated largely to contraband, there was not much civic pride in evidence. It was given over almost entirely to small, packed shops and stalls punctuated only by *parillada* (grill) restaurants and fast-food joints. Most people made the deal, had a meal and took the first bus out, usually back to Brazil. Smuggling goes on in the capital, Asunción, as well but there it is a little beneath the surface. Alfredo Stroessner, erstwhile dictator of Paraguay, controlled a coterie of generals who worked for 'Paraguay Incorporated', the country's largest and most successful industry – smuggling.[7] Everything from weapons to liquor to cars and electronics passed through Paraguay.

Twenty or so miles northeast of Asunción, set a little back from the River Paraguay, a tributary of the Paraná, is the town of Areguá where, in his novel *Travels with my Aunt*, Graham Greene's fallen/saved hero, Henry Pulling, ends his days. It has been quite a trip upriver from Buenos Aires. Henry passes through Formosa, another smuggler town, where he learns the reality of Paraguay Incorporated. A long and transformative journey nears its end for this retired Home Counties bank manager. It has been one of reinvigoration through travels with his eccentric Aunt Augusta. Ultimately he ends up as what else but a smuggler.

During the eighteenth century the River Plate was like a great funnel for smuggling towards Peru and, in the other direction, a slew of contraband silver spilled into the estuary zone. The Portuguese in particular brought in illicit goods from all over Europe but there was also an entwined local smuggling network. The trade was pretty covert: there were numerous islands in the Rio Paraná where contraband could be dropped off to be picked up by rancher-smugglers and sold or stored in Colonia del Sacramento near the mouth of the estuary. Timber-carrying boats were a favoured transport for the contraband. Once on shore goods were moved by night, ranch to ranch, abetted by some of the very men charged with stopping the trade. Colonia became the smugglers' capital. As well as being a market in itself, it was a distribution centre for contraband from Buenos Aires, which was then moved on to mix with goods coming from Brazil and traded on the renegade littoral between Montevideo and Maldonado.

The Brazilian Connection

Leather goods, wheat, oils and meat from the River Plate zone were exchanged for Brazilian tobacco coming from the east. Portuguese spirits were also part of the round trade.

Smuggling had begun early in the Amazon region. At the beginning of the seventeenth century a Portuguese merchant operating out of Cartagena was known to have moved contraband huge distances through the Amazon to supply this most defended of Spanish colonial towns. The Portuguese Companhia do Graõ was set up specifically as a trading firm for smuggling between Brazil and Quito via the Amazon and Matto Grosso. As in Buenos Aires, both rich and poor colonists benefited from the contraband trade. If the Dutch were the frontrunners in contrabanding in the Caribbean, the Portuguese, or rather Portuguese Jews, were the most dynamic free traders on the east coast of South America. In these regions the British were not far behind these 'New Christians' and the Dutch, and in Brazil in particular they often collaborated with them. The origins of this pact lay in the Inquisition.

There had been an exodus of Jews from Portugal fleeing religious persecution during the early part of the eighteenth century. Many were smuggled by boat to England. In terms of smuggling capital, it was a kind of brain drain. In tapping into their trade, knowledge and connections, the British gained access to the Lisbon-based Brazilian-Portuguese trading system. In large part this meant smuggling goods to Brazil as well as gold out of Lisbon, sometimes in Royal Navy warships but also in packet boats, particularly from Falmouth. This was made easier because all English boats had been immune from searches since medieval times, strengthened by a treaty imposed upon the Portuguese in 1654 by Oliver Cromwell.

Intensified Activity on the Sea of Contraband

In the eighteenth-century Caribbean the raft of contraband was still very much afloat. Today, as contraband ebbs and flows and mutates in places like La Guajira (as described in the last chapter), small ports, little more than encampments, have appeared to service it. Those renegade settlements – Nuevo and Portete – are not quite heirs to the old pirate havens of Tortuga and Port Royal but neither are they a new phenomenon. There were always ports like this around the Caribbean.

Monte Cristi on Hispaniola's Banda del Norte, more or less on the border between the Spanish and French colonies, was little more than a hamlet with some 100 Spanish inhabitants. But from the mid- to late eighteenth century it received several hundred ships each year, just like today's Colombian ports. Many smugglers came from colonial North America but there was also a thriving trade between the islands, which meant that French goods ended up in households on British islands. Much French sugar reached England repackaged as British. Contraband of war (Britain and France were frequently at each others' throats in Europe during this period) flowed both ways through Monte Cristi. For instance, sugar, molasses, rum, coffee and indigo leaked out of Sainte-Domingue (French Hispaniola), matching British contraband the other way. The lieutenant-governor of this smuggler port was the pivot of the entire operation, organizing licences for visiting foreign ships and facilitating distribution of contraband around the island and into the broader Caribbean on Spanish ships.

As detailed in Lance Grahn's study of the Guajira during the Bourbon era, *The Political Economy of Smuggling* (1997), the indigenous Wayuu continued their rebellious response to outside interference. Smuggling continued to be, in part, a necessity for the settlers as well – no registered ships came to Riohacha between 1713 and 1763. The main contraband was silks, taffeta and damask, which were exchanged for livestock, emeralds and gold. There were also playing cards, wheat flour, cotton, cloth and guns, but only good guns. During the spring of 1737 a Spanish captain, José Barón de Chaves, led fourteen soldiers to the smugglers' cove of El Pájaro on the peninsula where six foreign sloops were busy trading. They were disarmed by Wayuu warriors, and as if this humiliation were not enough, the Wayuu returned the weapons, saying they could get much better ones from the British and Dutch smugglers![8]

Smuggling was relentless there. In 1734, 25 smuggler vessels landed over a million pesos' worth of contraband, while in 1737 there were at least 35 vessels operating.[9] They were mainly Dutch but also British and renegade Spanish. Skirmishes were usually won by the smugglers. In August 1734, when a combined British and Dutch smuggling band encountered Domingo de Léon's small force of twenty Guajiro archers and Spanish soldiers, the latter were forced to regroup and rearm in Riohacha. The landing operation continued unabated: the very presence of the Spanish was ignored by the next wave of smugglers.[10]

The Guajiros became middlemen between all of these parties, escorting contraband cargoes even as far as Colombia's great waterway the Rio Magdalena. From here the goods changed hands, legal shipments of cloth from Cartagena to Lima being combined with contraband cloth.

Smuggling Across Continents

It seems that contraband was running across the continent, but is it realistic to speak of smuggling sweeping the world in this era? Can we begin to talk of a global economy of which smuggling was a part?

Consider its most breachable point, the Panamanian isthmus. Anybody sitting at the edge of Miraflores lock on the canal today, watching the huge 'Panama standard' ships sailing between two oceans, could be forgiven for wondering what illicit cargoes some of the containers might hold. For a long time now the isthmus has been permeable to any amount of intrigue. Guidebooks might bring us the touristic angle but other literature is more penetrating. Another passage from Greene in his book about his friendship with the Panamanian general Omar Torrijos, *Getting to Know the General*, describes the territory: 'the central *cordilleras* rise to 3,000 metres and extend to the Costa Rican frontier on one side of the Zone and the dense Darién jungle, almost as unknown as in the days of Balboa, stretches on the other side to the Colombian border, crossed only by smugglers' paths.'[11]

Scroll back a bit and with a measure of incredulity we might imagine William Dampier, that old pirate and sometime smuggler, in a planning room of budding empire. In June 1697 he was consulted by the Honourable Council of Lords of Trade in London about an interesting scheme proposed by a Scot, William Paterson. Paterson wanted to set up a colony in Darién that might bring together the lands of spice and silver in a thoroughly Protestant way – bypassing the meandering mule trains of the Spanish and connecting British trade directly and efficiently to the East Indies by cutting out the Cape routes. Dampier thought he knew the territory and advised that it was possible. Like Columbus reaching out for a more direct route to the Spice Islands than round Africa's Cape of Good Hope, this attempt to bypass Cape Horn would have been another form of geopolitical smuggling. It went ahead and failed. So, again the question arises how, in the eighteenth century, smuggling had become inter- rather than just pan-continental.

This book began with the story of smuggling spices. It is to this that one must turn for a story of contraband sweeping across the world: the story of Pierre Poivre.

Spice Dispersal: The Story of Pierre Poivre

Thomas Jefferson once claimed that 'The greatest service which can be rendered any country is to add a useful plant to its culture.'[12] This wasn't just an idle truism spoken by a great orator: he himself had been involved in smuggling rice out of Italy (in his pockets), a crime which carried the death penalty, and he had also facilitated the smuggling of hemp seeds out of China.

Hervé Joncour, Baricco's melancholy hero in *Silk*, operated for both himself and his investors in smuggling silkworms back from Japan. But during the eighteenth century Pierre Poivre, a generation ahead of Jefferson, set the standard for fulfilment of his patriotic duty through the transplantation of a 'useful plant' when he succeeded in smuggling cloves and nutmeg out of Dutch hands onto French territory and into fertile soil.

Poivre (whose surname means 'pepper' in English) gave his name to the entire genus of pepper plants, *Poivrea*. He was the son of a wealthy silk merchant and was a sometime missionary and adventurer, as well as, famously, the naturalist who conclusively broke the Dutch spice monopoly. He had the kind of resourcefulness and enquiring mind, like William Dampier before him and Alexander von Humboldt afterwards, and attention to the detail of fabulous exotic plants – potential resources little known to the West – that stirred the gruff merchant magnates as they sat around their long tables in the dark headquarters of various East India companies counting their profits and losses.

The problem that they all faced was as much horticultural as it was political and military. Commercial cloves are dried flowers, not a fruit or a seed which can be planted, and so in order to cultivate them one

A Bust of Pierre Poivre, Jardin de l'État, St-Denis, Réunion.

needs seedlings. These are particularly difficult to keep alive during transportation. The Dutch, of course, didn't make things easy – nutmeg was meticulously shelled, roasted and even coated in lime to prevent it from germinating once it was out of their hands. The export of seedlings was a capital offence. Nevertheless there was already a certain amount of scattered seed around the edges of the monopoly: locals had long traded spices to Mindanao and Kedah from areas little known to the Dutch.

Poivre's story is as fantastical as Jules Verne's *Around the World in Eighty Days* and he even has his own Passepartout in his daring lieutenant, Simon Provost, a clerk, or 'supercargo', in the French East India Company. Their path to glory was rather longer than 80 days and his adventuring did not begin auspiciously. Poivre was captured by the British in the Straits of Banka (beside eastern Sumatra), losing his lower right arm to a cannonball during the action. He was sold into the hands of the Dutch at Batavia but did not waste his time and learned Malay, just as he had learned Cantonese while incarcerated in Canton in a case of mistaken identity. Here in the heart of the Dutch stronghold he sensed another opportunity, lifted by the scent of spice that raised Batavia above the other European entrepôts.

On his odyssey back to France, and nearly home, he was captured again, this time by French corsairs off St Malo. They in turn were seized by British privateers off Guernsey. He finally reached France in 1749. Irrepressible, he soon headed off to the Far East again and, having gathered capital in Mauritius, Canton and Macao, sought further backing from the governor of Manila, Ovando Solis. Together, gathering maps and intelligence on the Spice Islands during 1751 and 1752, they plotted to destroy the Dutch monopoly. The mission was to begin at Pondicherry in southern India but the first hurdle Poivre had to overcome was the envy and rivalry of the governor, Dupleix, who himself eyed the prize. The expedition didn't get far but Poivre did manage to obtain nine rooted nutmeg trees that he took to Mauritius. Four died en route but he was able to show them to the acting governor, Bouvet de Lozier, who was a keen horticulturalist, and subsequently to get some small support in the shape of a just-about-seaworthy craft, the 60-ton *Colombe*. It made it to Manila before it had to be beached and extensively repaired. But now, with renewed purpose, he set out to trawl the Indies for spice plants and seeds wherever he could get them, perhaps even to raid the Spice Islands themselves under the noses of the Dutch. So fearful were the crew that he didn't tell them about this potential final destination.

They drifted without much good fortune, washing up in Lifao in Portuguese Timor. Poivre tried his luck here but the governor came up with just eleven nutmeg trees and a few clove seeds, which he took back to Mauritius. As so often seems to happen with competing egos, Poivre was soon in conflict with the company botanist, Fusée-Aublet. The five remaining original nutmeg trees had died and his small recent pickings were hardly going to bring down empires. When the remainder withered, Poivre accused his rival of fraud, claiming that nutmegs had merely been grafted onto shoots from entirely different species. Fusée-Aublet in turn alleged that Poivre had destroyed other nutmeg trees obtained from a different source.

Disillusioned, Poivre headed home via Madagascar. Although deflated and exiled from the scene of the action, back in France he obtained political and financial backing for his horticultural espionage from

Comptroller-General Bertin and the foreign minister, the Duke de Praslin. However he seemed to have lost some of his drive, spending it on a home, La Freta, a wedding and a botanical garden. He was drifting into pipe and slipper territory.

The French East India Company, corrupt and inefficient, was also languid, but when it was axed the Mauritius project was resuscitated. Poivre was persuaded by Praslin to return as Comissaire Ordonnnateur of the islands of Mauritius and Bourbon. In Mauritius he set about, as its new *intendant*, to build a great botanical garden, Pamplemousses, and a home to live in that he named Montplaisir. Just as importantly, around this time, he met Provost.

Now with resources at hand, the real mission could begin again in earnest and in May 1769 he dispatched Provost to the Spice Islands via Kedah and Manila so as not to arouse too much suspicion. The expedition consisted of two ships, *L'Etoile du Matin* and *Vigilant*, which sailed for Ternate. This time, however, Provost skirted round this island and landed on the uninhabited island of Miao, just northwest of Ternate, because he had heard that untended spices grew there. As it turned out this foray was in vain: the Dutch had been wise to this threat and destroyed all the spice trees. *Vigilant* then sailed south alone with Provost on board, arriving at Ceram. Here, after some frustration, he had a turn of fortune arriving in the form of a Dutchman with a grudge against the VOC who provided maps, intelligence and invaluable pointers to weak links in the Dutch chain of islands. Provost arrived on the island of Gueby in April 1770 and immediately hit it off with the local chiefs, who took him to nearby Petani. There they were given a good stock of nutmeg trees, although no cloves. The Frenchmen worried about the arrival of the monsoon and felt that they could tarry no longer but at the last minute, anchor almost raised, the Petani chiefs appeared bearing both clove seeds and trees.

As for Poivre before him, the journey home was an adventure. Before they could make the open sea, *Vigilant* was intercepted by a flotilla of small native boats commanded by the Dutch. However, the Frenchmen, crafty and determined, insisted that they had been blown off course in a storm and that they had only ever been heading for Batavia. Not only did the Dutch believe this unlikely story but they helped them navigate back through treacherous reefs. The crew waved to the Dutch as they feigned making a course towards the VOC's overseas headquarters. But they were no sooner out of sight than they turned for Timor, where they were to divide up the priceless specimens with

L'Etoile du Matin and head for Port Louis, Mauritius, which they duly reached on 24 June 1770. The intrepid Provost delivered to his boss 400 rooted nutmeg and 70 clove trees, along with thousands of nuts and seeds. Some were bound to survive. On a later mission he brought back more clove trees.

Pierre Poivre planted most of his specimens at Montplaisir. The irony is that Mauritius was an island that had been abandoned by the Dutch. He also sent some to the Seychelles and to Cayenne, French Guiana, to which he eventually transferred his ambitions because infighting in Mauritius impoverished the garden. From Cayenne, Poivre sent cloves to Madagascar, Zanzibar and Martinique, and nutmeg to Grenada, where it thrived even better than in Banda. This was the tipping point in the history of the Dutch spice monopoly, and was entirely brought about by smuggling.

Other Transplantations

The British, noting the French success, attempted their own horticultural smuggling. They tried early on to commission smugglers to obtain seedlings to be grown on their Sumatran colony of Bencoolen but the plants died. After many other false starts they managed to smuggle seeds out of Cayenne. Later, in 1801, the British invaded the Spice Islands while the Dutch were preoccupied with Napoleon in Europe. They gave them back in 1802 but this short window of opportunity enabled them freely to transplant spices wholesale to their own gardens in Ceylon, Bencoolen, Calcutta and Penang. Typifying the state–smuggler relation, a certain Captain Moore, a free trader, smuggled 6,000 pounds of cloves provided by Sultan Nuku of Tidore on his ship *Phoenix* to Bencoolen. But this covert transplantation – along with a more open one organized by Dr Roxbury of Madras, one of the grandees of imperial horticulture, that had delivered 21,000 nutmeg and 7,000 clove seedlings, also to Bencoolen – failed miserably.

The seventeenth to nineteenth centuries saw many acts of 'bio piracy', leading to great shifts in geopolitical wealth. John Rolfe smuggled Spanish tobacco seeds to Virginia from the Caribbean in the early part of the seventeenth century. Around Poivre's time other adventurers were smuggling plants from abroad to their own territories. In 1747 a Brazilian, Francisco de Melo Palheta, charmed the wife of a French governor in Arabia into giving him coffee seeds that he took home. Brazil's coffee industry originated from this theft. The British would become experts at this great smuggling game, transplanting tea, cinchona (whose bark is the source of the anti-malaria drug quinine) and rubber. It seems, however, that the French had the greener fingers when it came to spices, although others followed. In 1817 the British, who invaded the Bandas again, took hundreds more nutmeg seedlings along with soil samples and transplanted them once again to their empire, which once again involved Ceylon, Penang and Bencoolen with the addition this time of Singapore. Within just a few decades the new plantations were more productive than those on the Bandas.

NOW WE CAN FINALLY TALK of smuggling across the world. Whichever corner of the earth one looks at, there was business in contraband staple commodities and luxuries. There was a huge demand for smuggled brandy, tobacco and tea into eighteenth-century England. Boyars sold smuggled tobacco from Circassia and Ukraine, and pelts and furs went from Siberia to China. Prince Gagarin of Siberia amassed a huge fortune undermining the official caravans. In Defoe's *History of the Pyrates*, pirates operating out of Malagasy would freeboot goods between Asia, Europe and America, undermining official East India Company agreements. Everybody wanted to line their silken purses. From the 1780s onwards illicit trade blossomed in multifarious colours, and Bengal silks and cottons became as important as spice.

The result was that monopolies atrophied and, considering that smuggling was now so broadly entrenched, paradoxically there was much less need for illicit trade because the world was much more laissez-faire. Looked at from one angle, smuggling had been too successful. By the 1790s it was equivalent to only a third of official trade, although it continued to increase in quantity.[13] Even the Spanish changed their tune: rather like the Ming in China, they had pushed too hard and eventually had to retract their monopolistic regulations, removing the raison d'être for most contrabanding. This was the end of the golden age of smuggling entrepreneurship, which would now move to the forefront of imperial expansion. First, though, came an epoch of revolution, and smuggling was the perfect vehicle to spread and embody radical new ideas.

SIX

REVOLUTION AND RESISTANCE

Turning Over the Idea of Smuggling

'. . . confess what you are smuggling: moods, states of grace, elegies!'
Kublai Khan to Marco Polo in Italo Calvino's *Invisible Cities*

Smugglers were shallow. Such was the opinion of many adversaries of free trade during the nineteenth century.[1] Running counter to this viewpoint, we see laissez-faire themes emerging in literature in which not only characters but ideas travel freely; where they cannot, they are smuggled. How, then, given this apparent idealism, can smuggling be so readily conceived as one-dimensional? It has certainly plumbed the lowest depths but it has also carried the noblest of ideas. It can be amoral, or morally indefensible, but also heroic. It has often been behind idealistic causes: smugglers carried Voltaire's *Questions sur l'Encyclopédie* across the Jura mountains from Geneva into a restless pre-revolutionary France, but they also carried his *Candide*, which was considered mere pornography. Were these revolutionary smugglers, or free traders with profit the bottom line? Or should these two motives necessarily be considered mutually exclusive?

In some instances there clearly is a line: people smuggling might sometimes be considered a service but those who trafficked in slaves, *piezas de negros* (pieces or units of human currency), were never in this business. During the Morisco uprising and the subsequent War of Alpujarras (1568–71), the local noblemen around Almeria who were rebelling against coercion to become Christian used a similarly dispassionate and cruel logic: they smuggled in artillery, rice, grain and flour from Barbary and Algiers, as well as muskets, traded in the ratio of one gun for one Christian slave. Usually, though, the line is less clear, the exchange never quite so straightforward, and smuggling and smugglers remain somewhat ambiguous.

Pierre Poivre is either a thief or a patriotic man of action and hero, depending upon the context in which one looks at his ambitious transplanting of spices. He quite possibly saw himself as neither, given the title of his autobiography, *The Voyages of a Philosopher*, which was read by the esteemed American revolutionary Thomas Jefferson. But then Jefferson's recommendation of the 'greatest service to a country', as mentioned in the previous chapter, was not to create a land of the free but rather to steal another country's flora and smuggle it back to the home country. Smuggling, it seems, can be simultaneously noble and dishonourable.

Consider other sentiments around this question. José de Amendáriz y Perurena, Marquis de Castelfuerte, the viceroy of Peru, called smuggling an 'evil communication' in his *Relación de Gobierno* of 1736. Kublai Khan on the other hand, in the quotation above, senses a softer contraband of 'states of grace', while in the science fiction novel *Contraband*, novelist George Foy's main character, a smuggler, ponders over what he considers to be the only worthwhile cargo – humans and ideas.[2]

Some things seem certain: smuggling is efficient, works on demand and ventures where other trading, be it in commodities or ideas, dare not go. This makes it an important vehicle for people and for change. This chapter, then, will take a pause in the narrative of empire-building spearheaded by smuggling and consider its relevance to revolution, freedom and social inclusion.

Smuggling and Revolution

In 1756 a young Thomas Paine, later feted for his work *The Rights of Man,* was stopped by his father as he was about to enlist with the privateer *Terrible* at Execution Dock in Wapping. Had he succeeded in this venture he might have ended up like William Dampier, as a pirate and part-time smuggler, explorer and chronicler. Instead, remaining more socially entangled, he became a revolutionary. His rebellion came in the form of pamphleteering – a medium that, by its often illicit nature, has an affinity with contraband. His pamphlets *Common Sense* and *American Crisis* became fuel to the fire of the American Revolution. The irony is that he served as a customs officer during the formative years of his radicalism. Perhaps less surprising is that in June 1774, during a campaign for better working conditions for revenue men, he met Benjamin Franklin in London and soon after emigrated to North America. There is no evidence that Paine was involved in smuggling per se but he would have been a natural smuggler, as one ideal of smuggling is the principle of free circulation of ideas.

The touchpaper that lit the fuse of the American Revolution was a more concrete instance of smuggling. The *Liberty*, a ship carrying Madeira wine, was seized by the British in 1768 in Boston Harbor because its owner, patriot John Hancock, refused to pay customs duties. The authorities labelled him a smuggler but his act of resistance was so admired that it laid a significant paving stone towards the Declaration of Independence in 1776.

The second phase of revolutions in the Americas, the South American wars against Spain, saw another smuggler revolutionary in action. José Gervasio Artigas was a gaucho cattle smuggler who came out of the wild east of the Vicereality of Buenos Aires and descended upon Montevideo with dreams of creating a United Provinces of the River Plate. It was perhaps his skills as cowboy and smuggler that made him such a fine soldier and revolutionary. Although he was eventually defeated by a combined force of Argentinians and Brazilians, he is regarded as the founding father of the Republic of Uruguay.

There are other great smuggler generals who looked beyond the simple profit motive. Martin Zurbano was a rebel for whom smuggling served as a platform from which to launch a guerrilla surge during the Spanish Carlist Wars. He made his fortune in smuggling but, unlike the conservative and fiercely regional Chouans, a smuggler group from Brittany that fought against the revolutionary French Republic as described in Balzac's novel of the same name, his sympathies were with reformists. Zurbano fought for the 'Cristinos', the forces of the incumbent monarch, Isabella II, and her mother the regent Maria Cristina, against the conservative 'Carlists', who supported the pretender Don Carlos, Isabella's uncle. He brought together various renegade forces, including the Partido de Contra Aduaneros (the Anti-customs Party), into a formidable private army called the Compañia de Tiradores de Alava (the Company of Musketeers of Alava). They became much more than just a motley crew of smugglers, bandits and other chancers. Eventually, though, Zurbano fell out with Ramón Maria Narváez, one of Isabella's closer generals, who had him executed.

The legendary Louisiana pirate and smuggler Jean Lafitte was also a renegade spirit, although he is linked less with revolution than with intrigue, espionage and building his own contrabanding world. Like many real smuggler spy stories, however, there is much myth-building going on beneath the official history. One story about Lafitte is remarkably inventive, even if it is probably untrue. The death of Lafitte is officially recorded as 5 February 1823: his ship, *General Santander*, had been decoyed into an ambush the day before. He was buried at sea. But another story circulates that Lafitte did not die then, and that, no doubt helped by his smuggler skills, he went underground. Twenty-four years later he was to be found in Paris working for a group of subversive American bankers, meeting Karl Marx and Friedrich Engels and subsequently financing the Communist Party Manifesto![3] Smuggling culture and revolutionary ideology come face to face in this tale, although of course one might argue that by this time Lafitte would have retired from being a smuggler. Actually Karl Marx disliked smuggling because he thought it bandaged over the chronic shortages and deprivation of mainstream capitalist society, thereby delaying revolution. But he almost certainly would have approved of the clandestine dissemination of his 'dangerous' ideas.

Black Books

Dangerous ideas and their main vehicle, contraband books, are one obvious starting point for considering smuggling as a higher calling. Certain banned books seem to have a seditious energy secreted between every page, and historically this has sent the forces of conservatism into a paranoid frenzy. Although Marx's books had a direct relation to revolution, they were rarely banned. But in many cases the very existence of contrary literature was unbearable to authority. This, of course, only encouraged its clandestine distribution. The narrator in Czech writer Ivan Klíma's 'The Smuggler's Story', in his book *My Golden Trades*, debates this potency of smuggled literature: 'For years now I've had a running debate with those who liken books to explosives or drugs.'[4] There has been something about the printed idea that in itself gives it great value. But it is only as strong and durable as the paper it is printed on, and this carries with it a certain anxiety. Klíma makes this paradoxical power and fragility quite literal in 'The Smuggler's Story'. The smuggler of the title is stopped with a carload of books by police, and in the panic recalls the time that a friend had carried a letter for him across the border. Rather than allowing the customs officer to read it, he swallowed it. Caught with contraband literature, the smuggler now wonders: could I eat three whole bags of books?

In Hispaniola in 1607 – going back to a region already strongly featured in this book – foreigners were seen distributing heretical books along with other contraband, prompting the Inquisition to intervene. In the event, they turned the screws on those who blinked at orthodoxy in Cartagena instead. This doesn't alter the fact that the Inquisition was usually dreaded for its tyrannical stance but smugglers were equally persistent, particularly when it came to books.

In another Inquisition-related case, around the turn of the sixteenth and seventeenth centuries, Portuguese Jewish immigrants to the Basque country – *marranos* (a term of abuse, literally 'pigs') – carried heretical books from St Jean de Luz and Bayonne in France across the Dancharia pass into Spain as far as Pamplona. The Basque lands that straddled the border, French and Spanish, were ideal for smuggling, kinsman to kinsman. It was a competitive business: some Basques, even habitual smugglers, objected to outsider involvement, particularly if it was carried out by Jews.

Another term used in smuggling during the eighteenth century was *marroner*, to do a clandestine job, very often the smuggling of *mauvais livres* – bad books. The verb comes from the French *marron*, literally meaning sweet chestnut. One supplier of these books was the Société Typographique de Neuchâtel (STN). A common route for revolutionary or pornographic texts hot off the presses of Swiss printers in Neuchâtel was over the border through the northern valleys of the Jura mountains to Pontarlier and thence into the heart of France. It was a relatively honourable form of trade: smugglers offered insurance and money was paid back to the STN if the books were confiscated en route. Often the *mauvais livres* were 'larded' – hidden inside other books. John Cleland's erotic novel *Fanny Hill* became a gospel, while later *Fille de joie* became the New Testament. One of Voltaire's works might be found inside a law book. Other books were illicit because they were pirated, especially travel books.

There will be book smuggling wherever there is revolutionary intent. The book trade to Latin America around the time of the wars of independence was a quasi-smuggling operation. One of the key figures was an Anglo-German, Rudolph Ackermann, who spent four years in Mexico from 1825 onwards. He used the time-honoured smuggling method of undervaluing or misdescribing the goods, and employed an agent to make 'deals' with customs. He also kept things discreet by using smaller ports that were separate from but close by more important ones for importing his books – Tampico rather than Veracruz and Santa Marta over Cartagena – or those that were in competition with the main centres, like Valparaíso instead of Lima. These weren't all political texts but many were. Perhaps his biggest contribution to sedition was his supply of two portable lithographic printing presses to Simón Bolívar's rebels in Venezuela.

Besides political tracts heading straight for lands of revolution, in other places smuggling might circumvent the annoyance of pointless censorship. Sicily, for instance, had a prurience that worked against a very basic enlightenment of the people. The narrator in Giuseppe Tomasi de Lampedusa's novel *The Leopard* observes that 'because of a vexatious Bourbon censorship working through the Customs no one had heard of Dickens, Eliot, Sand, Flaubert or even Dumas.'[5]

A comparable situation existed in Lithuania during the latter part of the nineteenth century. Between 1864 and 1904 the *Knygnešiai* or 'book carriers' smuggled literature, primers and periodicals printed in the banned Latin alphabet from Lithuania Minor (East Prussia) into Lithuania, to counter Russia's insistence that all texts be printed in Cyrillic. To give just two examples, the Romantic liberal journal *Aušra* (The Dawn, founded by Jonas Basanvičius) and *Varpas* (The Bell, edited by patriot Vincas Kurdirka) were smuggled across the border. It was resistance against an enforced Russification of their lands and culture. Later on literature moved the other way. Boris Pasternak's *Dr Zhivago* might not seem terribly seditious now but during the 1950s it was considered too individualistic and implicitly critical of the Soviet system. In 1956 the manuscript was smuggled out of Russia by the philosopher Isaiah Berlin. Words and ideas that might have been purged from history were published in 1957 (in Italy, in both Russian and Italian), won the Nobel Prize for literature in 1958, and were adapted into a famous film in 1965.

Smuggling Ideas

There have been many other instances of smuggling manuscripts out of a censorious country for publication abroad, as well as visual testimony of grave events in such places, usually through photographs.

After he was interned in occupied France during the war, the Hungarian-Jewish writer Arthur Koestler had to smuggle his great novel *Darkness at Noon* to England, and he himself followed *sans papiers* after deserting the Foreign Legion. The German writer Hans Fallada was able to write anti-fascist works, even into the Nazi era, but as pressure mounted upon him to conform and his drug habits caught up with him, he was committed to a psychiatric hospital. Here he wrote *The Drinker*, a novel about alcoholism and insanity, and smuggled it out by writing it down in minute script between the lines of an innocuous short story. Photographs by the renowned Jewish photojournalists Robert Capa, David Seymour and Gerda Taro depicting the horrors of the Spanish Civil War were smuggled out of Vichy France by the Mexican ambassador but in this case the outcome was largely aesthetic because they only emerged, in Mexico City, some 60 years later.

There is a more general principle than revolution, or just cause, at stake here: the freedom of movement of ideas, not always in paper form. The film *Johnny Mnemonic* (1995), scripted by William Gibson from his short story, sees an unusual mode of portage of a data file – it is inserted into a chip inside the head of the main character. This is sci-fi but the idea of transforming knowledge to avoid its suppression has long interested academic circles: the art historian Aby Warburg created libraries in Hamburg and London that were so different to traditional systems that they could successfully evade what he called the 'border police' of disciplinary separation. In some instances ideas in isolation have been considered taboo and unfit for circulation. Robert Mapplethorpe, whose artwork was deemed dangerously homoerotic, had to smuggle some of his photographs from the U.S. in a Canadian diplomatic bag for a exhibition at the Institute of Contemporary Arts in London in 1979.

Neither should we just credit Western intellectuals with this kind of ingenuity. Pre-Columbian religions in Mexico and Central America smuggled their gods past the Inquisition by disguising them as Catholic saints. In her book *Idols Behind Altars*, written during the 1920s, the Mexican-American writer Anita Brenner describes the numerous practices of this smuggling of one religion inside another. The same happened with *Vodou* (Voodoo) in Haiti.

A further scenario of denied freedom in which smuggling thrives occurs when activists and other idealists are interned. Two recent examples are to be found in Burma. Between 1998 and 2004, the artist and political prisoner Htein Lin smuggled from his prison cell in Burma over a thousand critical drawings and paintings made on plastic bags and *longyis* (sheets of cloth that are worn like a sarong). He bribed a guard to bring in paint for him and secreted some of the artwork in mattresses taken out by his family. One guard who discovered one or two of them thought that they were maps and threw them away. The dissident politician Aung San Suu Kyi, who was under house arrest for many years, smuggled out her recorded Reith Lecture, which was broadcast in Britain in 2011.

A lot of these gestures, many of them by people who were or later became famous subsequent to the successful clandestine circulation of their ideas, are made on behalf of the oppressed and they tend to be idealistic. But a meeting of knowledge and smuggling does not always deliver up enlightenment or even liberation. This qualifier is poignantly illustrated in Iranian director Samira Makhmalbaf's film *Blackboards* (2000). In the film, set in Iran, a teacher tags onto a train of boy mules carrying contraband towards an unspecified border. This teacher, who tries to make a class out of the forever-on-the-move smuggling boys, represents sense and stability as a counterpoint to their restlessness. It is evident in the following exchange. First the teacher: 'Listen, my child, with education you will be able to read a book, or even better, a newspaper, when you're travelling, learn to read and write! You'll know what's going on in the world.' The smuggler boy replies: 'Us, we're mules, always on the move. How do you expect us to read? To read a book, you have to sit down. Us, we never stop moving.' Nevertheless there is a network of solidarity among the boys, an instinctive sense of social participation through smuggling that substitutes for the desperate economic realities that they are circumventing.

Another way, then, of looking at smuggling as a noble or at least a popular activity is to consider its earthy reality and principle of social inclusion.

Social Values: Smuggling as Resistance

It is easy to be dazzled by some of the apparently authoritative characters in smuggling – Artigas or Zurbano – not to mention some of the less principled ones such as John Hawkins or Captain China. But the bottom line has usually been financial profit in one form or another, and the only way to ennoble it from this point of view is to ascribe to it a motive of social inclusion – a sense of community produced by the involvement of all in smuggling. Actually, this is not that difficult to demonstrate because many people have been pushed into smuggling by oppressive economic decrees, and it has been the only work or means of survival available to them. Richard Platt in his book *Smuggling in the British Isles* sums this up very clearly, modifying the romantic image: 'Perhaps instead smuggling deserves to be re-evaluated on the margins of Britain's labour history. Maybe those hanged and transported should take their place alongside the Tolpuddle Martyrs and Wat Tyler.'[6]

So, are smugglers fighting in a tight corner or do they naturally migrate towards their vocation? A bit of both, it would seem. It depends upon where they are operating, and how society treats both them and their bread and butter customers, the common people. If you were caught smuggling you would have been much better off as a colonist in the Spanish Americas than as a European: there was a significant difference in the penalty. Comparing the geographically variant punishment for smuggling with that for religious heresy is illuminating. In Spain and its colonies, until well into the Bourbon period, religious dissenters were executed and smugglers were only fined, unlike in England, where smugglers were jailed or executed and religious dissenters gradually came to be accepted.[7]

In the colonial Americas toleration was largely a facet of social pragmatism. At first it was a matter of enabling more people to profit from trade, and an economic necessity for the smooth running of society. Habsburg bureaucracy tended to view laws as ideals that often went unfulfilled (in the real world quotas of slaves had to be met, and if legal supply was insufficient, illicit supply was tolerated). Smugglers would plead lack of enforcement of decrees as an excuse for offending: in other words, everybody is at it, so why shouldn't I? Even in Britain, attitudes were changing: by the end of the eighteenth century widespread distribution of contraband was sometimes considered a utilitarian, Benthamite gain for society as a whole. Smuggling slaves was always penalized heavily but other 'harmless' contraband much less so, except when it was contraband of war.

Moving further up the stairway of virtue, one begins to see smugglers in a new light. A character in García Márquez's *Blacamán the Good* states that smugglers are 'men to be trusted and the only ones capable of venturing out under the mercurial sun of those salt flats'.[8] George Foy, seeming for a moment to step out of the futuristic world of his novel *Contraband*, and bringing together both pragmatic and worthy summations, quotes from Harry Beck's *Folklore and the Sea*: 'For many people smuggling is a way of life. The smuggler feels he is performing a service to his community rather than committing a crime.'[9]

The ambivalent morality behind smuggling different types of contraband occasionally emerges. For Henry de Monfreid in his autobiographical account *Pearls, Arms and Hashish*, smuggling, in his case in the Red Sea at the beginning of the twentieth century, wavers between motives of romantic adventuring, resistance and profit. But Ray Milland's smuggler hero Captain Evans in the film *Lisbon* (1956) is emphatic: 'I don't kill people, not required, and I don't traffic in narcotic, not required.'

Probably no smugglers were saints but, unfortunately for law enforcers, this is usually ignored in folklore and stereotype. By contrast the image of customs is almost always negative. In the few characterizations of customs in literature, preventive men are invariably depicted as incompetent, boring, miserable or plain nasty. Nathaniel Hawthorne's *The Customs House* is pretty damning of the profession, which is depicted as a tired and torpid upholder of the ideals signified by the eagle above the entrance of the house. As Adam Smith pointed out, customs was old and set in its ways: a 'customary' burden on the taxpayer.[10] Hawthorne goes further, seeing only 'evil and corrupt practices, into which, as a matter of course, every Custom-House officer must be supposed to fall'.[11]

These 'evil' practices don't seem to have corrupted the cultured life of one customs official, Charles Henry Brewitt-Taylor. In 1885 Brewitt-Taylor joined the Chinese Maritime Customs Service, serving in colonial smuggling hotspots like Tianjin (Tientsin), where during the Second Opium War the treaty of that name came into being, forcing the Chinese to open so-called 'treaty' ports for legitimized smuggling of opium. He was also resident in Yunnan, a prolific smuggling state. In the early twentieth century and the later Indochina wars its proximity to the Golden Triangle of opium cultivation and heroin production, and to the Ho Chi Minh Trail, made Yunnan important for trafficking in arms and narcotics. Brewitt-Taylor is known not just for his publications rewriting customs regulations but more significantly for his translation of the great fourteenth-century classic novel the *San Kuo* (written by Luo Guanzhong), known in English as the *Romance of the Three Kingdoms*. However, this refined colonial official was something of an exception among customs men.

Alongside the more typically lacklustre image, many smugglers might seem to come across as Robin Hood-style heroes, and this more positive stereotype pervades large areas of representation – literature,

Robert Louis
Mandrin, in an
undated engraving.

song, film and even serious history writing. Smugglers are rarely demonized, a point that social historian Eric Hobsbawm makes in his book *Bandits* in relation to the smuggler Robert Mandrin: 'He was a professional smuggler from the Franco-Swiss border region, a trade never considered criminal by anybody except governments.'[12]

The story of Robert Mandrin is typical of the romance of smuggling. Sometimes known by his first name, Louis, Mandrin was a Dauphiné man, born and bred in St-Etienne-de-Saint-Geoirs near Grenoble. He became a big-time smuggler in response to an incident in which his brother was caught, tortured and hanged for the petty contrabanding that supplemented the family income. Motivated by vengeance, he was soon smuggling silk, muslin, tobacco, tree bark, jewels, watches and prayer books. As his smuggling activities developed, he was forced to flee to Switzerland but this only facilitated his raising a guerrilla army, mainly from the disaffected of Savoy and Switzerland. In 1754 they descended upon France, fighting running battles with the *gâpians*, the French preventive men. Significantly for the concept of smuggling as something more than profiteering, he soon became known as a bandit revolutionary and subsequently a folk hero. Smuggling was his resistance.

Following his first foray, and back in Switzerland, yet more recruits joined his rebel uprising and he returned to France with more than 2,000 men. His private army stormed the customs houses and jails of eastern France, setting free only smugglers and army deserters. Mandrin gained more popularity after he forced the hated farmers-general to buy his contraband themselves, even after they made it illegal to deal in any way with smugglers. This impudent action succeeded in several towns, although he encountered stiff opposition at Le Pûy after the *argoulets*, the regular army, were drafted in to defend the house of the farmers-general merchants. Having lost several men in a frontal assault, the rebels stormed the building from the roof, rather like a modern-day anti-terrorism squad.

During 1754 Mandrin made six sorties into France but eventually, although back in Savoy, his corps was infiltrated by government agents claiming to be army deserters. One night at the castle of Rochefort, the traitors opened the gates for the *argoulets* who poured in and seized Mandrin. On 26 May 1755, defiant to the end, Mandrin was executed in the marketplace at Valence.

One could look at this another way: as merely a small part of a social history of salt smuggling in which Mandrin, who began through informally trading salt, was just a colourful dot. We could go back to the Dutch arriving on the Araya Peninsula in Venezuela. They were not there to provide inspiration for the cast of future Hollywood epics: they arrived after their European salt provision, vital for preserving foodstuffs, was cut off by the Spanish. Taxing salt, so ubiquitous, was an easy way of raising revenue. The Chinese, particularly the Sung dynasty (tenth to thirteenth century), enthusiastically taxed salt production and trade. The British, quite fantastically, built a 1,500-mile-long hedge in India to act as a customs barrier for collecting salt tariffs. Gandhi's great salt march must be seen in the context of this history. Mandrin, as a salt smuggler, was at one with the people who resented above all the imposition of a punitive tax on a staple provision.

Alcohol, while not an essential commodity, has always been popular as contraband. Again one might approach this history in different ways. American prohibition and its attendant smuggling is, in popular perception, most often seen through the lens of gangsterism and the spirited response to it: Al Capone, Eliot Ness and speakeasies. But it can also be felt in, as Platt puts it, the 'margins of labour history'.

American mobsters were also in Cuba but there is another side to the liquor story coming out of this island. Enrique Serpa's *Contrabando*, a novel set in and around the impoverished but politically militant Cuba of the 1920s, gets beneath the skin of worker resistance as it portrays a spectrum of characters on the contraband boat *La Buena Ventura*, from the opportunist captain, El Almirante, to the anarchist Cornuá and the rest of the crew who 'work like mules'. In at least two ways it is a novel of collective resistance, going beyond personal rebellion. First, unlike most smuggler fiction that creates larger-than-life, melodramatic char-acterizations, it gets close to the distinctive ways of speaking of the *contrabandistas*. Second, smuggling at that time had a militancy in that it broke a broader agenda of U.S. Prohibition that aimed at squeezing more productivity out of workers while not really affecting the middle classes, who could afford the small amounts of contraband alcohol that were initially available.

Moving beyond romantic stereotyping, a case can certainly be made for the importance of smuggling within the histories of both revolution and social resistance. A further question might be: how is singular, personal identity produced out of smuggling?

Smuggling and Identity

How does one spot a smuggler? Well, it might be a little more compli-cated than the pirate-lite image that seems to colour much of our perception of smuggling. Take for instance the 'contraband' of Louisa May Alcott's short story 'My Contraband'. This is an account of an American Civil War nurse who falls in love with a wounded contraband (in Civil War parlance, a black Southerner who has gone over to fight on the Unionist side). This, however, is not the only interesting aspect to the story: contraband is also her illicit desire for the man. It is a bid to escape the path that seems to be mapped out for a New England girl from a good family.

Desire also seems to be more than economic in some stories more familiar to our times. Moroccan writer Mahi Binebine's *Welcome to Paradise* is a tale about migration *san papiers*. On the northern shore of Morocco seven migrants wait for passage across the Straits of Gibraltar to 'Paradise'. The narrator, Aziz, is a Moroccan youth looking for a better life. As they wait to be smuggled across, they are urged to burn their papers so as to become less identifiable as illegal immigrants when they get to Spain. Aziz thinks it a terrible thing to do:

What a waste, don't you think, all those red, blue, green and maroon passports mouldering in the pockets of all those ripped jeans. Ah, now if I had one, I'd have taken care of it. I'd have cosseted it, pressed it to my heart, I'd have hidden it somewhere the thieving and envious wouldn't ever be able to find it, sewn into my skin, right in the middle of my chest, so I'd only have to unbutton my shirt to show it when I was crossing borders.[13]

Even when our estimation of smuggling is at its lowest – usually around trafficking in narcotics – there is more to it than meets the eye. The cultural theorist Avital Ronell links it to subjective modalities of expression within capitalism: '[drugs] double for the values with which they are at odds, thus haunting and reproducing the capital market, creating visionary expansions, producing a lexicon of body control and a private property of self.'[14] In another fiction, it is more than just cocaine that is being smuggled inside the body. The dramatist Winsome Pinnock's main character, Allie, in her play *Mules*, proclaims: 'Every face that's ever scowled at me, looked down at me, denied me. Headmasters, teachers, shop assistants, petty officials. I walked through customs sticking two fingers up at them all and they couldn't do anything about it. One-nil to me.'[15]

Are smugglers more often than not performing an alter ego? There is one example in fiction that is precisely about this. Michelangelo Antonioni's film *The Passenger* (1975) is all about a television news reporter who is having a breakdown. Circumstance finds him sharing an evening with a somewhat nondescript man in the bar of a seedy hotel in Saharan Chad, where he is researching a documentary about the civil war. When in the morning he discovers the man dead, he adopts his identity, playing out the life of someone who, he begins to discover as he follows up a chain of rendezvous, had been a gun smuggler for a rebel group. Like Alcott's character in 'My Contraband', the secrecies and evasions of the smuggler mentality perfectly suit his flight from the path laid out before him.

It would be a legitimate criticism to state that of course this is all fiction and that these four characterizations created by Alcott, Binebine, Pinnock and Antonioni are merely performance, but nevertheless the implication that we are all smuggling something in the performance of our daily lives is a convincing one. Under unusual circumstances we might all become smugglers; subconsciously perhaps we already are. Sigmund Freud thought as much when he likened psychoanalysts to border guards searching not just briefcases and portfolios – what the patients offer up – but also what these 'spies' and 'smugglers' might have hidden away.[16]

Maybe these small smuggling operations are about holding ourselves together and, occasionally, projecting another side to ourselves.

THE MULTITUDE OF TYPES of smuggling show its complexity but also, I hope, move it beyond the merely black and white. It has been perceived as both base and noble, sordid and heroic, revolutionary and profiteering, an economic aberration and necessary alternative labour. It can be opportunist or, as in the case of salt, an historically ingrained response to over-taxation. And in personal terms it might be quite a natural way of maintaining or even enlivening our everyday lives.

All of this would be of little concern to most hardened smugglers. The Englishmen who smuggled for both the French and the English during the Napoleonic Wars would have had little time for such sentiments. Even the pirate smuggler Jean Lafitte, who became a patriot at the Battle of New Orleans in 1814 and occasionally played the part of a revolutionary, was at heart merely a freebooter. It is to these pragmatic smugglers caught up in events that I now turn.

PART TWO

SMUGGLING EMPIRES

SEVEN

PIRATICAL PATRIOTS

Fickle and Pragmatic Smugglers

'Hellish banditti'
General Andrew Jackson commenting on Louisiana smugglers and privateers

'Piratical Smugglers'
New Orleans newspaper editorial, 19th century

Barataria is a bay some 50 miles south of New Orleans. In 2010 it was hit, like most of the Louisiana coast, by the Deepwater Horizon oil spill. The islands here are largely mud and grassland, with a few small windblown oak trees. Very few people actually live here but the spill caused environmental devastation and ruined the fisheries. In 1810, long before this modern surplus filtered into the bayous, there was a thriving community. People came from New Orleans not to birdwatch but because on one of the islands, Grand Terre, quite a bargain could be had. The bay is named after the Spanish word *barato*, meaning cheap, and it was the smuggling world of Jean Lafitte.

The legend of Lafitte portrays a dashing, charming privateer smuggler, a leader respected and loved by his men. He also dealt in slaves and some considered him a pirate. What, then, was the moral compass of Jean Lafitte and his brother Pierre? One answer envisages a world of treachery and opportunism, betrayal of nation and pursuit of personal profit. Another is that smugglers like the Lafittes constructed new worlds with their own laws: justice, *égalité* and *fraternité*. There is clearly something of a paradox here. On the one hand these privateering smugglers seem be the heirs of Hawkins and Drake – out for profit under the guise of patriotism. They were caught up in empire-building similar to that of the spice race (only that now one can add the expansionist Americans and the battling Latin American revolutionaries to a mix of Spanish, French and British). On the other they created functioning alternative societies beside these cynical motivations.

Smuggler Patriots

There were often complex and ambiguous relations between smugglers and customs between the seventeenth and nineteenth centuries. This was especially true during the turbulent years of revolution in both Europe and America, beginning with the American struggle for independence and running through the French Revolution, the Napoleonic era and the independence struggles in Latin America. The spectrum of opportunity ranged between piracy, privateering, filibustering and smuggling. They all overlapped to some degree and each might be ascribed to the Lafittes at different stages in their career. It is not that there wasn't also the black and white of smugglers arraigned against revenue men but rather that between these two poles there were also the smudged lines of grey that ran like the ink on a ship's manifest left out in the drizzle.

One of the most colourful of the Cornish smuggling bands, the Carters of Prussia Cove, occasionally operated in this haze. From the safety of their stronghold on the south Cornish coast near Penzance, they were consistently defiant of authority. But they also operated in a milieu of shifting loyalties when they were caught up in the larger drama of the Napoleonic Wars. Even before this Harry Carter, with his vessel *Swallow*, had served the Crown, in a fashion, as a privateer in the American Wars of Independence. Later, on travelling to St Malo for repairs to his cutter *Shaftesbury*, he found himself in jail, suspected of being a pirate. John, his brother, arrived to bail him out but he too was imprisoned. At this point the story becomes more mysterious. An exchange was made, apparently at the behest of the Admiralty, for two French officers incarcerated in England. Surely this was recompense for work done that benefited the crown. Not long after, Harry was bailed out as a smuggling operation foundered, this time at the Mumbles in south Wales. His ship fled after being mistaken for a privateer, and in the panic he was left stranded, suspected of piracy because his papers were on the escaping ship. Again it was the Lords of the Admiralty who came to his rescue.

There is more tangible evidence of his service to the Crown. In 1782 Harry quite clearly demonstrated his patriotism by answering the call of the Collector of Customs in St Ives to confront the alien privateer *Black Prince* from Dunkirk, which was menacing the Bristol Channel. Commanding the *Shaftesbury* and aided by another Carter vessel, *Phoenix*, they damaged the enemy ship, which sought refuge in Padstow but eventually sank. Carter apprehended seventeen survivors.

Of course smugglers also knew that the fog of war might benefit their clandestine business. When the smuggler William Fenwick's ship *Rachel* was overhauled by the Jersey-based naval vessel *Aristocrat*, commanded by an emigré Frenchman, he stated that the reason he was lost in the Irish Sea was because while sailing round the north of Scotland he had become disorientated in a storm. He was actually at Cape Fréhel near St Malo, as he well knew.

On the other hand there are numerous examples of men who, though their smuggling actions defrauded the exchequer, nevertheless, cometh the hour, put the interests of the nation first. Two such were Hampshire smugglers Isaac Gulliver and Harry Paulet. Gulliver's claim to being a smuggler-patriot came after he foiled a French assassination attempt on George III, who was on holiday in Weymouth, by alerting a Royal Naval squadron of the approach of a French force. Another story claims that he passed information to Nelson about the whereabouts of the French fleet. Before him, Paulet is said to have escaped a French vessel during the Seven Years' War clutching a bag of despatches that he found in a cabin. Subsequently, on a smuggling run, he sighted the fleet of French Admiral Conflans, which had evaded the British blockade at Brest. Paulet alerted the British commander, Admiral Hawke, who, though at first sceptical, nevertheless set his course to intercept the French fleet, surprising it at Quiberon Bay in 1759 and winning a decisive battle. Paulet, who had assisted in the battle itself, was amply rewarded in gold guineas.

At other times this fealty seems a little suspect: after a whirlwind career as a smuggler and privateer in Britain and the Caribbean where he served on the *Terrible*, the Welsh smuggler Owen Williams briefly became a customs officer. It seems, though, that this was merely cover for more smuggling and he later returned to privateering, this time off the Barbary Coast.

Official Smuggling

Maybe we shouldn't be surprised by the proximity that the British Crown actually had to its smugglers. Yet another Hampshire smuggler, Temple

Simon Luttrell, from an old Irish gentry family, was reputedly a smuggler to order of fine wines and cognac for the aristocracy, and even for the king. He died in a French jail in 1803. Another renowned smuggler, Captain Yawkins, who operated around the Solway Firth, once took lunch with a revenue cutter captain. Before returning to his patriotically named smuggling vessel the *Black Prince* (apparently a popular name for smuggling craft), he presented the officer with his prized gun and a decanter.

There was also ambiguity in the relations between the Royal Navy and smugglers: sometimes bitter hatred but much respect. This latter is ascribed to admiration for smugglers' seamanship but it might also be explained as empathy: there had always been a certain amount of smuggling within the Navy itself. Sailors often bought illegal gold and silver coins, and captains sometimes refused customs men access to holds. When in 1767 HMS *Active* arrived at Spithead off Portsmouth, many crew were 'privately' running contraband rum from Jamaica. As they were transferring to the port in a Navy barge they were ambushed by a revenue cutter. A fight ensued but, with several customs men up-ended into the water, they made it to the off-limits naval dockyards for a party and a bonus. During the eighteenth century Royal Navy ships (for instance HMS *Gorgon* in 1794, according to its captain, James Gardner) smuggled silver dollars out of Cádiz. One ruse, associated with the English Hotel, was to secrete them in specially adapted waistcoats to carry them past the port authorities.

The State's Ambiguity Towards Smuggling in Peace and War

In times of crisis, when it came to actual battles, the state, and in particular the Royal Navy, needed its smugglers to be on side. The Act of Oblivion of 1782 offered amnesty to smugglers if they would fight in the American war, notwithstanding the fact that other smugglers who had been deported to the North American colonies might be fighting against them. Again in 1792, as war loomed closer to home, the government offered a free pardon to smugglers who would enlist in the Navy. Smuggling captains, as master seamen, were a boon to the service and most smugglers were more able than press-ganged men. Officers were to put the letters CP before their new service numbers, indicating that they had been enlisted via 'civil powers'. Some were recruited primarily because they owned their own vessels.

It had not always been like this: when smugglers showed principle it was sometimes for the other side. Evidence of this is found in Hawkhurst in Sussex, which is associated with the most infamous act of English smuggling brutality. Here a gang tortured and murdered a customs officer and his informant. They supported the Jacobite cause, distributing leaflets proclaiming the right to the throne of the deposed king, James Stuart. A pub in the village, The Oak and Ivy, was named after the emblem of the Jacobite rebels.

Perhaps this is one reason why the state clamped down on smuggling before the Napoleonic era. The Act of Indemnity of 1736 imposed the death penalty for smuggling (but even here a deal might be struck and informants offered a free pardon). Undeterred, smuggling escalated, becoming a major drain on the government's finances. This provoked a more systematic crackdown and the golden age of smuggling supposedly ended with William Pitt the Younger's anti-smuggling campaign of 1784–5. The Commutation Act of 1784 was the first real blow to smuggling. It slashed duty on tea and at a stroke rendered the smugglers' mainstay contraband unprofitable. Notwithstanding this, the Napoleonic Wars provided new opportunities.

New Worlds of Opportunity for the Lafitte Brothers

Unlike smugglers, pirates were rarely offered a free pardon, but privateering – corsairing in French terminology – was a powerful Faustian bargain that the state made with its piratical tendency. Privateering was actually considered quite honourable and patriotic. This became, not for the first time, the frame for smuggling. The extended European wars between Britain and France fought out in a colonial context in the Caribbean provided great opportunities for desperate, energetic and innovative men like Pierre and Jean Lafitte.

Before finding their niche in smuggling in Louisiana, the brothers, refugees from France, tried their hand at privateering. When they arrived, conditions were also favourable for the emergence of concentrated nodes of smuggling, particularly in or beside supposedly neutral or rebellious territories. At the time of the Seven Years' War, St Eustatius, then as now a Dutch colony, became one of these smuggling worlds. So too did that old smuggling settlement Spanish Monte Cristi which, being so close to French Saint-Domingue (present-day Haiti), was a good place for smugglers to trade indirectly with the French in defiance of British blockades.

Other places, such as Rhode Island, were hotbeds of smuggling within the mercantile system of the British colony. Another more obviously separate smuggling world was Fernandina on Amelia Island in Spanish Florida. It became an important landing point for illegal slaves. This is the context of conflict and illicit trading opportunity in which the brothers found themselves as these wars between the Bourbon French and British extended into the Napoleonic era, and as the colonial Americas fell into 50 years of revolution.

The Lafittes have always divided opinion. Were they smugglers, privateers, smuggler-privateers or simply pirates? At the height of their speculative informal trading, as they built a small empire from contrabanding, the local press in New Orleans was calling them 'piratical smugglers',[1] but they were also privateer patriots who were simply doing in public what the American government schemed to do in private. One complexity involved in labelling the Lafittes, or indeed many of the smugglers who appear in this chapter, arises from the fact that the authority with which they are faced in part mirrors them. New Orleans, the seat of authority from which these accusations of piratical smuggling emanated, was itself in a renegade situation in relation to the new United States. The city's population, which was around 25,000 in 1810, was largely made up of Spanish and French, many of them Creoles. The French contingent was swelled by refugees from the slave revolt in Sainte-Domingue. All relished the potentiality of New Orleans as a trading world, semi-autonomous beside its new straitlaced landlord, the United States.

But even the U.S., while striking a dignified neutral pose in public, was simultaneously playing another great game. Consider its official posture towards Spain, the traditional commercial power in the region. The U.S. government had imposed severe restrictions on commerce aimed at curtailing Britain and France's influence: in 1807, under Jefferson, trade with all foreign ports was banned, which also affected Spain. But from 1809, with the Non-intercourse Act, conditions were relaxed in an attempt to embargo only Britain and France, given that smuggling was now thriving as the only means of supply of vital goods. However, the U.S. duped Spain as well, often supporting revolutionary movements in South and Central America and Mexico.

Informal American policy helped the Lafittes' informal business. The brothers, whose dubious commissions for privateering came from revolutionary governments in formation, repeatedly survived U.S. attempts to eradicate smuggling because New Orleans was the headquarters for these nascent revolutionaries, who were secretly supported by the American nation-builders and expansionists. The laissez-faire and bellicose conditions that favoured privateering in Napoleonic Europe were amplified in this crucible of imperial and national ambitions.

Jean and Pierre Lafitte were particularly well attuned to this world, almost, it seems, from their youth. Brought up in Bordeaux, they did not have an easy life and from an early age, at times of scarcity during the period of the 'Terror' following the Revolution, they dabbled in smuggling across the Pyrenees. Now, in Louisiana via the French Caribbean islands, and still operating in a milieu of unrest, the brothers saw the possibility of making a smuggling world with laws unto itself within the New World. Pierre was the businessman, usually based in New Orleans, whereas Jean was the man of action in the field, which in this case was Barataria.

Barataria

It is thought that a brief career as captain of a privateer vessel served Jean well towards becoming potentate of Barataria. This rough-hewn colony is what the cultural theorist and activist Hakim Bey, writing about 'pirate utopias', might call a Temporary Autonomous Zone (TAZ).[2] Some of the characteristics of a TAZ are that it is short-lived, burns vibrantly while it lasts, makes its own laws and has a unique culture. Barataria was precisely like this; a kind of mutant American Dream.

Jean began operating in Barataria Bay around 1809, first on the island of Grand Terre, then Grand Isle and later occasionally from Cat Island. Privateers provided the contraband, bringing in hijacked vessels to be stripped and often reflagged as additions to a fleet of predatory vessels. The channel at the eastern end of Grand Isle was the only one deep enough for oceangoing vessels and so Lafitte fortified this point. The Lafitte oufit worked because it seems that they alone, among a crowd of opportunists, had the entrepreneurial ability and speculating courage to set up a smuggling world with a momentum that precluded its dispersal after each operation. It involved making alliances that could provide letters of *marque* for privateering which the Lafittes then dispensed, or subcontracted, to various associates and other adventurers. They provided both a port and the channels for forwarding the contraband to market.

The Lafittes very quickly got to know the bayous, and used them to ferry contraband northwards to points on the Mississippi below New Orleans, from where buyers would take goods into the city. Alternatively they used a route to the west of Barataria Bay, Lafourche Bayou. It was hardly a secret: rather like in today's Guajira, contraband was notionally subject to confiscation but still flooded in and was available to all.

Although Jean was referred to by some of the privateering suppliers as 'the governor', he was hardly an autocrat and, like Hakim Bey's pirate utopias of Tortuga and Salo, Barataria was in part run along socialist lines. It was a community with its own body of laws and discipline. Every man on a ship was entitled to a share of the prize regardless of their importance. If they were injured, there was compensation. The Barataria contrabanding community lasted only until 1814, when larger historical events swept it away.

Smugglers at the Battle of New Orleans

The Lafittes adapted just as smuggling had fluctuated during the seventeenth century: the operation metamorphosed into something else when conflict loomed. The British–American war of 1812 provided a stage and the battle for New Orleans (1814) a catalyst for change. In these circumstances they could opt for either piracy or patriotism. Barataria had been under threat for some time now because it had become too high-profile, too autonomous. The contraband economy of New Orleans also had powerful enemies, unlike the earlier contraband silver society of Buenos Aires or the smuggling republic of Paraguay in our times.

So how did the Lafittes' opportunistic patriotism emerge? Jean was approached at Barataria by a British naval captain, Nicholas Lockyer, representing Commodore Percy, who was in charge of the naval invasion force threatening New Orleans. Lockyer proposed that Lafitte take sides with the British against the Americans. For whatever reason – newly discovered patriotism, opportunism, potential monetary reward, because his brother Pierre was in prison for piracy or because he sought a pardon for his alleged misdeeds – Jean listened to and led on the captain while actually offering his services to Governor Claiborne and General Andrew Jackson, his erstwhile enemies. He communicated his offer through a banker, Jean Blanque, a member of the New Orleans legislature. Blanque was one among many in the New Orleans merchant community to have benefited from the smuggling world of Barataria. Lafitte offered to defend the bay, and was supported by the lawyer Edward Livingston, another influential friend who would continue to represent the Lafittes in New Orleans, in and out of court, in years to come. Jackson and Livingston were old friends. At the time of the crisis Jackson even wrote to President Madison urging that the Lafittes be allied to the cause and that all smugglers and adventurers with dubious privateering commissions be offered amnesty.

However, the Lafittes' overtures were a little behind unfolding events, because both Percy and an ambitious American naval officer, Daniel Tod Patterson, were determined to invade and eradicate the renegade settlement at Barataria as soon as possible. This duly took place when Patterson invaded Barataria on 16 September 2014. Now the Lafittes had another motive – to regain some of the $500,000 losses from this eviction from Barataria. Playing patriot enhanced their chances of success.

Andrew Jackson took some convincing of Lafitte's offer: although he would later relent, he considered the Lafitte operation to be one of 'hellish banditti'.[3] However, he needed people like them, not just for their bush knowledge of the bayous but because New Orleans itself was full of their kind: ethnically diverse immigrants who would need to be cajoled to defend the city. Given the signal, on 20 December 1814 Jean and Pierre Lafitte marched into New Orleans and met with Jackson. What finally persuaded the general was the approaching British invasion force and his lack of flints for his infantry's guns. The Lafittes conveniently had a stockpile and dutifully took the oath following the offer of amnesty to 400 renegades. With them came 7,500 flints. The irony was that at the time of the battle the British and Americans had already signed a peace treaty ending the war, although the news had not yet reached Louisiana or the British squadron.

The Lafittes' participation in the defence of New Orleans has persisted in legend but their contribution was quite peripheral. Jean was dispatched to help set up an artillery position to defend one of the main bayou approaches to the city. Meanwhile Pierre, a little more central, became a kind of on-the-ground consultant on the natural defences of the approaches, front and rear, to New Orleans: the swamps and forests that had provided such cover for smuggling and that might now hinder the enemy. Thus the elder Lafitte, utilizing his bush knowledge, made a useful although not pivotal contribution in winning the Battle of New Orleans. Then something quite bizarre occurred to the smuggler and erstwhile lord of Barataria. Pierre Lafitte was sent to the bay with the mission of clearing it of all human habitation, a small scorched-earth tactic that both deprived the enemy of a sustainable foothold and prevented a resurgence of smuggling and privateering.

Galveston Island

The patriotism of the Lafittes did not last long, although it played out fitfully in the courts as they attempted to recover some of their lost fortune. Pardoned and legitimized, they nevertheless found themselves impoverished. What they needed was a new world of smuggling.

It came on an undercurrent, not yet a wave, of manifest destiny as the Americans, pretending to support Mexican insurgents, eyed up Texas as a new territory. Galveston Island was an opportunity for filibusters (private, speculative revolutionary forces), smugglers and privateers, and a useful irritant to the Spanish that the Americans could use in their games of intrigue. For the Lafittes it would become their second autonomous smuggling zone, albeit – inevitably – a temporary one.

Galveston was a harsh place also known as *Malhado* (Isle of Doom) and *Isla Culebra* (Snake Island). Its potential emerged after would-be revolutionaries occupied the island as a stepping stone to annexing Texas and began to issue privateering commissions against the Spanish. Until now it had never been permanently occupied, although the Karankawa people came there to fish. At least at first, the island was not private or even remotely exclusive to the Lafittes. But around this time, Pierre purchased the ship *Presidente* and began fitting her out as a privateer. Operating out of Galveston, the old firm began to regroup and a second smuggling world evolved. They soon prospered, at least locally. It quickly became apparent that they were the most organized of a dissolute bunch of privateers, smugglers and filibusters, and could play one faction off against another. By April 1817 Pierre had played a decisive hand in re-mobilizing some of the old privateering band out of the chaos of the battle. Jean had outmanoeuvred everybody on the ground with a mixture of charm, leadership and provision, drawing manpower to his camp so that his became the dominant operation on the island, setting him above even the loudest and most bullying of privateering captains and wannabe dictators of Latin America. Among the opportunistic smugglers who allied themselves with the Lafittes at Galveston was James Bowie, inventor of the fearsome knife and hero of the Alamo, who along with his brothers traded slaves between the island and nearby Louisiana. Jean set up an admiralty court, which was typical of all privateering bases. Bizarrely for such a bunch of desperados, and for an activity that has a reputation for disregarding the law, it was an authority that regulated privateering and its fair execution. He even appointed a collector of customs. Nevertheless, despite operating under the flag of the Mexican revolutionary junta, they were actually a law unto themselves.

Looking a little more closely at this world, one might come to the conclusion that this was hardly a utopia – Hakim Bey's hope for a TAZ. The Lafittes and their clan were fiercely loyal to one another but they had few longstanding compatriots and would spy for whomsoever could provide them with the latest advantage in this game of snakes and ladders, including everybody's old enemy, the Spanish. Slaves were once again a primary contraband and were smuggled to New Orleans. The going rate was $1 per pound of flesh. This particular smuggling world lasted only until 1820.

The Death of the Lafittes

Galveston had not been blessed with the protection – political, geographical or even climatic – that Barataria had for a time enjoyed. The settlement was hit by a devastating hurricane soon after the filibusters and smugglers arrived, making an already desolate place even more difficult to inhabit. The pirate-privateer world was changing fast. From 1819 onwards the U.S. tolerated only privateers that were sanctioned by legitimate states. Jean Lafitte's only legitimate commission of his entire career came when all other avenues had been exhausted: following a protracted abandonment of Galveston, he took a commission in the fledgling Colombian Navy, at last becoming a 'legitimate' operator. But by now, for many, these subtle distinctions no longer mattered and they considered him neither a benign smuggler nor even a privateer but simply an out-and-out pirate. The lustre of folk heroism that held this judgement in abeyance at Barataria was blown away in the swirling dust of a disintegrating Galveston.

Piracy often overlapped with smuggling in this period but life expectancies in that world were inevitably short. Pierre, on the run, died in the Yucatán, Mexico, in 1821 while trying to set up a third smuggling world on Isla Mujeres. In 1823 Jean met his end at sea in a skirmish after being lured into an ambush by two Spanish warships.

BY 1823 VIRTUALLY ALL newly legitimated states that had once supported privateering and smuggling during their times of rebellion outlawed it. This virtually ended filibustering and privateering. Where would the contraband come from and where would it land now that there were no more Baratarias or Galvestons? And when the Americans reduced customs duties, what was the point?

The temporary smuggling zones at Barataria and Galveston burned brightly but they were snuffed out relatively quickly because they soon became isolated. In Europe at this time, between 1810 and 1814, a smuggling world came into being that had the backing of an emperor.

EIGHT

BUSINESS AS USUAL

Napoleon's English Smugglers

'Genti terribili'
Napoleon Bonaparte reflecting upon English smugglers

The English merchants and adventurers who clung on to desperate little trading settlements at Batavia and Aceh in Indonesia during the sixteenth and seventeenth centuries – de facto smugglers in a spice trade dominated by the Dutch – would have collapsed in disbelief were they to hear the invitation extended by Napoleon Bonaparte to English smugglers on 15 June 1810. At that moment, by imperial decree, Dunkirk was to be opened up for them. Subsequently, on 30 November 1811, he set up a *ville des smoglers*, a smuggler city: an enclave at Gravelines for these *genti terribili* who were ostensibly his enemy. On the smugglers' part, given that Britain was at war with France, this seems to have been blatant treachery. What was going on? It was the strange other world of Bonaparte's so-called 'guinea run', a means for him to pay for his mercenary army with British coin.

The smuggler quarter of Gravelines, contemporaneous with Barataria, was a much more ordered and organized – indeed official – version of the Louisiana smuggling world. The enclave was actually only the most visible aspect of smuggling. The proud guinea smugglers of Kent and Sussex had established a broader illicit culture straddling the Channel. This culture, in Gravelines but also in Deal and Folkestone, is the main focus here. But in examining the guinea run one must also consider its geopolitical extension, beginning in Latin America, running through London and Paris and beyond, as it oiled the wheels of Bonaparte's pan-European war effort.

The Raison d'être of the Guinea Run

The main reason that Napoleon needed British gold, most conveniently in the form of guineas, was to remain solvent, particularly given the expense of paying a large mercenary army. The secondary reasons were to boost his own manufacturing and banking sectors and to ruin the British economy. Britain needed to hold onto its gold as there had been a periodic run on its reserves, and in times of war one needed ready and reliable capital. Exporting gold had been illegal since 1797.

Why were guineas more desirable for Napoleon than other currencies, such as Spanish silver coins? The French were fighting the Spanish and British in the Iberian Peninsula and so that channel of supply was difficult. Guineas were easier: at the end of the eighteenth century, war had so devalued currencies that this coin, rich in gold content, became a solid and valuable currency. Perhaps just as importantly, smugglers were prepared to supply it. From the smugglers' point of view the emperor was prepared to offer 30 shillings per coin. The international transfer of monies was as shady, circuitous and multilayered then as it is today. Napoleon obtained money from Veracruz in Mexico that was then sent to London by agents via places like Amsterdam and Hamburg. This was then used to speculate on the fluctuating English currency and to buy gold when the rate was favourable. Hence the money markets seemed to float above political differences.

Conditions were propitious for the guinea run because there was already a diverse smuggling culture. Indeed, smuggling thrived through-out the Napoleonic Wars (1793–1814). In the later years conditions were particularly favourable because of the emperor's increasing reliance upon it, but from the beginning, with customs duties in Britain raised to finance the war, there was much incentive to smuggle. There was less risk than in William Pitt's day: only a threadbare anti-smuggling operation existed as all Navy and revenue ships were redeployed for war.

From 1809 there had been a licensing system for semi-licit trade between the two countries because both sides were, paradoxically, so reliant upon each other. That year Britain's harvest failed and it needed grain. After both economies dived in 1810, France needed the market in Britain for trading in wines, brandy and silk. The latter continued to compulsively expand its exports, despite the war. Ports on the Continent continued to trade: they included Flushing (now Vlissingen, in the Netherlands), Calais, Dunkirk, Boulogne, Dieppe, Nantes, Cherbourg,

Lorient, Le Havre and Roscoff. This grey market was, then, tolerated to a certain degree. The running of liquors and silks into Britain on the returning guinea boats could even be thought of as an extension of this semi-licit trade.

Nevertheless until 1810 English smugglers were still largely unwelcome in French ports, and were pursued in home waters. They avoided these ports by operating out of the Low Countries or by picking up contraband from neutral shipping in the Channel. Napoleon's offer was a game changer. Although supplying his armies through contraband was not a new tactic – Frankfurt became a major entrepôt for contraband during the wars – the strategic move of establishing an official smuggler haven for the supply of guineas most definitely was.

The Smuggler City

Dunkirk was the first haven alongside – to a lesser extent – Wimereux, but in November 1811 the *genti terribili* were all transferred to Gravelines because of their riotousness. Although they were no doubt thankful for the renewed calm, it was quite a blow to the citizens of Dunkirk to lose the informal trade, as it had little other commercial activity. At Gravelines Napoleon hosted the smugglers but at the same time wanted to corral them where he could keep an eye on them. Besides moderating their behaviour, his intention was that they should not know too much about the logistics of his war effort, for instance about the munitions factory beside Dunkirk. They were never integrated into society, although before their eviction from Dunkirk they had considerable freedom to socialize; indeed, this was part of the problem. They were 'welcomed' as cash cows but were still distrusted as citizens, no matter how renegade they were, of an enemy state.

At the guarded compound at Gravelines smugglers were regarded as legitimate traders, and even given paperwork. The city was actually quite small: a triangle with sides of just over 200 metres or so. Everything was bureaucratized, right down to food and dwellings. The smugglers would share the enclosure with their French military security escorts who were mindful of their previous behaviour in Dunkirk. There was even a customs office.

William Pitt's anti-smuggling campaign was designed to strike a mortal blow to import smuggling across the Channel but the guinea run provided empty boats at Gravelines that were begging to be filled with

French produce. The guinea operation was so extensive that this other smuggling soon took on industrial proportions. One figure or family, Haywood, recurs in the port records at Gravelines, bringing in tens of thousands of guineas on the boat *Hope*.[1] It wasn't just confined to the smuggler city port – at the height of the operation 40–50 ships went to Flushing each week. Smugglers were charged 6*d*. (old pence) for each cask of spirits taken out of the port. During 1813 some 600 or so smuggling vessels docked at different times in Gravelines.[2] It took eight or ten hours to row to France in a galley, five if it was calm, and a typical cargo was £30,000-worth of guineas. Every week an armed escort rode the gold to Paris. During the five years of this smuggling pact, five or six million guineas crossed the channel in galleys.

This was France, foreign soil, a smuggler community that was an aberration; surely the guinea run was less visible in England? It was certainly illegal here but in Kent and Sussex 'owling' was a centuries-old pursuit. The run gave smuggling here a more coherent identity, a sense of impunity and a mythology to match our popular image of Cornish smugglers.

Kent and Sussex Guinea Smugglers: Tactics and Technologies

The high duties on wool, and proximity to both London and the French shore, made the southeast coast of England an ideal smuggling territory from medieval times onwards. Later it was tea but now the main contraband, apart from French brandy and Dutch and French gin, was laces, silks and leather goods, as well as small luxury items such as perfume, watches and playing cards.

Deal and Folkestone were the key smuggler ports in the guinea run. At the former, a culture of resistance had hardened when in 1785 Pitt's revenue men burned the fleet of smuggler boats on the town beach in a show of intent. Other towns involved in the guinea run included Ramsgate, Dover, Hythe, Hastings, Bexhill and Eastbourne.

The success of the run, and indeed its character, was to a large extent built upon innovation and adaptability. Deal galleys were cheap to build but extremely effective. They were up to 40 feet in length, light, fast and crewed by five or six men. They had a large lugsail and five or six thwarts on which the rowers sat. They were so effective and evasive that the newly established but still severely stretched Preventive Water Guard began to build its own galleys for interception. Later on smugglers'

J.M.W. Turner, *Smuggler of Folkestone*, 1823–4, watercolour.

galleys were also built in France after raids on boatbuilding yards in England. One famous raid took place not in the southeast but at Christchurch in Dorset. The Black House at the entrance to the harbour is where galleys were built. It got its name after it was blackened by king's officers trying to smoke out the illicit boatbuilders within. The galleys that flew closest to the wind were the so-called 'death' galleys. These had virtually no cargo space and were prone to capsizing but they were very fast and had the advantage from an entrepreneur's point of view of being expendable. Clinker-built smuggling yawls were even faster than galleys. These were based on Viking drakkars and were up to 60 foot long with two masts and a crew of up to 30. 'Cocktail boats' were another vessel that smugglers used to evade detection. They had six oars, sailed out of Folkestone and went out to retrieve barrels of spirits that had been sunk on lines in the Channel.

Kent boats, like all galleys, were shallow in draught, and made good use of the physical features around and offshore. If pursued, they usually made for Goodwin Sands. Here they could lift the boat over the sandbar and launch it on the other side, leaving the revenue cutters out in the deep.

There were other shore-based tactics for evading revenue men. French shore authorities devised a warning system of flags and lanterns to ensure smooth, unimpeded passage. On the English side there is a story of an arrangement whereby women of Folkestone would light a large bonfire on the Durlocks to warn their men on the 'cocktail boats' that the revenue men had set out in their boats to intercept them. On one occasion, on seeing the warning beacon, the customs men returned to shore and confronted the women, leading to a fight in which the women gained the upper hand.

Safe in their smuggler city and confident in their home environs, the guinea smugglers nevertheless had to use smart tactics in the deep water. Names on galleys were sometimes changed en route to add confusion. Smugglers often flew Dutch and Prussian flags and carried foreign ship's papers, with the crew disguised as foreigners. If waylaid, multilingual seamen were pushed to the fore and pretended that English was not their first language. The tactics used in the guinea run were extremely savvy.

Treachery and Occasional Loyalty

Smugglers were cheered on by all sorts of members of the local community but regardless of this backing, we might still ask the question: didn't this amount to treason? After all, the guinea run was quite clearly funding the armies of Britain's arch enemy. And it gets worse: the smugglers brought guineas to France but also carried escaped prisoners of war, English newspapers, commercial correspondence and other intelligence. During the Peninsular War, Napoleon first heard about his own general, Marshal Messina, attacking the enemy lines at Torres Vedras through an English smuggler. They sometimes returned to England with French spies, even housing them and transporting them around the country. Their mantle of courage trailed a tag with a pound sign on it. As Napoleon put it in a revealing aside: 'They are people who have the courage and ability to do anything for money . . . They are *genti terribili*!'[3]

There were more than 100,000 French prisoners of war held in Britain during the course of the hostilities. Escape back to France might cost a POW up to 300 guineas. Many of the officers were on parole – a kind of limited freedom in a village or town of confinement. Smugglers courted business in these places but sometimes the Frenchmen absconded, either seeking out smugglers in London or rendezvousing with those already contracted by relatives in France. En route to the coast they would hide out in farmhouses, outbuildings or inns.

It was, on the face of it, a melodrama: the guinea run was peopled by bold but unscrupulous ghostly figures who only stood still for long enough to count their money. Smuggling lore around the time of the Napoleonic Wars doesn't really help us get into the minds of these men, who were prepared to sell out their country in one moment but defend it to the hilt in the next. The story of Tom Johnson is exemplary in this regard.

Johnson was a sometime participant in the guinea run. At the age of twenty-one he had joined a privateer operating out of Gosport chasing French shipping. He was imprisoned but cut a dubious deal with the French that he would spy for them. As he was returning to England on a smuggling cutter, he was intercepted and press-ganged into the Royal Navy. Unwilling to be pinned down, he jumped ship at Southampton and began a career transporting spies and information across the Channel.[4] Another time, Johnson was arrested by a riding officer near Winchelsea and forced to flee to Flushing. But soon afterwards he was to be found piloting a Royal Navy force intent upon driving the French out of Holland, for which he was not only pardoned but given a reward of £1,000, a sum which was insufficient to prevent him sliding towards a spell in a debtors' prison. His career is so ambiguous that at times it is difficult to know whether he was an opportunist mercenary or a double agent. If he operated as a double agent, was it out of principle or simply because it meant double the pay? True to form, he smuggled his way out of dire financial straits by taking up Napoleon's guinea run.

Johnson apparently saw no contradiction between this trade and his patriotic conscience, which always seemed to bring him back from the brink of out-and-out treason. Later he refused Napoleon's offer to pilot his invasion force and was once again imprisoned, this time at Flushing. On release he lent his great experience to the British cause, something he apparently only did when galvanized by an overwhelming imperative. In trouble again, he was forced to flee to New Orleans but on receiving another pardon returned to Britain and worked with the American Robert Fulton to develop mines to attack the French fleet at Brest. This didn't work but three years later he led a successful attack on Flushing harbour. He completed his seafaring life as captain of a revenue cutter, the *Fox* – chasing smugglers!

Finally, it seems, he knew which side his bread was buttered. He was given a pension of £100 a year and retired at 44, apparently intent upon whiling away his autumn years as an inventor working on designs for a submarine. It was one of the world's first practicable submarines and was part of the *Nautilus* project, the brainchild of Fulton when he had worked for the French. The outcome was a 100-foot-long submersible boat with stowable mast and sails. But sea trials didn't go too well, and he almost drowned. It was a lucky escape, but there is more to it than this – it seems that behind the scenes he had been commissioned by the French to the tune of £40,000 to use the sub for Napoleon's escape from St Helena! However, the emperor died before the craft was produced.[5] Would Johnson have seen it through? His smuggler soul that had seen him play a double game in the past might well have overridden his better judgement and tempted him into this outrageous technical challenge, patriotism cast once more to the wind.

Another famous smuggler from this period, Jack Rattenbury, is equally difficult to pin down. Rattenbury joined a privateer at fifteen but was captured and imprisoned by the French. He escaped and made passage on a smuggling brig but it was overhauled by a French privateer. There followed the most outrageous piece of single-handed commandeering. At first he acquiesced and steered the brig to a French port. But as the makeshift French crew became drunk below decks, a fog descended in more ways than one, and under its cover he steered for Portland Bill, convincing the crew that it was Alderney. He persuaded them to lower a boat to collect a pilot from a port that they presumably assumed was St Anne. He then dived overboard and made it into Swanage harbour, alerting customs as to the enemy at hand. They in turn despatched a cutter to seize the vessel.

As a career smuggler, such patriotic heroics were incidental. Rattenbury's primary concern was contraband alcohol, bought in the Channel Islands. But like Johnson he was not averse to profiting from the wars, ferrying the occasional French escapee to these islands, claiming that he thought they were simply displaced Islanders.

Loyalty to Community

In his own supportive community the smuggler had only to hide from the revenue men. The nuances of collective smuggling culture are sinuous but not impenetrable, and as one delves into it one discovers that it was not just individuals whose patriotism wavered.

The Channel Islands have always had an ambivalent relationship with the British Crown, perhaps never more so than during the Napoleonic Wars. The Islands had different customs laws to the rest of Britain, and this, along with their proximity to France, made them attractive to smugglers. At times the Crown must have wondered about their loyalties. In their territorial waters gun batteries sometimes fired upon revenue cutters as well as on Royal Navy vessels chasing smugglers who had violated mainland laws. During the Peace of Amiens in 1802, the Islands, like Dunkirk later, lost their informal trade. The smugglers and merchants' response was simply to move their homes, warehouses and businesses to Cherbourg and Roscoff, staying there even as war resumed.

Perhaps something similar was happening in Kent; after all, its foundries had supplied cannons to Spain that were used in the attempted Armada invasion of 1588. The smugglers themselves were only a part of a culture that implicated fishermen, labourers, landowners, merchants and even elements within the Preventive Force. Sometimes sailors in the new Waterguard service, established in 1809, were posted away from home to avoid the temptations of working near to friends and relatives who were either smugglers or colluding with them.

To sense the flavour of the 'respectable' or socially entangled dimension of smuggling one need look no further than Isaac Gulliver. Gulliver is remembered as a 'good' smuggler – he never killed anybody. His ostensible profession was innkeeper of the Blacksmith's Arms (later called the King's Arms) at Thorney Down on the Salisbury to Blandford road in Dorset. Later he moved to Longham Kinson and then to Bournemouth. He had the craftiness of a typical smuggler: the tower of St Andrew's church at Kinson was used for storing contraband, and supposedly a tomb was built specifically for this purpose. In 1776 he bought Eggardon Hill, a prehistoric earthwork near Dorchester, placing a conspicuous plantation on top to use as a marker for his ships. All this is quite familiar. But unlike many smugglers he retired a millionaire, becoming church-warden at Wimborne Minster, a pillar of society if he wasn't one already, so unlike the 'evil' clergyman-smuggler in Daphne du Maurier's *Jamaica Inn*. Portuguese and Spanish priests in Habsburg and Bourbon America were deeply implicated in contraband, and this was more of the same, although in a much more sedate, English kind of way.

Does this characterization bring us any closer to an understanding of the complex smuggling culture in Britain at this time? Probably not. We tend to be distracted because although he appears ingrained in the pattern of early nineteenth-century provincial life, Gulliver seems, like Johnson, to be, if not larger than life, then still a character in a melodrama. Perhaps we need to cast aside much of the romanticized image of British smuggling and consider it from a transactional point of view more to do with logistics and even strategy.

Hierarchies of Smuggling

Late eighteenth- and early nineteenth-century smuggling was never just confined to remote coves, overgrown tracks and secret stores: at the harbour front it was an overt market operation like any other. Shopkeepers, innkeepers and merchants placed orders with smugglers. Sometimes more covert methods were required: in France the merchandise awaited the English smugglers sensibly packaged, wine and spirits in kegs ready to be rolled and hauled up cliffs and dunes in Kent and Sussex.

However, the guinea trade that financed so much of this returning contraband extended far beyond the quay. At Gravelines there were 70 merchants, many Anglo-French by birth or even born in England, who were given licence to trade in contraband. But just four dominated the brokerage of guineas: Jean Castinel, Benjamin Morel, Henry Faber and Solomon Hesse. Behind them, in Paris and London, were figures like Nathan and James Rothschild of the famous banking family. In Paris the exchange of contraband gold wasn't a backstreet transaction. It involved the French banking firms of Mallet, Davillier and Hottinguer, among others; manufacturers, financiers and consumers of every standing in society were involved.

Does this social imbrication and political extension of smuggling point to the futility of castigating a few colourful individuals for their apparent treachery? Not necessarily. It is rather that contraband culture was complex and contradictory. Deal men, at times, were Napoleon's smugglers, but they were also pilots for Nelson.

A Twist in the Tale

There is a surprising coda to the tale of the guinea run that might even portray it in a patriotic light. It was not just Napoleon who needed gold. On the British side there was also need for a reliable currency that would be available for spending in the theatre of operations of the Iberian Peninsula. However, British gold could not be exported legally. Part of the solution was to buy up foreign gold both in London and abroad for use in the locus of the campaign. The demand raised its general value, making Napoleon all the more interested in shifting gold. Put these two facts together and something interesting emerges. The high finance side to the guinea run story might have been something of a double game.

One of the key players, as already mentioned, was Nathan Rothschild, who sent the guineas to Dunkirk and Gravelines, from where his brother James helped in its transportation to Paris, and to a lesser extent to Amsterdam and Lille. This is all very intriguing but nothing compared to the unexpectedness of where some of Napoleon's gold might have ended up. The transnational, semi-licit nature of the smuggling operation makes it likely that not all of the gold terminated in Paris in the vaults of the financial backers of the emperor. Incredibly some of this gold for *his* war effort, although it had been channelled through Napoleon's bureaucracy at his Channel ports, might have been siphoned off to Portuguese and Spanish banking houses in France by the Rothschilds, whereupon it could have been exchanged for bills to be smuggled across the Pyrenees to finance the British and Spanish fight *against* Napoleon on the Iberian Peninsula.[6]

TOWARDS THE END of the Napoleonic Wars smuggling became more difficult. By 1813, 105 Martello towers (small, round forts) had been constructed along the English coast as an anti-invasion strategy. These also served to deter smuggling. On the other hand, just like any other trade-restraining barrier, such as the blockade of the French coast that was imposed from 1806 onwards, they also increased the value of the contraband that did get through, thereby offering an incentive to the bold.

After the wars smuggling was dealt further blows. A blockade was placed upon the south Kent coast and was enforced tyrannically by Captain 'Flogging Joe' McCulloch. The Royal Military Canal impeded free movement around Kent's Romney Marsh. Pay improved in the Preventive Waterguard, eventually overtaking Navy pay. But at the end of hostilities there was also a flood of demobbed manpower, expert sailors and soldiers, to both sides of the smuggling/preventive divide. Options were limited, the obvious ones being blockade work – tedious and thankless – or more *plein-air*, often nocturnal pursuits.

In 1829 one Joss Snelling was presented to the young Princess Victoria as 'the famous Broadstairs smuggler'. He was no doubt a curiosity – one who had defrauded the Crown – but possibly also a patriot and loyal subject. The moral of this chapter, in the absence of straightforward morality, might be that smugglers might serve you in their own way, but they will not be controlled.

NINE

SMUGGLING WORLDS

From the River Plate to the Red Sea

'To me that other world, its confused objectives, its preoccupations, its stifling proximities, its "honourable callings" that permitted so many interpretations, seemed purposeless. My world, the clean world of the sea, was to the governor a secret garden, remote, shadowy, poisonous.'[1]

Henry de Monfreid

There are many examples in myth and literature of the mercurial smuggler. Jean Lafitte was a fleet and elusive operator, while Tom Johnson and Jack Rattenbury always seemed to have the wind in their sails. Sir Walter Scott modelled the character of Dirk Hatteraick, in his smuggler conspiracy novel *Guy Mannering*, on Yawkins, another flying Dutchman who operated around Scotland's Solway Firth from his ship the *Hawk*. In the novel, Hatteraick is a blazing, wild figure: 'half Manks', 'half Dutchman' and 'half devil', lording it over the stormy Scottish waters in his lugger, the *Yungfrauw Hagenslaapen*.

These smugglers had no need for secrecy because they had the speed of quicksilver (mercury). Hermes, the god of secrecy, is surely the most appropriate deity of smuggling. Hermes is actually considered the god of travel, commerce and border crossing, but no other ancient Greek deity so closely fits the profile of divine patron for covert trade. On the other hand Mercury, the Roman god forged out of the Hermes myth and giving us the adjective 'mercurial', is flighty and dashing, and in this sense open and showy. Cousin to Hermes, he represents a departure from the secrecy attributed to the other.

This difference – on the one hand the covert hermetic and on the other the extrovert mercurial (contraband in plain sight) – is a typical paradox in smuggling. As we saw in the previous chapter, orders for contraband at Deal in Kent were quite calm and everyday, transacted in plain sight on the quay. Such is the protection that comes with the involvement of the higher strata of society. But the actual run tended to be covert, although it was often a race involving fast galleys and pursuing revenue cutters. In the New Orleans of the Lafitte brothers contraband was illegal but was nevertheless sold openly in the markets. It seems that there are traces of both Hermes and Mercury in the DNA of the smuggler. It is perhaps not such an irony that the American War of Independence smuggler Silas Deane procured arms secretly in Paris, posing as a Bermudan merchant, and then shipped them to North America in a vessel called *Mercure*.

A question that arises out of all this, closer to home than either the spectacle on the quay or unseen smuggling (or at least the smuggler disappearing over the horizon), is not so much whether smuggling has to be visible or invisible, but rather: is the world of the smuggler a part of our world, or a world apart? It is a question that I shall come back to in Chapter Fifteen. Should we 'Watch the wall, my darling, while the gentlemen go by!' as Kipling relates in his 'A Smuggler's Song', or is this our world anyway, and it makes no difference if we turn our backs? This chapter will reflect upon this question through the lens of three examples. The first goes back to the contraband economy of early seventeenth-century Buenos Aires that implicated almost everybody. The second is the embedded smuggler world of the Carters of Prussia Cove who, two centuries after that River Plate economy, which was riddled from top to bottom with corruption, established a guarded smuggler world that was apart from and yet socially integrated into rural Cornish society. The third is the story of the 'decadent' French poet Arthur Rimbaud trafficking arms in what today are Ethiopia, Somaliland and Djibouti – a journey apart for him, but one that was still entirely within the context of empire.

Buenos Aires: A Contraband Economy Through and Through

A certain Juan de Vergara arrived in the River Plate region in 1602 from Potosí, after which nothing would ever be quite the same again for a struggling Buenos Aires. Gradually over the next fifteen years or so it would become a smuggler city. By 1618 the economy of the city, under the stewardship of the ultra-corrupt governor Diego de Góngora, had become almost entirely illicit.

How had contrabanding come to overtly characterize this royal town? Neglect and over-regulation of trade gave smuggling its first foothold, as it had done on the Spanish Main. Most official Spanish-licensed, transatlantic imports arrived in Buenos Aires via the circuitous route from Panama to Lima and then downriver, back across the continent. This was to avoid the piracy that beset direct routes and Brazilian ports, but it also bred resentment against Peru. There was a lot of poverty in this area around this time and the wretched settlement, founded in 1536 by Mendoza, was threatened constantly by native peoples. There was a fear that depopulation would leave it militarily defenceless and vulnerable to Dutch incursion. Although marginalized, it was still strategically important as a gateway to the richer parts of the Vicereality of Peru. The response to this desolation came from neither Spain nor Peru, nor even Charcas (now Sucre, Bolivia, the new judicial capital of the region). The response, instinct and necessity of the Porteños (Buenos Aires citizens) was to embrace contraband.

Smuggling had been prevalent, although not pervasive, since the refounding of the city, now named Puerto de Santa María de Buenos Aires, by Juan de Garay in 1580. The new city steadily became a conduit for illicit goods going out, particularly flour, dried meat, sebo (animal fat), hides and silver originating in Potosí. Slaves, along with timber (for furniture) and European contraband, came in via Brazil. At this stage smuggling was still peripheral and relatively insignificant, certainly not a panacea for the city's economic woes. With the closure of the port in 1594 the town's fortunes would seem to have hit rock bottom. Porteños, however, took matters into their own hands and ramped up illicit trading. Far from reducing trade, the closure spurred it on: the economy flourished on contraband. It now had impetus and became an industry; those who had made money out of smuggling wanted to maintain their lifestyles. After 1594 this tolerated vice became a realistic answer to the neglect of Buenos Aires but from another point of view was a larger problem.

The surge in contraband activity and the implications of closing the port rang a few alarm bells in Spain. Only two ships per year could supply the port, and those just to avoid it being abandoned. In 1602 export restrictions were relaxed a little, allowing some local products like flour, smoke-dried meat, sebo and hides to be exported to Brazil in exchange for essentials. But exporting silver was strictly prohibited, as was the importing of slaves. Smuggling quickly put down roots. Alongside the opportunity for black-market trading provided by scarcity, there were several other reasons why there was such a perfect storm of smuggling brewing. It was to be a web that ensnared all participants in commercial activity, from the lowliest peon to the governor. Rather like the neglected 'wild coast' of the Guianas at this time, the River Plate fell out of the official colonial economy and into its more realistic grey zone. Significantly this smuggling world did not simply relate to Porteño society: it *became* Buenos Aires society.

As we shall see, the poet Rimbaud and Henry de Monfreid escaped to a smuggling desert and a contraband sea respectively, remote from their 'civilized' homes, but Porteños made their civilization out of smuggling. People came together to trade illicitly out of both necessity and opportunity. Many of the *contrabandistas* were Jews expelled from Portugal who had been persecuted for their culture and religious beliefs. Aspirant citizens of the faltering settlement in the generations following on from the conquest era had no choice but to ally themselves with opportunistic informal traders. Only then might these *comerciantes confederados* avoid becoming isolated from real influence in the city. The second influx of migrants had more capital and there was only one investment path. New immigrants were inducted, rather like the fleeing Nazi technicians who were vital to Argentina's economic and military ambitions in a later period of economic growth in River Plate history.

What did this smuggler society look like and who was driving it? At the top were two men who became almost untouchable: Diego de Vega (Portuguese, originally from Madeira, deported to Brazil for his religious beliefs) and Juan de Vergara (a renegade Spaniard, a Kurtz-like figure in Joseph Conrad's terms but one who was inside rather than outside the system). Just below this the web configured itself over Vergara and Vega's extended families and associates. Most of the city's distinguished families were involved, many of whose heads were connected as members of the *cabildo* (administrative council), or as blood relatives. Intermarriage resembled a Borgia saga: Vergara was married to the niece of Vega, for instance. Every layer and interest group in society partook of the spoils. The clergy were involved, most notably in the person of the bishop of Buenos Aires, Pedro de Carranza, and Francisco Salcedo, an officer of the Inquisition. Imperial officials oiled its mechanism at all levels, including governor, most ignobly in the shape of Diego de Góngora (incumbent between 1618 and 1623). At the bottom were slaves, peasants and other labourers.

A bond of loyalty and sociability (in the sense of both business and kinship) was forged between each member of the top tier of the network, although everybody had to understand their own role. This was fundamental to the structure in that the main participants brought with them external connections: Vega to Dutch financial centres and Vergara to the imperial financial machine in Spain. Simón de Valdez, a veteran of the war on piracy in the Caribbean and now Vega's partner in slave trafficking, was the treasurer of the Real Hacienda, a post that brought with it links to Madrid and the heart of empire. Besides Spain and Holland, business relations stretched to Portugal, England, Germany, Flanders, Brazil, West Africa, Angola (the governor of Luanda provided slaves for Vega and Vergara) and other parts of the vicereality. The network functioned like a corporation: it was a varied and hierarchical system based on exchanges of favour and clientelism. Some of these roles were provided by the state but adapted to smuggling: the treasurer of the *cabildo*, Vergara's brother Alonso, was also effectively treasurer of the contrabanding network.

A succession of governors were implicated, and if they deviated from the firm's purpose they were eliminated. This corruption began to dig in its claws with Governor Fernando de Zárate, who encouraged Portuguese immigration to the port. Diego Marín Negrón, incumbent between 1609 and 1613, denounced this dimension of the smuggling network – its growth mechanism relying on illegal immigrant Portuguese involved in slave trafficking – but this was probably because he feared losing his own slice of the pie. He also tried to limit the entry of new slaves to the port. He was poisoned.

Vega and Vergara had few effective adversaries. Hernando Arias de Saavedra, also known as Hernandarias, the governor of Rio de la Plata, was one, but most others were ruthlessly swept aside, as were many who remained neutral. The notary of the *cabildo* Cristóbal Remón was seized and paraded naked in public and later exiled to Africa. Judge Matías Delgado Flores, minister of the Council of the Indies, had arrived from Spain to investigate the corruption of Góngora but was soon deported, while Nicolás de Ocampo Saavedra was thrown into a dungeon.

With the acquiescence of other governors, such as Mateo Leal de Ayala (1613–15) and Francés de Beaumont y Navarra (1615), and later Góngora, contrabanding became thoroughly institutionalized. All the same, a facade of governance was dangled before the Royal *hacienda* (treasury): Góngora sent it tame complaints about economic losses to smuggling but he ignored the one weapon that might have galvanized his absent masters into action – a denunciation of the 'New Christians' who were dominating business.

Almost from his arrival Juan de Vergara acted with impunity and self-confidence. Prior to Buenos Aires he had been in Potosí, the silver city, and before this in Tucumán (now part of Argentina). In both of these places he made useful connections with the military, civil service and judiciary. He was well placed from the start. In Buenos Aires he initially worked for Juan Pedrero de Trejo, who had been sent to investigate the problem of smuggling. He soon held the offices of *regidor* (member of the *cabildo*), notary of the holy office and treasurer of the *Santa Cruzada*, a system of financial indulgences conferred by the Pope.

Whereas Jean and Pierre Lafitte produced a precarious smuggling haven just outside New Orleans, Juan de Vergara's smuggling world was relatively stable and at one with society. Even more so than Gravelines, Napoleon's smuggler enclave, the Buenos Aires of Vergara was a smuggling society through and through. It was corrupt but effective. Most importantly, considering the desperate history of the colonial city up until then, it provided relative stability. His story, however, is not without incident and at one point descends into melodrama. It was a shock to Vergara when Simón de Valdez was arrested by Hernandarias. He was sent to Spain for trial but when the ship carrying him was detained in Brazil he was able to send advance evidence that would place him in a favourable light before the court, which led to his acquittal.

Vergara's own trials were much more dramatic. In August 1627 Governor Francisco de Céspedes pre-empted his own denunciation by members of the *cabildo* as being implicated in smuggling by jailing his erstwhile smuggler boss. However, Bishop Carranza, hearing rumours of a plot by the governor to assassinate Vergara in jail, facilitated his escape and gave him refuge in the church, and later with the Jesuits. The bishop had mobilized his clerics, armed to the teeth, to protect Vergara and threatened to excommunicate anybody who denounced him. In the event the bishop, standing on the steps of his cathedral, excommunicated the governor himself who was besieging it. The latter was promptly abandoned by his troops and expelled from the city. However Céspedes sought help from Hernandarias, who resumed the case against Vergara and now also against the bishop, both of whom were sent to Charcas for trial.

One might think this was the end for Vergara, and the unravelling of his smuggler world, but he escaped any punishment when the king, on the birth of his son Prince Baltasar in 1631, declared an amnesty for *contrabandistas* in Buenos Aires. He even went back to his old post of *regidor*. The near absolute power of the smugglers resumed and contraband continued to permeate all levels of society.

The Carters of Prussia Cove

The Cornish Carter family fulfil many of our romantic preconceptions of smuggling. They brought brandy, tea and lace into a wild but secluded smuggling kingdom, pulling their cargoes over slippery granite rocks and up mossy tunnels to an alehouse on top of wind-battered cliffs, from where the contraband was hauled off up sunken lanes. Local agrarian muscle helped out. But this is just one side of the story. Originally fishermen, the Carter family worked hard to make a fortified smuggling world and to foster loyalty among communities in the hinterland, as well as cultivating friends in high places.

The leading lights of the family were John, 'King of Prussia' (supposedly so named after a childhood game), and Henry (Harry) Carter who, unusually for a smuggler, has left us an account of his exploits in his autobiography, which was published in 1809. He calls them a 'speculating family'. John led the band – the 'Cove Boys'. John had a basic education and was a principled man known for his reliability and punctuality in fulfilling orders for contraband goods. A much-cited story tells of his raiding the customs house in Penzance to recover confiscated tea that had been promised for a customer but not touching any of the contraband that was not his own. Harry was self-taught with a particular interest in maths, becoming the accountant of the family business.

They operated out of three small secluded coves that were riddled with caves: Pisky's, Bessie's and King's, collectively known as Prussia Cove (originally Port Leah, beside Mount's Bay). In 1770, at the age of 33, John built the King's House, probably so named because the site had caves beneath it that had possibly once served as a customs store. Now, defiantly, it became a contraband depot. In Bessie's Cove he constructed a small harbour and a road up the cliffs. He even installed a gun platform on which he mounted eight six-pounder cannons. With the outbreak of the American War of Independence, five of the Carters' ships were given 'marque' – commissions to privateer – which now enabled them to strengthen their offshore weaponry.

The Carters flourished in their kingdom: they were smugglers by profession but not exactly informal members of their community. Prussia Cove's untouchability became infamous after a raid in 1792 by customs militia from Penzance was repelled by the community, after which customs could not recruit volunteers for any further incursions. They had their ups and downs. After the St Malo debacle mentioned in Chapter Seven, they lost their cutter, and when they arrived back at Prussia Cove they found that the business had run into debt without its two masters at the helm. But they soon bounced back. One of the great skills of the family was its flair and adaptability for riding the wave of whichever contraband was most profitable in any given moment, thus ensuring a constant flow of business even as the value of each contraband ebbed and flowed.

The Carters might be seen as a counterpoint to the Rothschilds: while the former family was rough-edged and aspirant, the other was refined, now old money. But in essence they were in the same business, opportunistically augmenting their fortunes during the turbulent Napoleonic era and its prelude. Looked upon as a family saga, the Carter story has no lack of excitement. If Juan de Vergara's career only eventually took a melodramatic turn, Harry's, if his memoir is to be believed, was dramatic throughout, albeit with a curious twist of homeliness about it after he became a devout Methodist. He always ran a tight ship on which swearing was forbidden and the torment between his agrarian, fisherman's piety and his adventurous roving spirit often comes through in his memoir. Melodrama, however, is the predominant tone.

By the age of 25 Harry Carter had his own well-armed ship, the 200-ton *Swallow*, crewed by 60 men, followed by the *Shaftesbury* which had a crew of 80. In 1788 another ship, *Revenge*, was ambushed by the revenue cutter *Busy* and HMS *David* off Cawsand. He was severely wounded by a cutlass slash but, by playing dead on the deck as his crew were herded below, he was able to bide his time and leap overboard. After a desperate swim he made it to the beach, and with the help of some other smuggling men he rejoined his brother Charles in the village. A £300 reward was posted for his capture but Charles managed to patch him up and spirit him away to various refuges near Prussia Cove. The first of these was Marazion and he then moved to Acton Castle, which was owned by a wealthy landowner and learned gentleman who had once employed John as caretaker. To avoid capture he took passage to America, where he discovered Methodism and dabbled in farming, returning to England in 1790. Back in Cornwall, he felt a calling to evangelize his new religion (at a time when he should have been keeping a low profile) – ironic given John Wesley's tirade against smuggling, a sermon that he had even delivered in person in Cornwall. To sequester him for a while, the family sent him off to that great smuggling entrepôt, Roscoff, where he continued to broadcast the Lord's word. When war came in 1793 he was placed under house arrest like all Englishmen but managed to return to Prussia Cove in 1795.

The smuggling operation ran on until 1825. It was a family saga that did not become a dynastic story. Gradually, during the early nineteenth century, the enterprise depleted and they no longer speculated with quite the same energy. John had died in 1803 and Harry, after his return to Mount's Bay, was now more interested in preaching his religion, farming and writing his memoirs. In 1825 the newly formed Coast Guard built a guard post here, and he died in 1829. The Carters had one foot in society but unlike the smuggler world of Buenos Aires of the seventeenth century it was not institutionalized and eventually, like the Lafitte's Galveston settlement, it yielded to the winds of change.

The prevailing element in the Carter story is its legend: mythologies like this inform our perceptions of smuggling, and it would be disingenuous to claim that most of us are not affected by them. Still today at Prussia Cove one can make out the wheel ruts carved by many a weighty shipment and the cottage that used to be the alehouse. An ambient romance still lingers at secluded sites like this along a haunted and beautiful Cornish coastline.

Arthur Rimbaud, Arms Trafficker

On 10 November 1891 a wasted, emaciated and agonized man, his right leg recently amputated, died in a small hospital in Marseille. The clerk dealing with the formalities of his death described him in the records with the succinct epithet 'trader . . . in transit'.[2] An anonymous death, and yet this man had had a brilliant and shining career in poetry before being shot by his companion and fellow poet, Paul Verlaine, and fleeing into apparent oblivion in Africa. The two decades before his death in Marseille are, to literary scholars, lost years culminating in this sad end.

But there are memories, traces of Rimbaud's African years, and even monuments to his presence. In 1938 we have a witness peering out of the anonymity of a crowd describing the renaming of the Place des Chameaux (Camels Square) in Djibouti City.[3] It was to be called Place Arthur Rimbaud (now Place Mahmoud Harbi). Until it was scuttled in 2005 a tugboat, *Arthur Rimbaud*, worked Djibouti harbour.

To observers of informal trading on the fringes of empire, these years are fascinating as an instance of trafficking in another world that is alien to the milieu of developed (literary and civil) society. Rimbaud cared nothing for the literary reputation that had grown during his absence. If asked how he might have liked to have been remembered, he would probably have said as a trader, not a poet. And, albeit not immediately, his trade became smuggling.

If the smuggling world of Buenos Aires during the seventeenth century was one of luxury and patronage, in the Horn of Africa trafficking was a desperate, sordid, intermittent speculation, and Europeans were certainly not its driving agents. There was no rush to smuggle, unlike for many of those involved in the diamond trade in West Africa during the latter part of the twentieth century. Strangely for such a rebel poet, Rimbaud remained for a long time a very orthodox trader.

He had always had an ambiguous relationship with trade regulators. He certainly had an aversion to customs men, as Charles Nicholl imagines it in his book *Somebody Else: Arthur Rimbaud in Africa, 1880–91*, 'their pipes clenched between their teeth, their axes and knives, their dogs on the leash'.[4] A year or two before this he had written a less than complimentary poem about them. Nevertheless, with his horizons closing in on him and financially at a low ebb as he travelled through British-Egyptian territory, like Thomas Paine and Robbie Burns before him, he considered applying for a job with customs. He did not succeed, and conversely and more realistically he quietly placed his hopes in the informal sector. On the other hand, as he actually says in a letter home, he has come to Africa to 'traffick in the unknown'.[5]

Perhaps trafficking is too strong a word for Rimbaud's foray into the arms trade. Both slave and arms trafficking in this part of Africa were quite unremarkable, everyday practices, and the genius poet was certainly not a mercurial smuggler. In the 1860s, on arrival, his profile was low and his plan barely formed. He noted the customs house/shed (known as the 'bender') in Aden, his base on arrival in the Red Sea region, but without dissent. His outlook continued to be one of hope and obeisance to the proper channels of trading at a time of belated colonial speculation (Africa was 'opened up' to trade much later than Asia or the Americas). Nevertheless his immediate experience was far from that of the bright young colonial. It was more about boredom and surrender to heat and humidity.[6]

Was it weariness with the inertia of official trading or the seduction of greater profits to be made in the informal sphere that brought Rimbaud to trafficking? As mentioned in Chapter Six, a burnt-out reporter in Antonioni's film *The Passenger* comes only very slowly to the realization that he has taken over the persona of an arms trafficker. Rimbaud slips into the role more consciously, and not entirely as a rebel: in extending French trading interests he was acting as a kind of informal agent of proto-empire.

Perhaps he became a trafficker simply because arms trading was always proximal to the formal sphere of petty trading. In this torpid world Rimbaud, struggling to make a living and a new life as a trader, slowly drifted towards the darker side of commerce because he was already in a marginal trading borderland, one a little like the smuggler territory of Guajira in Colombia – sand-blown, peopled by semi-nomadic tribes and onto whose shore all manner of contraband and opportunities wash up. Unlike slave trafficking, there were few moral hang-ups about the practice. Smuggling was certainly an important trade here, even quite an everyday one. At Tadjourah, where Rimbaud began his arms-trafficking venture, populous caravans arrived made up largely of slaves trafficked from the interior en route to Arabia. The mildly narcotic shrub qat was taxed but of course was also smuggled. The Danakil occasionally ran guns, as did French colonial officials.

For the former poet, as later for Hunter S. Thompson in Guajira, this kind of environment induced ennui and lassitude, but he was also curious. In 1884 his first impressions of a small smuggler settlement are remarkably similar to Thompson's when he arrived by boat in Puerto Estrella some 80 years later ('nothing but Indians and whiskey').[7] Rimbaud says of his village, Obock: 'It's a deserted scorched beach, with nothing to live off, and no trade. Its only use is as a coal dump, for refuelling warships on their way to China and Madagascar.' And in another letter the following year, Obock still 'consists of just a dozen freebooters'.[8] Thompson eventually moves on, but Rimbaud is caught here, a stage on an inexorable journey towards his death in the small hospital in Marseille.

It probably didn't feel like this as he prepared to carry his guns inland to the king who with such weapons would become ruler of Abyssinia. Rimbaud had to be resourceful: arms trafficking required considerable planning. One didn't just ghost through Somaliland: a caravan had to be arranged, handlers and guards contracted, camels procured, money invested in merchandise from Europe and permissions sought from local chiefs.

After months of delays his caravan got under way from Tadjourah, taking four months to reach Entotto. There were many hazardous stretches, including the desert between Lake Assal and Erer, raiding territory for rival Danakil tribes. Although he would later get on quite well with Menelik II, he came out a poor second in bargaining a price for the guns, and was palmed off with bonds redeemable (only with great difficulty, as it turned out) in Herar, a city that had been conquered just weeks before by the ambitious and belligerent king. Rimbaud had no smuggler base to which to retreat. This was a splayed out, nomadic smuggling world and he was an outsider briefly circulating within it; a passenger, a 'trader in transit'.

Rimbaud's 'trafficking in the unknown' brought him to some desolate places and desperate endeavours. Although smuggling can sometimes be associated with a kind of freedom, this wasn't the case for him. This harsh environment soon began to close in upon him. After a paralysing injury – probably cancerous – he was carried in great pain on a stretcher from Herar, his home for much of his time in Africa, to Zeilah on the coast, and then across to Aden. He had to be carried onto the ship, *L'Amazone*, that would take him out of Africa forever.

However, faint echoes of Rimbaud's struggle have survived. The observer standing in the crowd that day in 1938 at the renaming of Camels Square was a certain Henry de Monfreid, a hashish smuggler. His smuggling days, narrated in two books, *Hashish: A Smugglers' Tale* and *Pearls, Arms and Hashish*, to a certain extent represent a kind of freedom, what he called 'my world, the clean world of the sea'. But when Monfreid turned his hand to arms trafficking he also felt less free, caught in what was now a more defined colonial geopolitics dominated by Italians, British and Turks. While Rimbaud dealt openly in weapons, it was now much more covert.

Caught up in politics, playing the hermetic games of colonial redistribution of power and commodities, Monfreid nevertheless follows his own path. At heart he is a romantic and, in a sense, insists upon the mercurial nature of smuggling. As he states: 'Don't make the mistake of confusing smugglers with those who make their living out of smuggling.'[9] For him smuggling was becoming too geopolitical, too cynical, but then, wasn't it always thus?

WE HAVE COME A LONG WAY from the integrated smuggler society of Buenos Aires and the fortified bastion of Prussia Cove to reach the nomadic smuggling of adventurers like Arthur Rimbaud and Henry de Monfreid. Monfreid achieves his flight more successfully than the poet but in the context of a colonialism in Africa that in some ways prefigured the power games of the Cold War, he is perhaps the romantic exception that proves the rule of state involvement in smuggling.

The next chapter turns to something altogether more savage: the largest and perhaps most insidious state-sponsored smuggling project in history.

TEN

SHADOW EMPIRE

Addicting China to Smuggled Opium

'In short, the traders who operated a business for which their government still
refused any responsibility were de facto spies and surreptitious diplomats.'[1]
Martin Booth, *Opium: A History*

The menace was scarcely apparent in the early years. Later on it was
impossible to ignore, brutally apparent in the great hulks that
served as floating depots for the trade. If Monfreid's dhow, *Altair* ('soaring
eagle'), sailed lightly, as befitted its airy cargo of hashish, these immobile
vessels sank low in the water under the weight of their goods: wholesale
chests packed tightly with black-earth, white and red-skin opium.

The smuggling of opium into China began towards the end of the
eighteenth century. Lark's Bay near Macao was an early landing choice,
evading Portuguese and Chinese scrutiny of cargoes. By the 1830s the
trade had swelled enormously and penetrated deep into the Pearl River
estuary. Foreigners were forbidden from bringing their ships into Canton
but as the *fanqui* (foreign 'ghosts' or 'devils') appeared in ever greater
numbers at the permitted anchorage of Lintin Island, the fortunes of
the trade were rising like a storm surge. The city was addicted and the
door to the broader Chinese market was ajar. The seascape beside the
island had become foregrounded with, among other ships, *Merope*, a
Jardine Matheson vessel, *Samarang*, owned by Lancelot Dent, and *Lintin*,
an American vessel. Soon there were 25 sinister receiving vessels riding
permanently at anchor. Growth had been exponential: in 1805 some
3,000 chests were imported, rising to 40,000 by 1839.[2] The mandarins
seemed to have no response to this pernicious invasion. At the end of
that decade there were some ten million addicts in China,[3] and the
situation had become intolerable.

There was a response. A siege of the trading factories in Fanqui town, the European enclave at the edge of the walled city of Canton, stopped the trade and alarmed the merchants, and even more so the governments that backed them. But nothing could permanently halt this juggernaut of state-sponsored smuggling. At the end of June 1840 some seventeen Royal Navy warships, four armed East India Company steamships and 27 troopships rendezvoused off the Chinese coast. Like parasites, a swarm of opium-trading vessels moved in under their protection. The story of opium trading to China that had begun on a small scale with the Arabs, followed by the Portuguese out of Goa, was tried speculatively by the Dutch out of Bengal via Java from 1659, and now by the British East India Company (EIC) out of Patna, was about to enter its most intense phase.

The Early Years of the Opium Trade

Opium hadn't always been such a problem for the Chinese. Although not indigenous to China, it had been grown in Yunnan province since late antiquity, although it would always be of poor quality. The trade was boosted by the new fashion among Chinese of smoking opium in pipes mixed with tobacco, learned from Dutch sailors operating out of Java, who believed that this mode of consumption would ward off malaria. On the consumer's part, briefly enforced restrictions on tobacco imports had led smokers to take more of what was left over – opium.

There were few risks. Although possession and distribution of opium had been an offence in China from 1729, its importation, paradoxically, was not illegal, mainly because so many Chinese officials did very well out of the trade. If it remained relatively discreet then it would inevitably thrive. In fact it was only in 1799 that importing it was banned. Now it was truly contraband but this hardly registered on its growth trajectory. The EIC did not at first throw all its weight behind this new mercantile opportunity and Warren Hastings, the governor of Bengal, initially forbade the export of opium to China. But with vast profits on offer he relented and allowed the first official smuggling trip in 1782. Although it was unsuccessful economically, this reconnaissance mission was promising.

The logic of the trade easily overrode the governor's private scruples: in Britain the sums mattered above all. By the first decades of the eighteenth century tea was fast becoming Britain's national beverage and by 1785 it was importing around 15 million lb of it per annum from a very willing China. Britain needed the revenue from tea, which on import was taxed at a rate of 100 per cent. But the downside of this trade was that it drained the country of £26 million of increasingly scarce silver, while its exports to China were a mere £9 million (turbulent events in the Americas and Europe from 1776 onwards had restricted bullion flows, culminating in the Napoleonic guinea run described in Chapter Eight).[4] Much other British silver also went towards importing Chinese porcelain and lacquerware. If the Industrial Revolution were to thrive, and the empire to grow, it needed to address this negative balance of payments. Getting the Chinese addicted to opium, dominating the business and demanding payment in silver proved the answer. And this devious plan worked very smoothly: in 1773 the EIC earned just under £40,000 from opium sold in India or exported but by 1793 this had increased by a factor of six.[5]

The Indian point of the triangle, where the opium was grown, was also desperate to increase the trade. It needed income from exporting opium to China to pay for the cottons imported from Britain's expanding factory production. They too paid in silver and needed Chinese coin to compensate. In addition to the seepage of money towards the mother country, the EIC needed to pay for its internal ambitions as it expanded its territory fighting a series of wars in the Northwest Frontier province. When the British population at Patna in Bengal was massacred in 1763, General Clive's response was to end the Nawab's rule, including control over his opium yield. In order to pay for this new British hegemony these beautiful poppy fields might be turned to good use. The security of the empire was always problematical and policing it required considerable finance. It was a new economic opportunity, indeed a necessary one, without which Britain's entire eastern empire might well have collapsed.

Thus Patna, some 300 miles inland from Calcutta, along with districts around Benares, became the productive heart of the EIC's smuggling operation. An incredibly cynical aspect of the championing of this 'harmless' drug was that it was exported even as its consumption was banned in India for reasons of morality and its effects on productivity.

Now that the EIC sensed a green light, events started to move a little faster, although there was not yet a rush. The EIC handled the trade at one remove, licensing private operators to run the risks. These middlemen, known as 'country firms', made seasonal passage towards the leaking underbelly of the otherwise self-sufficient Chinese Empire: Macao,

The Stacking Room, Patna, c. 1850, engraving.

Canton and later Hong Kong in the Pearl River estuary were its weak points. Later, super-fast clippers such as *Red Rover* and *Sylph* overcame the perils of the monsoon season through their capacity to sail safely against the wind. The EIC sold its opium at auctions in Calcutta that took place three to five times between December and July, offering 5,000 or so chests for export. The key to profitability was once again to strive for a monopoly. It worked quite smoothly out of Bengal, although less so on the west coast, where Malwa region production and export out of Bombay could only be partially controlled.

Opium – *Lachryma papaveris* ('poppy tears') – came in various forms: Patna opium was known as 'black earth' because of its dark appearance, Bombay's was called 'white skin' and that of Madras 'red skin'. The trade flowered slowly during the first two decades of the nineteenth century as Chinese society gradually became more addicted, but three factors still restricted its growth. First, it was limited to the Canton (now Guangzhou) area. Second, when smugglers dispersed landings along the coast on coming under pressure after the latest Chinese edict against the evils of the trade in 1828, it weakened the industrial imperative of concentrated bulk supply. Also, the remoter spots were prone to piracy. Third, the monopoly of the EIC in China hindered the circulation of trade in general.

Free – 'Strong-arm' – Trading

The trade, now officially illegal but never more licit, took flight when the Government of India Act in 1833 abolished the EIC monopoly on China trading (it had already lost its Indian one in 1813). Free trade now became its mantra. By implication it was a multinational business, but was still largely British (80 per cent), spearheaded by Thomas and Lancelot Dent and William Jardine and James Matheson, the latter pair of whom set up their partnership in 1834. The Americans also had significant interest through Russell & Company and Perkins. Indeed, a Boston schooner, *Coral*, was one of the first ships to smuggle opium into China. Also involved were Greeks, Dutch, Swedes, Danes and Latin Americans, as well as Spanish operating out of Manila. It wasn't that the EIC was elbowed aside, but it officially lost control of the point of sale.

It was certainly smuggling, although hardly clandestine. Whampoa island (local name – Huang-pu), 10 miles downriver from the city and little more than a malaria–plagued swamp, was as far as foreign ships could penetrate but Western opium magnates had created a comfortable lifestyle for themselves on the edge of Canton itself.

Just before Canton is an island known as Dutch Folly after a failed episode of micro-empire-building. The Dutch attempted to smuggle 400 cannon onto it after they had been given permission to set up a hospital there, but the barrels in which they were hidden had burst open. The city itself was secretive and fabled, forbidden to *fanqui*. It was walled, with a large billowing skirt of river boats known as Sampan City. Another of its parasitic fringes was this traders' enclave, which was both wretched and luxurious. It was situated beside a creek that functioned as a sewer for the city. From the river it looked prosperous, with white neo–classical facades, but behind these were blocks of enclosed rectangular factories whose only access to the busy, shabby streets was through these narrow, albeit elaborate, facades. Nevertheless, as Amitav Ghosh depicts it in his novel *River of Smoke*, it was addictively lively, and the most successful merchants had fine apartments, dining together in splendour. It was most likely a place of intrigue; this is certainly how Ghosh imagines it. In the novel subterfuge comes naturally to the expatriates: the Gujarati opium merchant Bahram hides his identity by wearing Indian garments over his Parsi ones; Robin, a painter, infiltrates a hint of Velásquez into a formal Victorian portrait of Jardine; and flower girls (prostitutes) are smuggled into the factories.

George Chinnery, *View at Canton (Chinese Police Station and Foreign Factories)*, 1838, pen and ink.

The opium magnates had very cordial, albeit business-like, relations with Chinese merchants. The most prominent among the latter was Wu Bing-jian, aka Howqua, leader of the Co-Hong or Hong merchants – some eight to twelve privileged traders. A polyglot, he not only dealt in opium but in tea and silk, and even invested in the American railroads. By the mid-1830s he might well have been the richest man in the world.[6]

The Frontline of Smuggling Opium

The first part of the Pearl River run was entirely licit. Through the channel between Macao and Lintin Island and then past the most prominent fort of the Bogue islands, the narrow strait known as *Sher-ka-mooh* (Bocca Tigris or 'tiger's mouth', as the Portuguese called it) awaited receiving vessels moored all year round off Whampoa (and later Lintin after the Chinese turned up the heat around the former). As the trade grew, the number of receiving vessels, floating castles, multiplied. The next stage in the operation was oiled by the payment of bribes to officials, for instance at customs on Whampoa. There was immediate payment on receipt of the opium, now out of its chests and bagged up, which was then transported speedily into the backwaters around Canton in two-masted, shallow-draught, 50- to 60-oar vessels. These were larger

Canton and the Pearl River Estuary at the time of the Opium Wars, also showing modern-day Shenzhen.

than but in other ways similar to the Deal galleys that took guineas across the English Channel during the Napoleonic Wars, and were known as 'centipedes', 'fast crabs' or 'scrambling dragons'.

This frenetic nocturnal activity, at first appraisal, might seem to have been the main smuggling part of the opium trade, but it is not that simple. It is difficult to conceive what actually constituted smuggling during the growth years of the trade in the first half of the nineteenth century. Was it this hands-on Chinese portage, or was it the extensive business, at a remove, of the EIC? Was it the independent merchants such as Jardine, Matheson or Dent who took over from them but in part operated on their behalf? In Ghosh's novel, William Jardine distances the traders nested in Fanqui town – their opium-laden ships at anchor some distance away – from the smear of being called smugglers, suggesting that whatever smuggling was going on was either Chinese or EIC (the 'father of all smuggling and smugglers').[7] In addition the self-righteous traders also look down on less hypocritical merchants such as James Innes, who seemed to want to bypass the system by running opium entirely covertly, without bribery, into Canton.

There was occasionally a show of displeasure from the mandarins of Canton: on departure, the EIC-licensed ships leaving the estuary might run a gauntlet of Chinese war junks. The foreign vessels slowed down to allow the Chinese vessels to keep pace, keeping them just in range of their deliberately misaimed salvos. In the main the trade was guaranteed by the profit motive on both the Chinese and the European side. However, this modus vivendi was not to last.

Chinese Action

In 1836 the Chinese emperor definitively banned the import of opium, and even arraigned Jardine and eight other merchants on trafficking charges. The edict was of course ignored, there having been little will to implement such restrictions in the past given that so many powerful Chinese traders, politicians and even courtiers were either addicted to opium or made money from the trade.

For the first time, though, the emperor sensed a moral decline and diminution of energy among many of his subjects and resolved to see it through. Some of the less arrogant of the merchant class took note of this hardened stance. Superintendent of Trade Sir George Robinson had the specific task of monitoring the smuggling of opium as it passed through Lintin Island. He detected a change in the Chinese position, a response to the heedless and headlong escalation of the trade. But his forthright report to the foreign secretary led only to his dismissal. Relations worsened when a provocative group of traders bypassed Lintin Island and fed opium straight into Canton, cutting out all the backhanders along the way.

Tasked with implementing the Chinese hardline was newly appointed High Commissioner and Imperial Plenipotentiary Lin Tse-hsü (Zexu). He was chosen for the job because he had cleared up the opium problem in Kiangsi province where he was known as Lin Chi'in-t'ien – Lin 'clear-as-the-heavens' – for not taking bribes.

Lin, following the imperial edict, demanded the surrender of all merchants' opium supplies. Unrepentant foreign traffickers would be beheaded. Turning to his own citizenry, he proposed that addicts might at first be offered rehabilitation: they were given eighteen months to hand over their opium, and if they did so might escape punishment. But dealers would be strangled. There began a series of demonstrative executions of opium dealers. One of them, den owner He Laojin, was executed in front of the American factory. A few Chinese smugglers were also despatched in the ensuing months. The factories (hongs) were assailed by hysterical mobs.

In March 1839 the British traders were ordered to surrender their opium by the new Chief Superintendent of Trade, Captain Charles

Elliot. They complied because Elliot, on his own initiative, had promised that the British government would reimburse them for their losses (to the value of the drug, not for lost profits). But this was a good deal in any case because the besieged factories were currently unworkable and, as stated above, traders faced execution if they carried on as before. Besides, there was too much opium sitting in the factories. They delivered millions of pounds worth of opium, 20,000 chests, into Elliot's keeping and he duly passed it on to Lin who in May took it to Chen k'ou (now part of Humen, near Canton). There he had it mixed with salt and lime and turned into slurry in three large holes from where it was allowed to drain abjectly into the China Sea: the crisis dispelled and dispersed, so it would seem.

But Lin, a learned and in many respects a very reasonable man, did not lift the siege, instead bricking up the entrances to the factories. Elliot and his men could not even communicate with the outside world until they managed to smuggle out letters with Chinese workers, rolled inside cigars or hidden in shoes. Bread, water, sugar, oil and chicken, as well as feed for livestock, were smuggled the other way. Eventually the British were allowed to leave.

The Build-up to War

There was a range of possible responses to the events around the factories in the Canton enclave. Elliot was ambivalent. He was morally against the opium trade but as a representative of Her Majesty's often hard-up government he gave in, faced with a tsunami of a profit motive and operating at the vanguard of free trade. During this period just before the first opium war the British exchequer gained about 10 per cent of its income from trafficking the drug.[8] Even as he prepared to defend British interests, he likened the trade to piracy in a letter to Lord Palmerston, the foreign secretary, in November 1839.[9]

The British government put a different spin on Chinese outrage. It justified the renewal of the 'popular' opium trade as relatively harmless, suggesting that the Chinese government's attempts at ending it were merely intended to protect its own silver reserves. Such provocative comments were inflammatory, to say the least. Meanwhile smuggling continued along the coast in Fukien and Kwangtung provinces.

The traders themselves, while rattling sabres in mock outrage, were quite pleased that they had succeeded in rousing the government at home and simply carried on as before. Jardine, Matheson & Co. was already preparing new cargoes, and with the transfer of all foreign opium operations to Macao the industrial smuggling operation was up and running again within a month of the seizure. At first profits skyrocketed because supply had been halted and demand had not faltered. These traders never really expected a war and blithely assumed that things would naturally reset to the former status quo with a dose of gunboat diplomacy and the power of the market. However it was still a crisis because the Chinese were playing a zero sum game and, emboldened by their success, were in no mood to relent. By the end of June 1840 a mini armada of almost 50 British ships lying just outside the Pearl River estuary considered how best to teach the Chinese a lesson to allow the opium trade to continue to expand.

The First Opium War, 1840–42

One of the first actions of the war was the storming of Dinghai on Zhoushan Island, about 100 miles south of Shanghai. It was taken relatively easily. Elliot had denied the area to opium ships but this did not deter the smugglers who offloaded the drug at loss-leader prices hoping to entrap new addicts – future customers. The embargo was largely symbolic anyway: Elliot allowed unmolested opium trading on the mainland beside Zhoushan. His quandary was largely economic because he raised money for the war by selling bonds, and the only people who would buy them were the opium traders; in a sense he was in their pockets.

Further one-sided battles took place, culminating in a massacre at Chuanbi Fort at the mouth of the Canton River in January 1841. In an action appropriate to the true nature of this war, a naval detachment blew up a customs house near Anson's Bay in the Bogue. A truce was declared in March following more conflict around the Bogue forts in February. Elliot's peacemaking, and his exchange of Zhoushan for Hong Kong, led to his sacking by Palmerston.

The war was a mismatch mainly because of Britain's superior and more modern weaponry and technology, but also because opium had made a once disciplined society into an empire of lassitude. When the fort at Xiamen (Amoy) was easily overcome, the Irish assailants found opium pipes beside the defenders' discarded guns. This was not quite headlong flight: Chinese officials found time to smuggle out the city's silver bullion reserves in hollow logs.

The Treaty of Nanking ended the war and granted Britain the right to trade in the so-called 'treaty ports' of Canton, Xiamen, Fuzhou, Ningpo and Shanghai. Lin was exiled to Turkestan in 1841.

Business as Usual

The war itself was fought not so much to reinstate the trade as to guarantee its continuation. Throughout the conflict it continued to grow. Immediately after the siege at Canton, Jardine Matheson had intensified their operation. While the war was being fought just to the north, the firm imported more than 6,000 chests to the city, with half as many again waiting in the holds of its ships. At Lintin opium trading took place in broad daylight. The market was flooded in a swift reversal of the state of affairs of the year before. Nevertheless everybody made a good profit, even though the price was depressed by the sheer amount of opium now coming in.

As an indicator of how tenacious and pernicious the trade was in wartime, one need go no further than the irony of the clinic on Zhoushan set up by William Lockhart of the London Missionary Society. This field hospital aimed at alleviating the depradations of addiction was protected by the British Army and Navy. However the very presence of these protectors allowed state-sanctioned opium smuggling to take place. By November some 40 ships had offloaded about 12,000 chests of opium onto the island.

There were also collateral implications of the war for smuggling further afield. The illicit slave trade from Africa to Brazil and the southern states of America made a minor recovery after so many preventive vessels were diverted from the coast of West Africa to China. Closer to Canton, Hong Kong thrived because it had none of the bureaucracy and corruption of the former. It became the new centre of illicit opium trading alongside the smuggling of salt in contravention of the attempted imperial monopoly over that oft-smuggled commodity. So much money was now circulating that opium ships were used as banks.

Opium importation grew apace and by mid-century an estimated one in three adults in China was addicted. By 1856 opium accounted for about 22 per cent of British India's revenue,[10] and Chinese imports were approaching double those from before the war. The trade seemed unstoppable; life was being sucked out of the formerly self-sufficient empire, not least in the form of its silver reserves.

But is this the whole story? As Julia Lovell has argued in her book *The Opium War*, China continued to have a trade surplus, and in 1857 its balance of payments with Britain was £9 million in the black.[11] Imports of tea and silk still outvalued sales of opium and other British and British-Indian goods.

The Second Opium War, 1856–60

The British government favoured a belligerent approach to facilitate broader trading and thereby tackle the deficit. From the traders' viewpoint there was an horizon of even more fabulous wealth to be made. A new war, for some, was the answer, although this generated heated debate. In response to letters from merchants denying even the existence of an opium trade, read out in parliament by Samuel Gregson, chairman of the East India and China Association, William Gladstone retorted: 'Your greatest and most valuable trade in China is in opium. It is a smuggling trade. It is in the worst, the most pernicious, demoralizing and destructive of all the contraband trades that are carried upon the surface of the globe.'[12] Matheson, now at home and MP for Ross and Cromarty, was dubbed 'member for opium' by the press but he kept his counsel for fear of presenting too high-profile a target for the anti-opium lobby.

The second war was more of an international affair. France and America were also heavily involved in opium smuggling while at the same time, like Britain, denying their involvement. This time they actively defended their interests. The second war took the same irresistible course as the first. The main British protagonist was James Bruce, 8th Earl of Elgin, son of the 7th Earl, provider of the Parthenon frieze – the Elgin marbles – to Britain.

On 3 July 1858 Elgin signed the Treaty of Tianjin. It took a long time to complete, not only because of Chinese protocol but because so many of the imperial negotiators were addicts. The treaty allowed for a 5 per cent tax on trade goods imported to China, including opium (later raised to 8 per cent on the drug alone), effectively regularizing trading in the latter. Although moral outrage on one side and denial on the other continued to make it highly controversial, it was no longer smuggling at all, legally speaking. However, since opium was repeatedly taxed as it was transported inland, there was still an incentive for evasion at the China end. The Americans wanted to make the trade illegal but their ambassador realized that realistically this would simply encourage even more smuggling.

The peace didn't last after 700 British marines were massacred in the countryside around Canton in February 1859. It led to the invasion of Beijing, culminating in the sacking and burning of the Summer Palace just outside the city by British and French forces – a suitably barbaric ending to a spurious *casus belli*.

In the twenty years following the Second Opium War imports of opium doubled and it became even more valuable to the exchequer. In a distant echo of Drake and Hawkins's 'strong-arm trading' – contrabanding by another name – the British forced other exports upon the Chinese, such as Manchester textiles, a crude insult in the land of silk.

ONLY IN THE 1880s did opium exportation begin to decelerate, and this continued during the 1890s when production costs rose in India. Jardine Matheson had ceased trading it in 1872. In 1909 India stopped exporting opium.

The insidious trade did not end there. Opium dens flourished in places like Shanghai and the drug was never made illegal there until the end of the Second World War. When the Japanese invaded Manchuria in 1931 they began systematically to traffic heroin, morphine and cocaine along the coast so that when the Sino–Japanese war of 1937 broke out they had already weakened their enemy. Smuggling only ended when the Communists came to power in 1949.

Jardine Matheson Holdings is today a hugely influential multinational company linked with Rothschilds (two of whose number, James and Nathan, were influential players of the guinea run). The Honourable East India Company's opium venture established the benchmark for state-sponsored smuggling. This model for projection of state power through smuggling continues to flourish.

ELEVEN

REFRESHMENT AND RESISTANCE

Too Much Opium, Too Little Tea

The Royal Botanic Gardens at Kew is one of the more peaceful corners of London. Its expansive collections, housed in various pavilions, glasshouses and orangeries, attract amateur and professional gardeners alike. Its serenity and scientific authority conceal a mildly sinister past. Kew stored contraband plants that would in many ways bring the British Empire to fruition. Under the auspices of the esteemed botanist of empire Joseph Hooker, it cultivated rubber seeds stolen from Amazonas, and before this, under his father, William, cinchona that had been smuggled out of Peru by Clements Markham, later president of the Royal Geographical Society. Even today there are 'dangerous' plants at Kew Gardens: cannabis and opium plants not on view to the public.

In an echo of Pierre Poivre's clandestine spice dispersal of the previous century, contraband flora stored at Kew were marked for transplantation around the empire. Smuggled rubber seeds would create a boom on reaching Southeast Asia, while cinchona's bark would be useful all around the empire (quinine, whose counter-malarial effects allowed for greater industry, comes from cinchona). The opium trade represented another strain of organic smuggling by the British, though there were attempts at biopolitical resistance. Chinese mandarins, exasperated by the addiction of their subjects to opium or, looking at it more cynically, envious of the money swirling around the trade and wishing to limit the devastation of its silver reserves through its purchase, transplanted opium poppies to China, potentially undermining the Indian monopoly based in Patna.

The British feared such a move. Robert Fortune, a botanist and an old East Asia hand, was in China shortly before the outbreak of the Second Opium War. It was his third trip, and his second for the East

India Company. The EIC had their man *in situ* on a mission of tea espionage and asked another favour of him: that he smuggle back some Chinese opium for examination – plants and seeds – as well as tools associated with it. He duly obliged, becoming in the process not just a tea trafficker but another narcotics smuggler.

The British had reason not to be complacent, for they had another example of smuggling undermining their hegemony. Just beyond their reach but at the heart of their own empire was yet another narrative of the opium trade. The 'white skin' of Malwa was smuggled through and beyond the great state-sponsored opium trafficking enterprise of the Company. Malwa is a territory in west-central northern India (covering the plateau region of central Madhya Pradesh and southeastern Rajasthan) that in the nineteenth century supplied opium for shipment to China from the west coast of India. The Company simply couldn't bring it under the umbrella of its monopoly. It was a case of smuggling beyond smuggling.

Untouchable Malwa: Its Relations with the East India Company

A well-established group of opium growers and traders worked out of Malwa even before the British monopoly got underway in Bengal, gaining further impetus when ousted east coast traders came across to this side of India. Seth Bharamji, the main protagonist of Ghosh's *River of Smoke*, was a west coast merchant. He shared the Canton enclave with not only the Bengal-based free traders but his Malwa associates, and by mid-century men of his class were almost the equal, in wealth at least, of Jardine, Matheson, Dent and co.

The British were frustrated in their efforts to suppress the Malwa trade. Part of the problem was that in addition to the important players, as in many smuggling zones then and now, there were multiple small-time operators who acting together could also turn a substantial profit. The variety of routes meant that the British forces were spread thinly, and as they could only administer the empire through local rulers in the years before the Raj, they also resisted aiming at complete territorial domination. An additional problem for all the European firms was that they lacked direct or effective contact with the opium heartland of Malwa and so were always at a commercial disadvantage. Jardine, chief among the free traders, explored the possibility of broadening his firm's interests in western India but had to admit defeat. The variety of routes and personnel involved across much of northwestern India meant that market values predominated, undermining the artificially high EIC prices. Ultimately the British could not impose their own prices.

For the EIC this was the shady side of India in contrast to a Bengal brought under the 'civilizing' influence of British rule – the western India smuggling operation was only dark because it was not British! Actually, in Bombay, some of it was British – private firms daring to compete with the EIC, such as Remington Crawford & Co. and Forbes & Co. They operated alongside the Portuguese Pereira's and the Armenian firm of Gregory Apcar. Often, though, the British smugglers were out-contrabanded by savvy indigenous traders. For instance in 1822 a trading firm, Premji Purshottam, secured the handling of a substantial proportion of the season's Bombay share of Malwa opium and offered an EIC representative named Taylor much of it at a moderate price. The sum was low enough to interest him but just high enough to make him defer purchase and continue to barter. Meanwhile Premji, at the same time as dangling this carrot before the EIC (offering to connect them directly with suppliers in Malwa) and pretending to make arrangements behind the scenes, sold almost the entire supply to indigenous traders. He had never intended to supply the British. The whole thing was a charade from start to finish, intended to distract the EIC's purchasing operation so that not only would they not get this supply but their usual contacts would look elsewhere, leaving the Company with nothing but a few expensive scraps.[1]

Smuggling Malwa Opium: Ruses and Routes

How did the smuggling operation function on the ground? Amar Faroqui, in *Smuggling as Subversion*, gives a detailed account of the operation. A typical clandestine transport might entail concealment of the opium in cargoes of grain, cotton or hay, or secreted between folds in horsemen's saddles. Generally smugglers would try to avoid British territory.

In the same way that in the eighteenth century books carried across the Jura mountains into France were insured against seizure, the opium businessmen of central northwestern India would minimize their risks by taking out insurance policies. Sometimes the insurers would be the *hundabharas* or *hundeeekurrees* – fixers – who would negotiate toll payments at customs houses (*nakas*) and protection money for safe passage

Opium trails out
of Malwa during
the first half of the
19th century.

over designated expanses of territory. Transporting contraband opium
was a relay operation. One of the big bosses of the Malwa opium trade,
Appa Gangadhar of Mandsaur, provided protection for his and others'
transports to the coast, but even his influence did not extend to Rajasthan,
where traditional armed escorts were drawn from the warlike Charuns.

The main towns around which production centred were Ujjain in
the south of Malwa (important early on) and Mandsaur in central Malwa,
whose market-fed smaller traders operated out of Pali and Kota in the
north of the region. There were two main groups of middlemen: the
Marwari to the northwest who controlled the clandestine Rajasthan
routes, and traders out of Ahmadabad in Gujarat to the west of Ujjain.
Broadly speaking southern routes were important early on before northern
ones came to surpass them.

In the south two routes were popular with smugglers, either because
the jungle and hill territory offered good cover or because political control
was weak, making inland borders extremely porous. With the first of
these routes transports went south through the Gaikwad of Baroda's
territories. The second started slightly to the north and went through
the (anti-British) Sindia-held Panch Mahals east of Ahmadabad. More
often than not the destination was the Gulf of Cambay in Gujarat. Here
there were several small ports that served the trade. Jambusar was a key

early exporter before the British occupied it, pushing its business to Cambay town. Also important were Surat, Tankaria and Bharuch.

As the British gained more control the trade shifted to the north through Rajasthan via Pali territory. Pali became a major transit point and Marwari involvement in the trade became crucial. It is most associated with the Rajasthan smuggling trail but also became the junction for other routes, for instance from Jaipur and through Kisingarh, bypassing British-held Ajmer.

Other places grew in importance alongside Pali, such as Mandsaur. Here Appa Gangadhar was a kind of regional godfather. He drew large revenues from the family's extensive landholdings and channelled his substantial revenues from this into his other business – opium export through the deserts of Rajasthan, conveniently close to his vast poppy meadows.

The Rajasthan route had become the most important by the time of the Opium Wars in China but the first challenge for the Marwari lay in crossing the Thar Desert. The route went via Pali, Jodhpur and the beautiful fortress of Jaisalmer, and then out across the desert and, assuming survival, into Karachi (then a small town with a busy port). Bullocks would often be used for transport to Pali, whereupon loads were transferred to camels for the desert crossing. Each camel carried two to three chests. As with Rimbaud's caravans in the Danakil deserts of Abyssinia, it took a lot to organize beasts of burden that were also in demand for agricultural tasks. In both places armed escorts were a necessity.

There were one or two other routes that made up the fan of opium export out of Malwa. Chief among them was a central line that overlapped with the northern route. This was the trade from Kota (a northern opium-producing town), dominated by Bahadur Mal Seth, the 'Rothschild of Malwa', who was particularly prominent in the 1820s;[2] and by an outsider, Lakshmichand Panjray – Mahajan of Ujjain (Mahajans were a financially savvy people from Punjab) – who ran the family opium smuggling firm. The central route ran more directly westwards to the coast than the Rajasthan trail, via Patan (in Gujarat, further north than the Cambay route). Since it was still quite northerly, it also served as a strategic alternative spur to the northern routes that converged on Pali and led into the Thar.

There is one final route to be noted and this one headed directly south towards Bombay. It avoided the British by pausing in Pune southeast of the city. Then the opium was carried to Alibag Creek on the coast before being shuttled up to large oceangoing ships in Bombay. This Deccan trade, though, was of much less significance than the Rajasthan–Gujarat trade, particularly as the British increased their presence and hold on the region. However, what this last trail does point to is the importance of using a major port, even if it was a British one, in the last leg of the relay – to China.

Export

Coastal mafias took over to bring the opium to export ports. These included long-established Indian traders as well as Armenian, Portuguese and even private British firms, all operating in the interstices of the British 'monopoly'. Small ships, *patimars* (couriers) with a crew of ten, made their way down the west coast from the small settlements mentioned above, for instance on the Gulf of Cambay, to ports like Daman and Diu on the other side of the gulf.

Portuguese Daman, some 150 miles north of Bombay, was the most important opium export port until the British opened up Bombay for the transit of opium in the 1830s. Even before this, opium passed covertly through Bombay, but it was only with its semi-legitimization that it could come to rival Daman. Bombay, although now British (and later often thought of as the 'gateway to India') was a key factor in the challenge to the EIC's grand opium plan centred on Bengal.

Although it rivalled Bombay, Daman didn't turn its back on it. A typical transport might take on opium at Daman and then cottons at Bombay, both destined for the great trading centre of Macao. The Portuguese had sensed an opportunity to enter the opium bonanza through the looser trading possibilities on the west coast. Merchants like Roger de Faria and J. F. Pereira of Pereira and Co. made huge fortunes out of what might be called doubly illicit opium (because in the early stages of its journey it was smuggled around the channels of the British monopoly smugglers). There were also private British interests operating in alliance with the Portuguese: for example, the founder of Crawfords had captained Pereira's flagship, the *Angelica*, built in Daman in 1798.

Reflection, with a Cup of Tea

The renegade opium traffickers of Bombay and Daman managed to divert supplies that might otherwise have been directed to the likes of Jardine Matheson by their Indian agent, the opium merchant Seth Jamsetji Jejeebhoy. They were a relatively minor irritation compared with the Malwa exporters who resisted and evaded British channels completely, thereby puncturing its hugely profitable monopoly. Capitalism here, be it through the EIC monopoly or the new doctrine of free trade, needed to continue to expand and diversify, not deflate. Growth could only be maintained through adding another ingredient to the Britain–China equation. This was *Camellia sinensis* – tea.

The British government, not yet strictly speaking the hands-on masters of Asian trade (the EIC continued to be the major economic force until the mutiny/rebellion of 1857), looked at this in terms of macro-economics. China had tea and Britain's opium trading balanced the deficit of importing so much of it. The Treasury already offset its expenditure on tea by taxing it massively upon import and sale. Now a more devious strategy began to emerge: if Britain could grow its own tea in India it might turn tea, as well as opium, into pure profit for the empire. It would tip the trade balance Britain's way.

But how to create a tea industry when it wasn't even known, for all the cups that were drunk in England, exactly what tea was? It was assumed that black and green tea were different species (later it was proven conclusively that green tea leaves were actually just dyed black tea) and, rather like the nutmeg, mace and cloves consumed in Europe in medieval times, nobody in these regions had any idea how or precisely where they were cultivated. At least this time they knew the approximate location of production. China at the time was, to the outside world, a secretive, closed society that was dangerous to explore. After the First Opium War China had opened up a little for foreigners, although it would be a brave man who would take advantage of it, and anyway travel was still banned much beyond the walled treaty ports, in part precisely to protect the secrets of its tea and silk production. It was strictly forbidden to visit the tea cultivation areas and the Chinese merchants in cities were far from being repositories of knowledge about them.

Nevertheless China's administrators in a land of abundance were complacent, unlike the ruthless and crudely ambitious plant hunters/smugglers of empire. Victorian explorers were genuinely interested in knowledge – although knowledge itself was part of a more general Orientalist project – and had an asset-awareness ingrained in colonialism.

Places like Kew might have sent out its most learned botanists to barely explored parts of the world to broaden its understanding of the biosphere, but it was always also a patriotic mission. One such patriot was Robert Fortune, a dedicated cultivator and scholar, who in 1848 was chief gardener at the Chelsea Physic Garden in London. He had a comfortable, although not lucrative living. So how is it that we find him in 1857 obliging the EIC, as mentioned in the introduction to this chapter, by secretively bringing Chinese opium for them to examine? The answer is probably that Fortune craved adventure as relief from his simple bourgeois life in London. In essence, he was almost as much an adventurer as he was a scientist.

Robert Fortune's First Tea Smuggling Mission

When Fortune arrived in Shanghai in September 1848, he was not a novice traveller in China. His first adventure/scientific mission to East Asia had taken place between 1843 and 1847, and had the backing of the Royal Horticultural Society. On his return, he wrote a popular book, *Three Years' Wandering in the Northern Provinces of China*, which was not so much a dry scientific account as a colourful anecdotal travelogue describing, for instance, encounters with pirates. More importantly, though, in this botanical offshoot of the Great Game, he also laid the groundwork for his first dedicated mission of industrial espionage and for participation in this entanglement of opium and tea. While in Hong Kong he visited mysterious opium-trading quarters of the city where he met colonists who would help with difficult arrangements in the near future.

An opportunist, he seems to have sensed on that first trip that there were greater pickings to be had, both for himself and for his employers. Already in January 1848 tea cultivated in the Himalayas from seeds smuggled out of Canton (nothing to do with Fortune) had been tasted in East India House and had the merchant grandees enthusing at the prospect of profitable Indian production. This early Indian operation was actually somewhat desultory: the product lacked the fragrance of Chinese cultivated tea and productivity was not good. Indeed many Assam tea pickers were addicted to opium. Nevertheless the vision of massively expanded profits, should a transplantation succeed, nestled snugly among the gathered merchants in the Company's headquarters. It was a vision reminiscent of the spice-laced one that more than 200 years before had so motivated the Heren XVII of the Dutch East India Company in their headquarters in Amsterdam.

Fortune had a specific commission: he was sent to find and smuggle out the finest green and black tea seeds and plants. An incentive was that he would hold the intellectual, or at least cultivar, rights to all the other exotic or new hardy species that he might traffic back to his Physic Garden. He came well equipped for smuggling plants, which was a much more difficult operation than transporting neatly packed chests of opium. He carried Wardian cases (known today as terraria) – sealed vitrines whose internal moisture circulation freed them from the perils of the soiled but not green fingers of neglectful sailors. Plants could be kept alive for months if not years in such cases.

That this was espionage is obvious from Fortune's disguise: he put on silk robes and braided a 'queue' (pony tail), the Manchu symbol of subservience, to his own hair, taking on the persona of a mandarin. He travelled in a river junk, a flat-bottomed boat. The inland waterways of China were perilous places at this time, worked by opium and arms dealers, rebels and outlaws. He was taking quite a risk. Along the way his guide, Wang, convinced a succession of tea cultivators and transporters of the importance of his master as a merchant, giving him 'face', as the Chinese say. His small party made its way to Xiuning province where he picked tea plants and collected seeds on the Wang family's land. Then he drifted downriver over a number of months to Shanghai, whereupon the plants and seeds were repackaged over several more weeks before transfer to Hong Kong.

With the plants apparently safe in their Wardian cases, everything seemed in hand. But then it all fell apart. The ship carrying them to India was diverted to Ceylon. Worst of all, many of the cases were opened. Almost all the tea plants apparently died and only 80 seeds survived – there was little hope of a successful transplantation.

Fortune's Second Journey Inland

Undaunted, Fortune's second attempt was even more ambitious than the first.[3] His goal this time was to seek out the source of the legendary Bohea tea that he knew to be cultivated somewhere in the Wu Yi mountains in Fujian. He travelled to the town of Wu Yi Shan and engaged in some local fact-finding. His small party climbed up to a monastery, where he received great hospitality. But in return, ruthlessly and with great focus, he set about his industrial espionage. The monasteries of the region guarded the secret of fine tea production, but unknowingly, or perhaps because they lacked any financial motivation to keep them, they gave away their secrets. Fortune took painstaking notes on all aspects of production, from rainfall and soil type to field size, and picking and packaging of the precious leaves. Through his assistants, Wang and Sing Hoo, he managed to obtain samples of all the equipment that the Chinese cultivators used – tables, pans, ovens, spatulas and specialist agricultural tools.

Replete with knowledge and equipment, he made his way back to Shanghai where he picked up more expertise. Fortune somehow gathered together Chinese tea experts to relocate to India to oversee the trans-plantation (effectively to people-smuggle them given the Celestial Empire's introspective views on migration). It is not certain how he convinced them but it is thought that he used the *compradors* (buyers) of his compatriot Thomas Beale of the firm Dent and Beale to recruit them in the countryside. They managed to get six experts from the prime tea country that Fortune had been travelling in. Two more were experts in the packing of tea in lead boxes.

For some time now coolies – indentured labourers (effectively slaves) – had been trafficked to British sugar plantations in the West Indies and to Australian and Californian gold fields. Sometimes they were even kidnapped – 'Shanghaied'. Fortune's tea experts, bound for the fields of Darjeeling, were not exactly press-ganged – they were promised a degree of autonomy and responsibility – but the restrictive terms of their contracts meant that they were only one step above indentured labour.

On this second mission, Fortune had thought of everything, regard-less of the rights of his tea experts. His own expertise both as botanist and smuggler now came to the fore. For this shipment he put not just the plants but the seeds in the Wardian cases, creating an eco-environment for them as well. He took every precaution, burying hundreds of tea seeds in the soil of mulberry plants (which were now not quite the con-traband that they had once been when China guarded its silk production), adding another ingredient to the melange of deceit. Silk, once the closely guarded treasure of the Han dynasty, was simply the husk for a new and now much more valuable seed.

In 1851 they all sailed together in the *Island Queen*, a kind of cross between an ark and a booty-laden longboat. According to Fortune, 12,838 seeds germinated en route, and many more were to follow. The cargo's destination was the Calcutta Botanic Garden and ultimately the Himalayas.

Once in the mountains prospects were good, particularly under the care of the Chinese experts. So favourable were the conditions for cultivation in the Himalayas that, against expectations, even the 80 original seeds had germinated. In 1860 cinchona, the plant from which the anti-malaria drug quinine derives, began to be cultivated beside the tea of Darjeeling. Fortune had put the Kew ethic into action and despite numerous difficulties had smuggled the empire into a new era of profitability.

The Effects of Tea Transplantation

The smuggling of tea had been a patriotic action. It is no exaggeration to say that the implications of Britain seizing the cultivation of tea through smuggling were felt worldwide. Tea was subsequently transplanted to Ceylon, Burma and East Africa, assuring them as vital colonial interests. The need for sugar in tea meant that the West Indian plantations remained vital to the empire – often now worked by Chinese coolies. The empire spread with cups of Darjeeling tea in the hands of its righteous, upright, driven men and women: missionaries, soldiers, civil servants – and smugglers.

Fortune's own path later deviated from the Company/empire mission. He made two more journeys to China in 1858–9 and 1862 (taking in Japan on this last trip). He had the backing of the American government for the first of these trips, having lost his employer, the EIC, after it was decimated by the revolt of 1857. It seems that Fortune, a plant-hunting fanatic, also had the blood of the smuggler running through his green veins. He delivered tea plants and technology to Washington, whereupon the response was thank you very much and your services are no longer required (a bit like the attitude towards the Lafitte brothers after the assault on New Orleans). The American attempt at transplantation actually failed, partly due to expensive overheads, but also because it coincided with the outbreak of the Civil War.

SMUGGLERS HAVE ALWAYS BEEN USEFUL for state development but they are ultimately expendable. To look at this another way, even as they work within and for, or in the same line of business as, national and transnational entities, they will always remain outsiders in some way. West coast opium merchants shared an enclave in Canton with the Bengal-based Europeans and Americans but as the endpoint of the Malwa trade they were actually representatives of a resistant and rebel element in the industry. The complexity and vulnerability of monopolies was once again exposed. It is a principle of smuggling that the more one guards something, the more likely it is to be smuggled. There is a built-in obsolescence in all monopolies – that is, if such things are ever achievable in the first place. China was unable to fence off its own bio-riches and Britain could not quite control its cultivation. Malwa remained beyond its purview even as British tea came into production.

TWELVE

INDUSTRIAL REVOLUTIONS

Slaves, Cinchona, Rubber
and Technology

In Istanbul the small parts of manufacturing spill onto the streets. This is quite noticeable in the shops at the foot of the hill on which the Galata Tower stands in Beyoğlu overlooking the stretch of water known as the Golden Horn. Not so far away, it is much the same story in Tahtakale market in Emimönü district on the other side of the Galata bridge. *Tahtakale* means fortress, and the keep at the heart of this market is a large former hammam built in the fifteenth century, covering an entire block. It has been used variously since its closure for office space, an art exhibition and now the storage of machine parts, among other things. Unlike in Beyoğlu, much of these are small industrial contraband. Smuggling's contribution to manufacturing will be the topic of this chapter.

Armed with the terminology of economic science, one might break this contribution down into categories like 'knowhow', 'labour', 'productivity' and 'resources'. But in addition I want to enliven them by considering each through a globally important narrative in which smuggling has provided a shot in the arm for industry. I shall draw on four developments. First is the American Industrial Revolution and its illicit origins. Without the smuggling of machines between Britain and America – and, just as importantly, the knowledge of how to use them – its manufacturing would have lacked the technological impetus to develop quite as quickly as it did after independence. Second, smuggling is discussed as a component of industrial growth: the supply of surplus labour, to use a Marxist term, that was the trafficked slave workforce. The story here is one in which three industries in particular were to a large extent built or developed by the smuggling of slaves: rum production, textile manufacturing and shipbuilding. Third, regarding productivity, is the example of the smuggling of cinchona, which was hugely effective in the battle against the malaria that struck down colonial administrators and decimated native workers. Finally I shall explore the secretive transplantation of the plant that provided a resource so crucial in manufacturing during the late nineteenth and early twentieth centuries: rubber.

The business logic of accelerating industrial progress through other means can draw heavily on the smart practices of smuggling, enabling a country to get ahead of its competitors. Perhaps this is where smuggling and state entrepreneurship most obviously coincide, and where free trade lends its doctrine to both (relevant here in terms of universal rights to intellectual property – ideas – and resources for manufacturing). Sometimes this forging ahead is defended as duty, as it was in the cases of the third and fourth examples above, in which the British Empire was strengthened, or as a kind of manifest destiny, as in the first, in which American modernization began and expanded. The second area of discussion, contraband slaving as a means to maximize profits, is, from any angle, indefensible.

The Illicit American Industrial Revolution

Who could have predicted that the land of the Pilgrim Fathers would become a nation of smugglers? Perhaps it is an assertion too far; this irregular way of doing things could simply be put down to the rebel spirit that all revolutions require, or to necessity of supply both in the lead up to and during the War of Independence. Regardless, much of the success of the American Industrial Revolution derived from smuggling, which provided machine technology and knowledge of how to use it.

George Washington, Thomas Jefferson, Benjamin Franklin and Alexander Hamilton were at the heart of this strategic theft. Operating out of Philadelphia, Hamilton, Secretary of State for the Treasury, and his assistant Tench Coxe were the linchpins of the plan. The organ for facilitating a modernizing revolution was the grandly titled 'Society for the Encouragement of Manufactures and the Useful Arts'. Hamilton also headed up a company called 'Society for the Establishment of Useful Manufactures'.

What they were evading was a series of trade restraints on technology dispersal by a protectionist British government. In 1749 there was a ban on the export of silk and woollen manufacturing tools and in 1774 on cotton and linen machinery and on free migration of relevant technicians to the colonies. During the 1780s textile printers were forbidden from leaving the British Isles, let alone Europe, and between 1780 and 1824 the war on knowledge diffusion reached new heights.

Although there was a gestation period, the American modernization programme swung into action after the defeat of the British in 1783. For years before this, American smuggling in the Caribbean and Atlantic had contributed to economic prosperity in the colonies, thereby providing capital for industrial investment when the time came. Certain contraband fed directly into this manufacturing trend. For instance, iron, paper yarn and spun hemp, all used in industry, were supplied illicitly by the Dutch. Even in the approach to war, there had been a campaign to create an autonomous manufacturing base: Benjamin Franklin, on his tour to Britain in the early 1770s, tried to recruit artisans for the colonies (as well as revolutionaries – he succeeded in persuading Thomas Paine to give up his customs job in England and emigrate to America in 1774).

One of the early exponents of this game of industrial espionage was Joseph Hague, who brought back a carding machine to Philadelphia. But it was one thing to steal the parts or plans for a machine, even to smuggle an entire machine, and another to build or operate it. Moses Brown, anti-slavery campaigner and brother of slave trader John Brown, imported illicit machinery, although he had no idea how it worked.

Some of the operatives were far from illustrious: Abel Buell was a convicted counterfeiter, and the most successful of them, Thomas Digges, was only employed at the overriding behest of George Washington. As so many times in history, a pragmatic bargain had been struck between smugglers and statesmen, leading to the effective redistribution of resources and shifts in geopolitical power.

In 1792 in Dublin Digges managed to print Hamilton's *Report on Manufactures*, effectively a recruiting manual, and to disseminate it both there and in industrial towns in northern England. He persuaded around twenty artisans and machinists to emigrate covertly, including a skilled mechanic from Yorkshire, one William Pearce, who had worked with Arkwright, the renowned inventor of spinning machines. An even more important recruit was Samuel Slater, who smuggled himself to America in 1789 pretending to be a farm hand. He was later called by some the 'Father of the American Industrial Revolution'. He looked over Brown's machines in Pawtucket, Rhode Island, and although he could not work these he was able to dismantle them and build his own. His brother John followed, bringing more technology. Samuel set up the earliest spinning factories.

Another industrial spy was Francis Cabot Lowell, who toured Glaswegian and other northern British factories in 1811, bringing back knowledge on how to create integrated manufacturing with all functions under one roof. He was searched on departure from Britain but had already committed the ideas and schemes to memory and carried no notes. His Boston Manufacturing Co. set up its first operation in Waltham, Massachusetts, in 1813 and a town was named after him in 1822.

Beside friends in high places there was further encouragement for intellectual property theft in that only citizens could hold patents in the U.S. One could register a stolen invention there with the foreign 'owners' of it helpless to intervene.

The American Industrial Revolution was now taking on momentum and, realizing the futility of prohibiting emigration, in 1824 Britain lifted its bans. Some machines were now even legalized for export, while others were simply mislabelled as legal. By 1825 the U.S. had managed to obtain much of the knowhow for building and working all of the great cotton-weaving inventions pioneered in Britain during the 1760s and '70s. Britain's greatest revolution had been stolen!

The Illicit Slave Trade and Manufacturing

U.S. involvement in slave trading was twofold. It imported slaves that were initially brought from Africa to places like Cuba and Brazil, and it also brought in Africans directly, adding to American-born slaves and thereby maintaining the boom in cotton production. The cotton plantation economy of the southern U.S. was of course built on slavery, and to a large extent after 1820, when all such trading was banned, it was supplied with contraband slaves.

In 1787 Rhode Island had been the first to ban the slave trade but it was the main participant state for long after this. John Brown (not to be confused with the abolitionist pre-Civil War hero) was one of the main slave traders in this post-Independence period despite the attention of abolitionists, not least among whom was his brother Moses. At the very end of the eighteenth century Rhode Island traders expanded their business, initiating slaving passages directly out of Africa, and by the mid- to late 1810s the majority of slaves came here. American slave trafficking expanded as other players withdrew, particularly the British, who then made it their business to deter others. New York financiers and merchants were the main backers. The boom years of slaving out of Rhode Island were between 1830 and the Civil War, even running into the war years that for the North were ostensibly about abolishing slavery. This was because cotton was very important for the North, not just the South.

Southern cotton had two main manufacturing destinations. First, on a grand scale, was northern England – the Lancashire mill towns which were at the heart of the British Industrial Revolution; and second, and almost as important, was New England, particularly Massachusetts, where cloth and garment factories were developing. Northern industry was to a certain extent reliant upon the labour of Southern slaves smuggled by Northerners.

As is so often the case with trading – illicit as well as regulated – there were profits to be made on the side as other small industries grew up around the main slaving business. In the case of American slaving there were two manufacturing sectors that particularly benefited besides cotton.

Rum was a currency of the slave trade in West Africa, where it was often part of the exchange for slaves. This liquor was itself the product of a two-way contraband run. American traders, feeling disadvantaged after British restraint of trade in the Caribbean through regulation such as the Molasses Act of 1733, smuggled molasses out of the West Indian islands in exchange for contraband provisions that substituted for goods that the British failed to supply to those islands. Molasses spawned a rum distillery industry in Rhode Island, particularly in Newport. The channel for contraband slaves to the South was therefore interlinked with a smuggling-enabled industry in the North.

Later on, after the American Revolution, there was another manufacturing boost from the slave trade. Fast Baltimore clippers were the preferred vessel for the illicit trade, leading to a small boom in shipbuilding in this Maryland port. American vessels were also the preferred carrier for illicit slave traffickers of all nationalities, because flying the U.S. flag sent a message of defiance to the British. The U.S. was the only nation that stood up to a Royal Navy tasked with enforcing Britain's newly discovered and quite zealous anti-slavery campaign on the high seas. Only American-built ships could be registered under a U.S. flag and so they were in some demand.

During the mid-nineteenth century, the British government, speaking through its naval might, was at the height of its policy of trade regulation.

It might be seen as a kind of global seaborne customs officiary. Why, then, in another context, did it act out what it saw as its right to exploit the spoils of the world? This was the ongoing story of plant smuggling.

The Cinchona Smuggling Project, 1859–61

William Jackson Hooker had become the first director of the reconstituted Kew Gardens in London in 1841 and immediately set up the 'Museum of Economic Botany', a kind of nursery of empire. A decade later Fortune's China tea theft was complete. Buoyed by this success, Kew was ready for more clandestine work. A pact with the India Office (the successor to the East India Company after the Indian Mutiny of 1857) made it a powerful political force: depending upon one's viewpoint, it was either a rich scientific store or a dispensing house of 'acquired' flora whose recipients were largely plantation technicians and entrepreneurs in as yet insufficiently profitable parts of the empire. It was the plant smugglers' reference point, their state sanction and often the transit site for their barely surviving seeds and saplings.

The mastermind of the cinchona theft was Clements Markham, a retired naval officer who was now a junior clerk in the India Office. The theft was justified as the saving of an endangered species but it was actually all about combating malaria in the colonies and thereby increasing productivity in the cultivation of raw commodities for manufacture. The mission was three-pronged, with groups searching for different terrains for variant species of cinchona. Each group was given £500 and told to achieve their goal within a year. Markham was a hands-on participant.

Markham went with Kew gardener John Weir to Carabaya province, north of Lake Titicaca in southern Peru, to research and acquire the yellow bark version of cinchona. An expatriate, G. J. Pritchett, was called upon to find grey bark cinchona in the forests of northern Peru, while the hardened plant hunters Richard Spruce and Robert Cross would look for red bark. All except Spruce (who had trained at Kew ten years earlier) were tutored at the great botanical garden in London in the delicate arts of imperial exploration, plant preservation and smuggling. Each went about their smuggling missions with righteous determination.

Markham's expedition ran great risks in its quest for plants. First they narrowly escaped imprisonment in the Andean town of Sandia for their blatant botanical thievery. After they managed to flee the region clutching seeds – Weir heading north as a decoy and Markham southwest over the mountains for the coast – they ran into more trouble, this time with a local customs officer at the small port of Islay. However a bribe to the finance minister in Lima countermanded a presidential decree forbidding the export of flora and the requisite permissions were forwarded to the official. Soon the seeds were successfully on their way to Kew.

Spruce and Cross meanwhile rendezvoused at a small, cold, damp place called Limón on the lower slopes of Chimborazo in Ecuador, a mountain still at that time believed by some to be the highest on earth. Uncomfortable but at least unharried by local and regional *caudillos* (bosses), they managed to collect over 100,000 seeds, which they hauled and rafted downriver to Guayaquil: 637 cases of cinchona were sent to Kew. In May 1861 Ecuador banned the export of cinchona, but it was too late.

Dispersal Around the Empire

The ultimate destination for all three shipments was the Nilgiri Hills in southern India, and some were also to be sent to Ceylon. Pritchett's grey did reach India but its initial diagnosis in Ecuador and Kew as useless as an antidote for malaria was confirmed here. Markham's yellow might have prospered in the cool hills but ill-fortune continued to beset this arm of the project when a case of seeds fell overboard during transit to India. Many of the plants wilted in 42°C temperatures in the Red Sea, and on arrival in Nilgiri those surviving were too far gone to recover. There was one last hope – Spruce and Cross's red cinchona.

It actually all went pretty smoothly. By the time of Ecuador's export ban the red bark plants had been successfully planted in India and Ceylon. By 1880 it was in industrial production, augmented by an even better species brought to Kew in 1865 by Charles Ledger, a sometime alpaca smuggler who also took it, opportunely, to the Netherlands. Malaria, the terrible fever of the tropics, was henceforth held in check and Britain's plantation economy of tea, indigo and jute in India, coffee in East Africa and rubber in Malaya and Ceylon could now be managed more effectively by the erstwhile sickly white colonials and produced by a more robust workforce.

As for the smugglers themselves, Pritchett was largely ignored in the official narrative, Weir succumbed to disease, Cross contracted malaria and Spruce went bankrupt after his Ecuadorian bank collapsed and his health was broken by the subsequently deferred retirement. Markham, on the other hand, began his rapid climb to a position of influence culminating in his presidency of the Royal Geographical Society, while Hooker became a much better-funded patriarch of the great plant smuggling project that would continue to feed the expansion of imperial manufacturing.

Resource – Rubber

The redistribution of cinchona was the outcome of an organized smuggling expedition orchestrated from Kew and, as in the case of tea, there were massive benefits in terms of productivity (tea, brewed from boiled water, was a safer drink for factory workers than others, and so helped to combat cholera and other waterborne diseases). Regarding rubber – the *Hevea brasiliensis* variety, sometimes called 'Pará fine', the most suitable for manufacturing – it was the control of a key raw material in industry that was at stake. Arguably its transplantation would be the biggest coup of all.

Rubber seems to have attracted empire-builders. In the Putumayo (southern Colombia and parts of northern Peru and Ecuador) there existed a murderous rubber fiefdom that relied on the forced and expendable labour of indigenous people. Roger Casement, Joseph Conrad's friend and fellow traveller in Congo, was sent by the British parliament to investigate its excesses. Werner Herzog's film *Fitzcarraldo* (1982) draws on the life of a rubber baron, Fitzcarrald, who opened up a new territory of rubber production in southern Peru. Famously in the film (and in real life – it was filmed without special effects) a river steamer is hauled over a mountain into another watershed so that Fitzcarraldo can bring cargo possibilities to a stretch of river above rapids, thus giving access to another vast reserve of rubber.[1] It fails when the boat's mooring lines are cut by the indigenous people and it crashes down through the rapids. By way of compensation Fitzcarraldo turns the boat into a floating opera, and although he doesn't create another Manaus with its latex riches oozing in from distant tributaries, he consoles himself by emulating its culture.

There is another maverick associated with the story of rubber exploitation, and his story is one of smuggling. Heir to Pierre Poivre and Robert Fortune, the hero/villain in this rubber story was also an adventurer, another Fitzcarrald(o) – Henry Wickham.

The Rubber Odyssey of Henry Wickham

In January 1869 the 22-year-old Henry Wickham, the Hampstead-born son of a solicitor father and milliner mother, took passage from Trinidad with smugglers bound for the River Orinoco. The brackish water of the delta was soon lapping against the bow. Wickham already had some experience of Latin America, having previously visited the Mosquito Coast of Nicaragua gathering colourful feathers to be sold to adorn ladies' hats back in London. But it hadn't been a great success and he was still looking for viable commercial opportunities. He had only a vague plan but time to think as the boat glided slowly between the sand spits with only the occasional squall of startled wading birds to break the monotony. It must have been rather like Arthur Rimbaud's approach to Aden and Djibouti on the Red Sea, with mixed sensations of dread and excitement. Finally Angostura would appear, mirage-like, out of the grasslands.

This town was the birthplace of Simón Bolívar's revolution, giving it a certain fame, and it must have seemed like a jewel compared to the poet's abject, dusty trading ports. It offered hope of profitable trading. Just over the hills there were rumours of gold, and the hinterlands of the upper reaches of the river promised rich botanical bounty. It was a gateway port, not only to the rainforest of the Orinoco but, for the very adventurous, to the Amazon Basin. Wickham's hope was that rare and exotic commodities might be rafted, boated and shipped out of these great river systems and across the Atlantic to the now burgeoning consumer markets of Western Europe.

As described in Joe Jackson's book *The Thief at the End of the World*, Wickham enquired about the sources of all sorts of potentially profitable plants. He considered, for instance, a trade in tonka beans, a substitute for vanilla that could be used for aroma in soaps, perfume and tobacco. Perhaps it was as he left Angostura that his mind turned to rubber, some of which he may have come across in small quantities in the port. And it was only after he had struggled upriver past the unnavigable cascades of the Raudales de Maipures, and arrived at the small end-of-the-line town of San Fernando de Atabapo, that he came to realize the commercial possibilities.

But this was not to be his breakthrough trip: the rubber here, *Siphonia elastica*, proved to be of low quality. In addition fever and fatigue almost destroyed him. Eventually, deserted by his workers and companions, he

Henry Wickham, c. 1925.

abandoned his settlement, crossed to the Rio Negro watershed and was able to drift through the heart of the continent, washed through the Amazon back whence he came, like so many before him.

However, his spirit was not broken: on his passage downriver to the Atlantic, he passed through the large town of Manaus, so fabulously wealthy through its rubber boom that it had built a fabled opera house. He was dazzled. Further downstream, in the Pará region's main city, Belém, he met the British consul, John Drummond-Hay, who had written a paper on the commercial possibilities of rubber production. The two men got on well. Wickham was impressed by this cosmopolitan colonial administrator and by his polished but realistic study of the Brazilian rubber regions. It particularly focused on the hinterland of Santarém, in which, in passing, Wickham had sensed great potential. In Wickham Drummond-Hay saw a rough diamond, possibly with the determination and knowledge to set up some form of rubber plantation in the jungle (rather than just dealing), which could link up with the shipping transport business that Britain had already established in Amazonia. He was the first British prospector that he had encountered who had actually tapped rubber upriver and gained prolonged experience as a *seringueiro* (a rubber tapper or gatherer – rubber was harvested from rainforest trees by methods that were unknown outside of the Amazon jungle).

It might have been during these civilized discussions about planting that the germ of another, more daring plan – a smuggling operation – began to hatch at the back of his mind.

A Planting Life or a Smuggling Adventure?

In 1872 Wickham published his account of this trip, *Rough Notes of a Journey Through the Wilderness from Trinidad to Para, Brazil, by Way of the Great Cataracts of the Orinoco, Atabagao and Rio Negro*. Drummond-Hay added his report to the book. By the time it was published Henry Wickham was already back in Amazonas, this time with his wife, mother, brother, sister and brother-in-law, and various English labourers. He intended to live the life of a planter and gatherer of rubber. They settled at a place called Piquiá-tuba on the Rio Tapajos, a tributary of the Amazon that flowed out at Santarém, a day or two's ride away.

As he laboured Wickham heard news about the publication in London of his book, and his ambition swelled. He continued to struggle as a planter but also began to envision working with Kew's useful and profitable plant-gathering project that had now turned its attentions to rubber. He wrote to the new director of the Royal Botanical Gardens, Joseph Hooker, the son of William Hooker, who had died in 1865. Hooker didn't reply at first but on reading Wickham's book, with its convincing sketches of *Hevea brasiliensis* (something even one of Kew's own, Spruce, had been unable to provide), he saw in him what Drummond-Hay had discerned earlier – a useful man on the ground. Clements Markham once again became involved and, via the consul, Wickham was contacted to procure and ship rubber seeds back to Kew. The illicit transplantation of rubber had become an imperative mission.

Wickham's Smuggling Mission

Wickham wasn't to be the first smuggler of rubber seeds out of the Amazon. In 1873 Charles Farris of Cametá (some 60 miles south of Belém) brought 2,000 seeds to London, smuggled downriver inside two stuffed caimans. On arrival the seeds were immediately bought up by Markham's rubber advisor, the chemist James Collins, who had written extensively on the need to start up a British rubber industry now that vulcanized rubber (a technique invented some 30 years earlier for refining it for multipurpose use) was essential for so much machinery and equipment, from guns to vehicles to boots and raincoats. Some of the seeds were planted at Kew but they all died, as did those sent to the Royal Botanical Gardens in Calcutta, recipient of Robert Fortune's stolen Chinese tea.

Now the India Office commissioned Wickham to obtain up to 10,000 seeds, at a price of £10 per 1,000, although they didn't have much faith in him, particularly as he had delayed collecting the seeds for a season. He still held out hope of succeeding as a planter. But even as the India Office/Kew sent out Robert Cross to take charge of the transplanting operation, he made his own decisive move towards smuggling.

In February 1876 he headed to the Tapajós region to collect seeds. He bought them from the trading houses at Boim, which at that time was as important commercially as Santarém, and gathered them from the jungles of the higher plateau beyond the town, near a village called Agumaita. He reaped thousands of seeds from the black bark tree, much more fruitful in its rubber yield than red or white. He dried and packed them into baskets and crates for the journey to Boim, carefully avoiding damp and striations of excreted oil, both of which would lead to premature germination or rot. Wickham found himself with about a ton of biomatter to ship: 70,000 seeds packed in banana leaves in scores of wicker baskets. He now needed to work out how he was going to transport them to England.

This is where a smuggler's instinct took over. Through good fortune, for him at least, a small steamship, the ss *Amazonas*, had her import cargo stolen. With no money to buy rubber for the return it looked as though she would have nothing to transport back to Liverpool. Wickham jumped at the chance, chartering cargo space in the vessel. He had the ship come to the Tapajós river at Boim to secretly load the conspicuous cargo, eliminating the need for chartering a vessel at Santarém where questions might be asked on the busy quay.

Wickham and his wife Violet, along with an adopted boy, sailed with the cargo. There was now only one more obstacle to surmount before the open sea: the *alfândaga* – customs house – at Belém, 800 km downstream. It wasn't illegal to ship botanical specimens for scientific purposes but to transplant an entire industry certainly was, particularly as memories of the cinchona theft were still remembered. Rather than deny that the hold contained any plants, Wickham and the captain of the *Amazonas*, George Murray, decided to encourage a perception that it needed to be kept closed because it contained delicate scientific specimens. This both hid the cargo and explained why no new commodities were being loaded. The new consul, Thomas Shipton Green, backed up this story as he and Wickham met with customs.

There are probably embellishments and exaggerations as to the cloak and dagger nature of the passage down the Amazon, making it look something like a Tintin adventure. It was certainly stealthy but perhaps not quite so dramatic. Wickham claimed that they faced great danger upriver from a Brazilian gunboat. A story circulated that, as an insurance after submitting requests for clearance at Belém, he created a diversion by calling on the governor at his mansion and entertaining various guests with upriver tales even as his ship quietly put out into the estuary.[2] Then he stole away from the party, boarded a coastal vessel that ferried him to the *Amazonas* and they were on their way. There is great poignancy in that some fifteen years later Arthur Rimbaud was carried on to a vessel of the same name, *L'Amazone*, as he retreated out of Africa, a dying, broken man. By contrast, in 1876 Henry Wickham's horizon looked bright and clear. At sea the hatches were thrown open and the rubber seeds, germinants of a new, final phase of the British Empire, were nurtured all the way to Kew.

Global Ramifications

Only 2,000 of the 70,000 seeds would germinate but that was easily enough, and after their transplantation to Singapore, Malaya, Burma and Ceylon the end of the Amazonian rubber boom was inevitable. The rise of the eastern rubber empire and the demise of the western one would have come sooner had Kew not followed Robert Cross's advice to plant the seeds on floodplains, where he had collected his inferior specimens, and instead taken Wickham's advice to avoid river banks and plant on the slightly elevated, drier plateaux where he had found his own.

In 1913 the Amazon rubber industry was ruined in a single year when Britain's super-productive Southeast Asian plantations flooded the world market with rubber, which antagonized the by now largest industrialized country in the world, the United States. So important was a ready supply of rubber to the latter that in 1928, the year that Henry Wickham died, there was an attempt to claw back control of the industry when Henry Ford set up his own rubber industry town, Fordlandia, near to Santarém.

The Amazon rubber industry was later blighted by a fungal parasite, *Dothidella ulei*, that particularly affected plantation cultivation, and less so tree cultivation dispersed in the jungle (the modus operandi at the time of Wickham's Amazon adventures). Although the new British rubber industry perfected the plantation technique, they avoided this scourge as it remained confined to the Amazon. The disease attacked trees, not seeds, and Wickham had smuggled only the latter. Fordlandia was not so lucky.

Should we consider Wickham as a smuggler or a planter briefly charged with imperial zeal, a sort of Kiplingesque character? Jackson, in *The Thief at the End of the World*, gets into the mindset of the time in considering this question, discerning no mutual exclusivity here. According to 'contemporary definitions', Wickham and his wife were smugglers, working for more important smugglers who were dedicated to the cause of empire.[3]

Smuggling and Manufacturing Today

Smuggling as an element of the manufacturing process continued apace into the twentieth century. During the Cold War the doomed Soviet 'Concordski', the Tupolev Tu-144 that crashed at the Paris air show in 1973, was widely believed to have been designed with the help of plans smuggled out of Aérospatiale, the French company building the West's supersonic airliner. One of the most successful weapons of the twentieth century, the Kalashnikov AK-47 assault rifle, has been copied and smuggled all over the planet, both officially and unofficially. More dangerously still, Pakistan's nuclear weapons capability, a programme made possible by the theft of knowledge from a centrifuge complex in the Netherlands by the father of the 'Islamic bomb', A. Q. Khan, was covertly disseminated by him to China, and perhaps Libya and North Korea.

Henry Wickham, a maverick, was co-opted by his nation. The same, to a greater or lesser extent, can be said of many of the examples above – informal smuggling initiatives developing along more formal channels. Ikeja Computer Village is a massive informal electronics market on the edge of Lagos. Several firms here began as street sellers peddling illicitly obtained goods but as they grew they became largely legitimate. The journalist Robert Neuwirth, in his book *Stealth of Nations*, gives the example of BRIAN Integrated Systems, which began as a pavement vendor and is now a large operator building its own computers. It is still based in the market, and so remains informal in that sense, but it is now in partnership with Microsoft.[4] In a world that is dominated by transnational corporations, there is still room for such informal development paths.

There are also individual smuggling initiatives out of rather than into the factory. Over seven years, between 1998 and 2005, a worker in the luxury motor yacht firm Sunseeker, based at Poole in Dorset, England, smuggled out parts from its factory with the intention of building his own luxury yacht.[5] Perhaps he had listened to Johnny Cash's song 'One Piece at a Time', which tells of a downtrodden Detroit automobile worker who, at the end of his shift each day, smuggles car parts, piece by piece, out of a General Motors factory to be assembled later at home into a brand new Cadillac. In a sense it is the fable of Fitzcarrald(o) all over again – a vessel is smuggled across a divide in order to build another world, but of course it is likely to end in ruin, leaving only cultural traces.

WHEREVER THERE IS MANUFACTURING, there will be both formal and informal ways of putting things together. The Tahtakale market in Istanbul, like Ikeja in Lagos, is a complex mix of the legitimate and the illicit, as was the path to American modernization and the redeployment of bio-wealth to sustain the British Empire. Theft of flora and intellectual property have often been part of nation- and empire-building projects, a continuation of the systematic reordering and reassembling of the world by means of smuggling that had begun with Poivre, or perhaps much earlier with a deceitful princess along the Silk Road.

The examples put forward in this chapter indicate that the kinds of industrial espionage and smuggling that we see today have had a long historical lineage. And of course other modern smuggling has had its rehearsal – the heroin and cocaine trades echoing opium supply to China, for instance. But most telling of all, however, is recognition of the principle that anything and everything can and will be smuggled.

PART THREE
A SMUGGLING WORLD

THIRTEEN
SMUGGLING CULTURES
Looted Treasures

The 1860s and '70s were energetic times, decades during which things, people and ideas began to become unmoored and more mobile. The wider world felt smaller – the Suez Canal opened in 1869 and in the same year the Union Pacific Railroad from the east met up with the Central Pacific from the west in the state of Utah, completing the world's first transcontinental transport link. The industrial nature of the American Civil War had boosted, not ruined, transportation infrastructures. In 1872 Giovanni Battista Pirelli opened his rubber workshop in Milan and Thomas Cook arranged the first tourist trip around the world, publishing his account of it, *Letter from the Sea and from Foreign Lands, Descriptive of a Tour Round the World*, the following year. In 1873 Jules Verne's *Around the World in Eighty Days* came out, the account of Phileas Fogg's attempt to outwit the sedentary gentlemen of the Reform Club in London by circumnavigating the globe in record time. Cultural objects and trends might also more easily and rapidly travel the globe. The year 1863 had been a big one for art, with French painting upsetting tradition in the Salon des refusés, not only challenging realist painting but now infused with Oriental style and fashion. A delicate and beneficial borrowing, one might think, cultured and enlightening, but only made possible, as politicians might say (after the shock passes), by the new industrial energy that accelerated the dissemination of ideas and trends. But this period was also important for other borrowings and circulation, not least the twin sports of looting and smuggling of other countries' ancient artefacts.

While America was preoccupied with moving contraband of war around the continent, the Old World was reviving its arrogant habit of acquiring the culture of distant lands, a high (or low) point of which was the acquisition of the Parthenon marbles by Lord Elgin during the first decade of the century. In 1860 the Summer Palace outside Beijing was looted and torched by his son, the 8th Earl, in alliance with the French at the end of the Second Opium War.

In the same year as Phileas Fogg's fictional exploits, another well-heeled gentleman traveller who had made his fortune in import and export made his way rather suspiciously over the Turkish border into Greece. He smuggled across a golden hoard and hid it in barns, stables and farmyards until he could successfully transport it to Berlin. His name was Heinrich Schliemann, and he was a wealthy and hugely enthusiastic amateur archaeologist. In April 1873 he had discovered the city of Troy, hitherto presumed mythical, underneath a hill on the coast at Hissarlik in northwestern Anatolia in Turkey. More significantly for him, he had found what he presumed was its treasure. He was wrong in this: it was not, as it emerged later, King Priam's gold. In fact it predated Priam by some 1,200 years. However, believing it to be so, he did his very best to keep it out of the hands of Turkish and Greek customs officers. In 1881 he gave it to the German people and into the custody of the Museum für Völkerkunde in Berlin.

Perhaps this bold cultural transplantation by Schliemann was the artistic equivalent of the smuggling of spices, tea, cinchona or rubber that so fundamentally altered the economic and political geometry of the world. There are certainly similarities in the justification of these actions. Many have been defended as merely the dispersal and dissemination of God's gift to mankind, or as dealing in things that pertain universally to a more modern, cosmopolitan world (following this argument through to today, the classical ruins of Greece are world heritage, the ancient Greeks not being the modern Greeks). Some have argued that these items are *res nullius* (nobody's property). At the time these acquirers were not, contrary to some current thinking, condemned as disregarding national property, original habitat or cultural context. A principle of freedom of access to 'world heritage' has often been invoked; sometimes, as in the case of cinchona or the Elgin marbles, it is reinforced by claims that the perpetrators were saving something from extinction for the benefit of mankind. Whatever the rights and wrongs of this, what these controversial acts have brought about is the dismantling of one part of the world and its re-assemblage somewhere else.

Of course some of this is simply pillage and theft, even if the exhibition of contraband objects in magnificent palaces of culture in

Europe or North America might have seduced us into thinking that they are somehow in the right place, that they have almost always been a part of our developed world civilizations. There is a power in this right of possession (counter to claims of origin of objects) that should not be underestimated, and I shall go on to talk more about the significant real and symbolic effects of cultural artefacts being installed in wealthy nations' museums and private collections. But first another question: how has the profile of the artefact smuggler changed over the years? A lot of dust is disturbed in the looting and smuggling of art and archaeological artefacts, but between the grave robber, the smuggler on the ground and the wealthy private collector or unscrupulous acquisitions officer of a great museum there are a variety of ways of getting your hands dirty.

Smuggling Archaeological Treasures

These days there is often a long chain before a smuggled artefact arrives in a museum or collection. For the gold of the Moche Lord of Sipán to appear on the international antiquities markets after the discovery of his tomb by local *huaceros* (grave robbers) in northern Peru in 1987, it had to pass through four or five persons – ever more important dealers – during its travels. It wasn't always like this. Previously not only were the 'cultured' cogs in the smuggling wheel prepared to get their hands dirty, but they were often quite refined hands at that.

When in 1923 the French writer André Malraux, later Minister of Cultural Affairs under President de Gaulle, set sail with his wife Clara for Indochina he did not have literary research exclusively on his mind: he had another cultural agenda. Not long after arriving in Saigon the couple set out for Cambodia via Hanoi, their objective the ruined, neglected, ancient Khmer temple of Banteai Srey, nearly consumed by the jungle. Here they would lever off beautifully carved stone bas-reliefs and attempt to smuggle them out of the jungle by ox cart and river steamer and thence out of the country. They were apprehended. Malraux was tried but received just a one-year suspended sentence after Clara, able to travel home, enlisted as character witnesses such literati as André Breton, André Gide, Max Jacob and the Gallimard brothers.

Undeterred, in 1931 André and Clara, now travelling along the Silk Road, acquired Graeco-Buddhist terracotta heads from the Tashkurghan region of Afghanistan and managed to smuggle them across the Khyber Pass overland to Lahore and eventually to Bombay for shipment to France. Malraux's publisher, Gallimard, exhibited them in a gallery at its head office, attracting much interest regarding the dissemination of Greek culture by Alexander the Great against the current, to the east.

Clearly collectors came in varying shapes and sizes. One common figure was the aesthete at the marble face. Lord Elgin began the dismantling of the frieze and metope sculptures from the Parthenon in 1801. They were all in London by 1809, although some had to be brought up from twelve fathoms down after the ship carrying them sank off the island of Cythera in 1802. This initiated something of a frenzy of opencast mining of other peoples' culture. In 1811 Charles Cockerell, an artist and very active Grand Tourist, excavated the marbles on the island of Aegina that are now in the Glyptothek in Munich. He also removed reliefs from the Temple of Apollo at Bassae, which now reside in the British Museum. Statues dismantled and successfully shipped out of Greece following on from the acquisition of the Elgin marbles mobilized still more marauders in the region, a surge leading eventually to Schliemann and no doubt exciting other refined collectors around the world, as well as inspiring later adventurers and fortune hunters like Malraux. This pillage, of course, was veiled in respectability. Usually there was a veneer of academic interest, often some diplomatic involvement and either a museum or a wealthy individual patron waiting at the end of the road. Sometimes it is difficult to ascribe motives.

John Lloyd Stephens was a respected diplomat, explorer and scholar of Mayan culture who in 1839–40 hacked down swathes of jungle in Guatemala, Honduras and Mexico to reveal the glory of Mayan culture, much of it sketched brilliantly by his English travelling companion, the artist Frederick Catherwood. He narrated it in his much admired travelogue *Incidents of Travel in Central America, Chiapas and Yucatán*, and he is generally considered to be a champion of the culture. But even Stephens considered dismantling much of the magnificent Honduran site of Copán and shipping it back to the United States. In his footsteps, and inspired by him, another diplomat-archaeologist, Edward Herbert Thompson, bought the land on the Yucatán peninsula on which stand the Mayan ruins of Chichén Itzá. Among other excavations, between 1904 and 1910 he drained the huge natural well on the site, the Sacred Cenote, and removed many of its treasures, controversially, to the Peabody Museum at Harvard University. There is something of a recurring theme here: one year later, in 1911, Hiram Bingham uncovered the magnificent ridge-top Inca ruins of Machu Picchu and removed thousands of artefacts for his sponsors at Yale University, which only recently has agreed to return them to Peru.[1]

Recent transhipments of artefacts have been either more obscure or more obviously criminal in nature. Covert smuggling – now reflecting tighter laws against the export of archaeological finds – is often necessary for obtaining desired objects. This smuggling is not merely a by-product of opportunistic, dilettante adventuring in exotic lands; rather it is an integral part of supply and demand.

The Middle East has continued to be fertile territory for tomb raiders, smugglers and collectors. During the 1990s an English restorer, Jonathan Tokeley-Parry, turned to smuggling, fooling customs by altering the appearance of Egyptian artefacts. In one of his most audacious alterations he painted a sculpted head of Pharaoh Amenhotep III with bright, modern-looking colours over a false plastic skin to make it appear like a cheap souvenir. In 2001 fourth-millennium BCE ruins were discovered at Jiroft in southeastern Iran. In this case the tomb raiding was orderly and organized. Each family had a plot and the police did not intervene for a year, by which time most of the artefacts had been smuggled out of the country. A similar process occurred in Isin in southern Iraq after the fall of Saddam Hussein in 2003. In the majority of cases it is not known who most of the personnel are at the centre of the chain of these artefact dispersals, nor indeed where most of the treasures have ended up. But investigations into the smuggling of gold objects from the Lord of Sipán's tomb have revealed a few of the middle men – the white-collar smugglers who carry the objects.

The journalist Roger Atwood, in his book *Stealing History* (2004), tracks several of the known travels of looted artefacts from the Moche site near the town of Lambayeque in northern Peru which, before it was secured by police and archaeologists, lost much of its treasure to *huaceros* in the village beside it. One such channel was masterminded by a collector-dealer, David Swetnam, and a former diplomat, Fred Drew.[2] They initially arranged for airline crews to carry small quantities of contraband antiquities. It was easy to smuggle textiles as they didn't show up in X-rays, but customs officials were also bribed at South American airports. U.S.-bound looted Peruvian artefacts generally travel via Chile, with those for Europe going through Ecuador. But Drew and Swetnam chose Bolivia as a place of transit because its customs controls were particularly lax. The artefacts were smuggled overland to the capital, La Paz, with some of the ceramic pieces disguised in much the same way as Tokeley-Parry had done, this time adding false mud bases inscribed with *hecho en Bolivia* (made in Bolivia). They were then flown to the airport of Vancouver, which was relatively easy to enter, before being transported across the border to California. Later on, after this route became unviable, they sent them to London where a down-at-heel British dealer usually resident in Santa Barbara, Michael Kelly, who worked for an 'art conservation' company, would receive them. If questioned Kelly would say that his father, who had travelled in South America during the 1920s, had collected them. Between London and Los Angeles they were wrapped in English newspapers and, for at least one shipment, in an old raincoat that had belonged to Kelly's father. The first loads to arrive via this channel were ceramics and textiles, followed by the Sipán artefacts, all of them listed as 'personal effects'. It is quite possible that Kelly did not even know that the pittance that he was being paid was for smuggling part of the greatest archaeological find of the late twentieth century.

After the operation was exposed Kelly turned informer, feeling used by Swetnam and his wealthy collector-connoisseur backer Ben Johnson. Only Swetnam took the rap but even he managed to regain almost all of his collection, which had initially been seized by customs. He allegedly even paid his lawyer with a golden Sipán jaguar head.[3]

The middle section of the chain in antiquities smuggling is very much a white-collar affair. In Lima there is a hierarchy of fixers, collectors and smugglers, but at the top the dealers, people like Enrico Poli and Raúl Apesteguía, form an oligarchy. These are refined and respected members of society, despite having previous form in some instances (Apesteguía, for instance, was implicated in 1968 in a smuggling case after artefacts that were being smuggled out of Lima airport were seized).[4] Diplomatic involvement was also apparent in the Sipán trade – the advantage of immunity from search has often made embassy officials suspects in smuggling cases. Francisco Iglesias, Panamanian Consul-general in New York, was arrested for smuggling a magnificent gold piece from the Moche tomb.

Markets, Legalities

Peru's desert coastal hinterland is pockmarked with small tunnels made by *huaceros*. Initially tomb raiding was akin to a national sport, practised by enthusiastic moonlighters, but it has become more professional, even though pickings are increasingly scarce. Colombia has experienced similar individualist tomb raiding in the past, and it too has connected with a larger market. Not far from the Museo Nacional in Bogotá, which among other exhibits has artefacts from indigenous cultures past and present, there is a commercial showroom/exhibition space, Galeria Cano, that displays something similar. This business, which is now international, produces replicas of iconic gold statuettes housed in the city's famous Gold Museum, some of whose collection was donated by the Cano family itself. The family's involvement in antiquities began four generations back when Nemecio Cano raided a tomb in the department of Antioquia. There was never any question that this was a crime and Galeria Cano is proud of this family heritage. The Indiana Jones image of tomb raiding is rarely played down.

The antiquities shops that display much Khmer art in Bangkok's River City complex on the Chao Phraya river probably couldn't boast this tradition. And nor could the dealerships of Hollywood Road in Hong Kong that take in Chinese art, particularly Han and Tang figurines and ceramics. The worldwide trade is worth hundreds of millions if not billions of dollars a year. These are hard-nosed dealers servicing fashionable Western markets in places like Paris, New York and Chicago, some of whose customers care about neither the provenance of the desired sculptures nor the vandalism that might have occurred in their acquisition.

Most of the statues at the major Khmer site of Angkor Wat have been decapitated by looters, much of the damage done prior to the Khmer Rouge revolution. Sometimes the desecration that preceded smuggling was carried out by individual agents but in Malraux's day it was also systematically done by the occupying French authorities. This latter was hardly considered a crime, despite the fact that the authorities later made an example of the future French Culture Minister.

Huacero culture, although it might have directly fed certain 'respectable' outlets and collectors in South America and Asia, still seems quite far removed from the prestigious public and private collections of antiquities in North America and Europe. However, public museums, auction houses and collectors have always had some discreet connection with the smuggling business.

In North America even large museums have sometimes been embarrassed. Only in the last few decades, most significantly following the return to Turkey in 1993 of the so-called Lydian hoard from King

Croesus's reign looted in the 1960s, have claims for repatriation met with much success. For years entreaties were made to the Metropolitan Museum of Art in New York for the return of a rare Roman silver service looted in 1980 or thereabouts from Morgantina in Sicily. It was finally repatriated in 2010. Another contentious issue had been a Roman sculpture, the so-called 'Weary Heracles', the top half of which until 2011 resided in the Museum of Fine Arts in Boston while the lower half remained rooted to the floor of the Antalya Museum in Turkey. There are contested Mayan glyphs and stelae in many American museums including the Denver Art Museum, the Kimbell Art Museum in Fort Worth, the Art Institute of Chicago, the Cleveland Museum of Art, the Boston MFA . . . and so the list goes on.

The problem for curators of public collections is that their contacts, by the very nature of the dealing business, must be familiar with both the licit and illicit sides of their trade. Perhaps some of these providers spend a little too much time on the shady side, even as they present a respectable face to the art and antiquities world. One such was the New York antiquities dealer Michael Ward who, on being compromised, was forced to cede a hoard of almost certainly smuggled Mycenaean gold artefacts to a Friends of Greece society that could then repatriate them. Nevertheless he still managed to save $125,000 as the return constituted a tax deduction.[5] The scandal was that he was a member of the Cultural Property Advisory Committee that was tasked with advising the government on malpractice in the antiquities business.

In some places there is a certain kind of immunity from prosecution, while in others, where it is sought, the consequences can be dire. For instance, dealing in smuggled antiquities is tolerated in Hong Kong while in China looters are known to have been executed. Where you are, spatially and hierarchically, along the chain of looting-gathering-dealing-shipping-collecting-exhibiting of ancient artefacts affects the perception of your crime. After the Second World War attitudes would change, broadly speaking, and looting on a grand scale was thereon considered to be an act of aggression, but this did not slow the smuggling trade and had little relevance for *huacero* culture, which is sometimes considered simply a more exciting cousin of metal detecting. Until recently it was regarded as just another way of making some much-needed extra money and unearthing artefacts that 'belong to the people'. (This is the same logic used by the big collectors, incidentally, although for them 'the people' translates as 'humanity'.)

There have been a number of laws passed on an international level designed to slow the smuggling trade. The UNESCO Convention on the Means of Prohibiting the Illicit Import, Export and Transfer of Ownership of Cultural Property of 1970 was aimed at the markets of the signatory countries. It led to a series of bilateral treaties between the U.S. and other countries, including Canada, but European countries were less committed and France was the first to ratify it in 1997. This inertia on the part of some of the signatories, and its partial nature, compounded another more fundamental weakness in the legislation. The problem was that anything transported out of its original context before 1970, or on the international market before then, was exempt. There also had to be secondary national legislation for it to be enforced within any individual country. Despite reticence to legislate in the U.S., some regulatory authorities were set up, for instance the American (later National) Association of Dealers in Ancient, Oriental and Primitive Art. But this was just a lobby group cooked up to protect market freedoms if Congress ever became too litigious. It certainly had no ethical stance, and at least one of its number, its president, Frederick Schultz, was convicted in 2002 for his part in smuggling and selling Egyptian artefacts.

The sphere of (il)legality of transplanting artefacts – which sometimes, as in the case of the Parthenon frieze and pediment in the British Museum or the Pergamon altar in Berlin, were quite literally rebuilt somewhere else – remains confusing and contentious. Legislation is generally considered inadequate in terms of rights and repatriation. In addition, approaching smuggling cultures dealing in antiquities exclusively from the point of view of criminality generally points to a pure profit motive and this is to overlook what else is at stake for society.

Paranoia and Prestige: Real and Symbolic Effects of Smuggled Art

Why do we put so much store by our manifestations of others' culture? How do art and artefacts in some ways constitute our identity, society and culture, even if they were made neither by us nor anywhere nearby?

Smuggling is rarely neutral: whether it is caught up in discourses of romanticism or criminality, it tends to induce a certain excitement. Contraband art is no more immune from this mythification than, say, trafficked guns or opium. Indeed, it is worthwhile comparing art with opium in terms of their projected aura.

In Sax Rohmer's novel *Dope* (1919) opium is the poison that ensnares a good lady of England. By the end of the story a wily London detective has triumphed over the sly Oriental, who is stereotyped as alien and menacing. Nevertheless paranoia persists in this, even for the period, quite racist discourse of the 'yellow peril'. It is not just about psychological terror. The effect is also to project self-image. It attempts to define British character as upright and decent through pointing at what it is not – secretive, poisonous and dissipated. But there is also fascination. As Rohmer put it: 'Those who control "the traffic" control El Dorado – a city of gold which, unlike the fabled Manoa, actually exists and yields its riches to the unscrupulous adventurer.'[6] This fascination runs against the grain of paranoia. Like Rohmer's mysterious masters of 'the traffic', those who control circulations of cultural artefacts also wield a certain power. Objects of high culture bring us material riches but also, beyond this, great symbolic capital, and so there is much incentive to keep the artefacts arriving by whatever means.

The argument that contraband has materially transformed society is one of the main threads of this book. Some contraband items have also acquired a kind of sacred aura: spices, tobacco and tea have not only created wealth running through the veins of society but have conferred status and prestige and stirred the imagination. Wandering around institutions like the British Museum, we admire the treasures before our eyes, but then wonder about the stories behind them all: where they all came from, how they came to be here, and perhaps a further question – aren't we lucky to have them? This applies just as much to contraband objects in circulation. Practically speaking, the leakage of silver out of the Spanish imperial treasury created the first world economic system, affecting everybody. However, at the same time, imagining 'pieces of eight' in the hands of Drake or Hawkins evokes other, rather more romantic worlds.

Prestige feeds off the myth but there are other paths towards self-esteem through the acquisition of contraband. One way to use smuggled goods is to define or develop a new society, away from an older world. This could be what Buenos Aires saw itself as doing during its silver-plated contraband years – the city might well have been corrupt but its social fabric developed with smuggling and its institutions relied upon it when the motherland Spain seemed to have turned her back. Contraband has also started new fashions and engendered new possibilities across society, not least for the expression of self and societal identity.

We have seen how a contraband style could appear in eighteenth-century Bourbon Peru: it was Orientalist and Francophile. Chinese silks, satins and ribbons arrived in Lima from the Philippines, alongside Carcassonne fashions. Most of it was acquired illicitly but was worn with aplomb. The city became dandyish, decadent and exhibitionist: a refined performance of luxury beyond necessity, so different from the desperate smuggler towns of the Banda del Norte of Hispaniola and the 'wild coast' of the Guianas during the late sixteenth and early seventeenth centuries. There they had suffered shortages of official goods that were only redressed, not supplemented, by contraband imports.

This all seems quite harmless, and in many instances even quite necessary. But smuggling in the field of fashion has not always been about innocent superfluousness on the one hand or sheer necessity on the other. Often it has been much more pernicious. Jade leaking out of war-ravaged China in the nineteenth century, and more recently ivory and diamonds from Africa, as well as antelope fleeces from Tibet, were and are luxury contraband that prove that the business of cultural enhancement can be stained in blood. But of course that is no hindrance to their being refashioned as the must-have commodities of the desiring developed countries, now of course including China itself. Often this is simply about conspicuous consumption but, even where this exhibitionism is not possible, the desire simply to possess and hold close to the chest has sometimes been motivation enough for the collector of illegally imported cultural objects.

This was probably the case for Pablo Escobar, the Colombian cocaine smuggling kingpin. He was a complex individual. In some ways he might have desired to be another person – a latter-day Sun King perhaps – but even he could only fashion this to a certain degree through flaunting his wealth, and so his very private collections developed. He famously smuggled elephants and rhinoceroses into Colombia for his zoo at his ranch, Hacienda Nápoles.[7] He bought Picasso and Dalí paintings as well as those of Colombia's foremost painter, Fernando Botero.[8] His associate in the Medellín Cartel, Fidel Castaño, brother of the paramilitary leader and occasional *narcotraficante* Carlos Castaño, was also a cultured collector, perhaps even more so than Escobar, who sometimes bought art to launder drug money.

Showing smuggled art and archaeological artefacts, even if they are laundered through more and more respectable dealers, is becoming increasingly difficult. But this has hardly deterred some curators: Sipán objects lent by buyers would show up in places like the Santa Barbara Museum of Art just weeks after the smugglers handed over the goods. The contradiction is that these objects might be hot in a legal sense but they are also dazzlingly attractive for bringing in crowds to museums. There is a compulsion to have the objects on display in their new domain, and their reinstallation creates a kind of propriety that goes beyond the mere physical holding of the contraband object and its economic value.

Controversially acquired antiquities, beside the sense of loss at their place of origin, usually have an effect in their new context. There will always be a response to these objects, particularly when they are conspicuously exhibited, as the Elgin marbles are. They may confer identity; the classical Greek and Roman sculptures and architectural fragments in British, French, German and North American permanent collections add prestige to national museums that are often built in a neo-classical style. They project a notion of civilized society. As such, each smuggled artefact is more than just a treasure; beyond even its romantic, almost animist qualities (every object 'tells' or contains a story), it is cultural capital.

Generally today overt ideological demonstrations of cultural superiority are neither accepted per se, nor so easily carried off. It is not so long ago, though, that precisely this chain of looting, smuggling and exhibition of art and artefacts was, in some quarters, a matter of public policy.

Soviet Trophy Brigades

For the advancing Soviet armies in Germany and Eastern Europe loot was fair game, as it had always been in war. The difference now was that it was organized by the men at the top, whose tastes were rather more refined.

The Soviet Trophy Brigades were set up towards the end of the Second World War with the express purpose of carrying off much of Germany's cultural wealth. They were at the vanguard of operations detailed to seal off museums and private collections so that art and artefacts could be catalogued, crated up and then shipped off to Moscow and Leningrad. Most of them were hoarded away in these two cities, although some of the less important treasures were sent to distant provinces, places like Turkmenistan and Tajikistan.

The brigades were made up of art historians, museum curators and academics, who were looking for anything that might be termed 'cultural artefacts' – paintings and sculptures, of course, and architecture that might be dismantled, but also coins, medals, medieval maps, textiles, furniture, ceramics and ancient manuscripts – literally millions of objects. Konstantin Akinsha and Grigorii Kozlov, in their book *Stolen Treasure* (1995), call it a 'trophy crusade'. In other respects its execution was more like an inquisition: once it was up and running and many of the treasures were back in Moscow, the correctness of the transportation and the probity of the archiving process were scrutinized in minute detail and at every turn by the Stalinist anti-corruption police. These included General Ivan Serov, later head of the KGB under Khrushchev, and Stalin's personal secretary Alexander Poskrebishev.

In contrast to Hitler's alleged use of Baedeker guidebooks to plan destructive bombing raids on English cities that had clusters of 'three-star' cultural attractions, such as Bath and Exeter, the Trophy Brigades used the guidebooks to 'save' art. The guides also served as propaganda tools: Breslau (now Wrocław, Poland) was described in one such publication as an old Slavic city, not a German one, as Goebbels's ministry proclaimed. It had only been annexed by the Germans during the Middle Ages and so its culture, in this narrative, was essentially Soviet.

The Ministry of Culture struggled to defend this systematic looting using the justification of 'repatriation'. Yet they even used this terminology when they were talking about recovering art after centuries of exile. For instance, anything associated with Slavs, Central Asia or the Caucasus was simply regarded as coming home. There was also an argument that acquiring artworks was redress for earlier German looting: Russian cultural sites had been pillaged by the Nazis, including the Empress Catherine's palace in St Petersburg, the fabulous Amber room (actually built in Prussia) and the Peterhof Palace in the same city, as well as museums in Moscow. However it is much more difficult to make a case, except as unofficial war reparations, for the looting from German museums of African, South American, Indian and East Asian art objects, or the many Renaissance works, like Raphael's *Sistine Madonna*, that found their way into Soviet vaults. Behind the justifications, this was largely just another exercise in building prestige through appropriation but on a massive scale. It was a projection of cultural power and an accumulation of cultural capital; in a Cold War context it would be seen as an attempt to match the Louvre, the British Museum and the Metropolitan Museum of Art.

One might argue that this was more about overt looting than trafficking, but from the beginning there were also suspicions of covert smuggling by individuals going on within this great looting operation. It is tempting to appraise this as simply the small man resisting a larger entity (the state), perhaps a little bit like the relation between the *huacero* at Sipán and the archaeology museum at nearby Lambayeque that formally took possession of the finds, leaving the locals out in the cold. More cynically, one might frame it as private greed versus public prestige. But in the case of the Soviet Trophy Brigades it is perhaps more complicated than this. For one thing they played out this individual/collective smuggling drama within the same context, and for another there was a diverse interest in multifarious contraband. Not everybody was after an overlooked Renaissance painting, although some people obviously were: when six 'legitimate' boxes of loot reached the Pushkin Museum of Fine Arts in Moscow there were found among them 350 unlisted gold objects and Manet's portrait of Rosita Mauri. Were these art and artefacts that were being smuggled beneath the radar of the state? What was their intended destination?

Even if the Trophy Brigade actions were not strictly speaking smuggling – they were perhaps too officially sanctioned, although secretive, to be precisely described as such – there was plenty of contraband circulating around its consignments, and its cultural significance was often quite unexpected. There was another kind of contraband, or cultural capital, that the state considered dangerous for the general public: the possibility of picking up knowledge of Western consumerist luxuries.

It came first in the form of the radio. During one operation hundreds of radios were found in the cellar of a hotel in Gleiwitz (now Gliwice) in Silesia. Many were accused of selling them on the black market when Trophy Brigades took these luxury items back to Russia. Radios and other goods were often hidden in the crates containing works of art. In addition Western goods were to be found in the railway wagons bringing looted art from Germany. For instance, as well as Telefunken radios, a scooter accompanied the Pergamon Altar and Raphael's *Sistine Madonna* from Dresden. Other less refined loot on these trains included bicycles, coats and musical instruments. Almost all the Trophy Brigades were accused of smuggling. Pilots carried all sorts of things in their bomb bays. There is an account of one young pilot who, on replacing the regular one who was drunk, and not knowing about the cargo, opened the bomb bay doors for a test, raining porcelains, furs, cameras, typewriters and paintings onto a hitherto culturally unremarkable German town.⁹

It wasn't simply a case of impoverished individuals following the example of the state: some in the upper echelons of the hierarchy seem to have succumbed to the opportunity to secrete a little, or a lot, on the side. The home of Marshall Zhukov, the great hero of the Soviet victory, was found to be adorned with stolen treasures – some 2,000 objects were subsequently confiscated. But it was the man on the ground, or in one case in the air, who was generally most tempted. In July 1945 a plane sent from Berlin by Major Kulakovsky of the Trophy Brigade attached to the Fifth Shock Army was found to be carrying, alongside a hoard of gold and other treasures, crates full of textiles, shoes and raincoats.¹⁰

The gold in the aircraft was Schliemann's hoard. In 1945 the Troy gold had been removed by the Russians from the massively fortified anti-aircraft tower (*Flakturm*) beside the Tiergarten Zoo and loaded onto a Soviet plane for this latest stage in its contraband travels. For years the Russians denied ever having taken it and this, even if most of the other loot may not, might quite accurately be described as smuggled culture.

THE AESTHETE-ARISTOCRAT, the amateur archaeologist, the writer, the *huacero*, the white-collar mule, the diplomat, the cultured Soviet – they were all links in chains that have ended up with the collector and the curator and, ultimately, new homes for cultural capital. Much of this would have been unlikely, if not impossible, without smuggling, often with state backing. The Soviet Trophy Brigades brought looting to another level at the end of the Second World War. The Nazis had no choice but to abandon their cultural bunkers and as their treasures were carted off eastwards they began to think of saving themselves: they went west, and for them too the only option was smuggling.

FOURTEEN

BONZENFLUCHT

The Third Reich Smuggles Itself to Argentina

onzenflucht, roughly translated as the flight of the bosses or bigwigs, refers to what happened as the Third Reich began to unravel in 1945. Many Nazis headed south over the Pyrenees to fascist Spain. These mountains are unusual in that they form a seamless natural barrier along an entire border between two countries, France and Spain. Until the latter part of the twentieth century the main valleys such as the Roncesvalle, the choice of leaden-footed invaders over the millennia, were easily guarded but those adjacent were the run of mountain goats, wolves, bears and smugglers.

One of the favourite crossings for Basque smugglers had always been the Ispegui pass, with its narrow and precipitous mountain paths etched out of gloomy grey granite. Not far away, near the mountain village of Sare, beside St-Jean-de-Luz on the coast, was another crossing, the preferred one for smuggling downed Allied aircrews. This route followed the lower Nivelle valley, brazenly passing the Gestapo headquarters at St-Pée-sur-Nivelle. Beyond Sare the Pyrenean forests offered cover all the way up to the pass, which was known to be guarded only by sleepy Austrian soldiers. Before we come to the so-called Nazi 'ratline' and its international ramifications, let's consider this aircrew lifeline.

Operation Comet

Basques were integral to the actions of 'Operation Comet', also known as *La Ligne*, set up in 1941. It was an escape line in a very literal sense, in that the airmen were often brought into Brussels, from where they travelled by train all the way down the coastal line to St-Jean. They were escorted by women who would pretend not to know them but step in to help should the need arise. On arrival at St-Jean station, the last step often entailed slipping into the men's toilets on one of the outer platforms, which had another door out onto the street.

But this of course was not the final scene in this drama, because they still had to cross the border. This they would brave under the guidance of seasoned Basque smugglers such as Florentino Goikoetxea, perhaps the most celebrated of all the people-smugglers in the Pyrenees. He was personally responsible for taking 227 aircrew across the border. Typically they would set off from the Hotel Eskualduna or from the nearby Ocean Hotel, both in the historic, quiet and intensely proud fishing town of St-Jean. In almost complete darkness they would traverse a small mountain called Xoldocagagna, a last gasp of the Pyrenees range before it peters out into the Atlantic Ocean. Usually there would be a break at a farm in the hills where they would rest and prepare for the final stages of the journey in daylight. Towards the end, on the tram between the small town of Rentería and San Sebastián, they would nervously pose as Basques. From here they might more easily make their way to Bilbao where the British consulate could legitimately arrange passage for them back to England via Gibraltar or Lisbon.

La Ligne's masterminds were Andrée de Jongh, a Belgian, and Arnold Deppé, who before the war had lived in St-Jean, where he had smuggler connections. What they did was to tap into existing channels of smuggling and simply switch the contraband from consumer goods to downed airmen. This wasn't a compact cell of small operatives; instead it involved some 1,700 agents who managed to relay 700 or so Allied flyers into Spain. In fact the Basques were so prolific that they even sometimes aided German army deserters over the border.

The F Route

At the eastern end of the Pyrenees people-smuggling was equally active. Here the contraband items included persecuted intelligentsia. The route was set up by the American Varian Fry, and was known as the 'F route' after Hans and Lisa Fittko, its main operatives on the ground. Fry, a New York writer and journalist who had spent time in Nazi Germany and Vichy France, was fluent in both German and French and was recruited by the American 'Emergency Rescue Committee' to help artists, writers, former politicians and union leaders get to the Mediterranean border beside Portbou, and there to place them in the hands of the smugglers. It didn't always go smoothly. Lisa's first covert crossing had been with the writer and intellectual Walter Benjamin. As is well documented, it ended in tragedy. Benjamin was detained and committed suicide at the border with an overdose of morphine. Many took the same option before or on the border, as most carried it in sufficient quantities. Despite this failure, the Fittkos were recruited by Fry to run the 'F route' that followed a famous smugglers' crossing, the Lister Route, named after a Spanish Civil War Republican general who, like Hannibal, led his troops across this border in momentous circumstances. The escape line was successful, and Fry kept up the momentum for thirteen months before he was deported.

Bonzenflucht: Nazi Flight

Back at the Atlantic end of the Pyrenees, people-smuggling continued apace until the end of the war. One of the last actions of de Jongh and Deppé's Operation Comet was to smuggle out a captured list of Gestapo personnel who themselves were preparing to run for Spain at the end of the war.

Some groundwork had already been done. In Madrid the Horcher restaurant was a meeting place for many who had recently fled Axis territory and were looking for onward clandestine passage. It was set up by the Berlin restaurateur Otto Horcher in 1943 and decorated with furnishings and silverware from Germany. Göring and Himmler were part of the Berlin branch of the business. A determined middle-aged spinster and expatriate Nazi, Clarita Stauffer, ran another escape line from her Falangist office in the Spanish capital.

The Atlantic Pyrenean borderlands were not entirely the fiefdom of the Basques. ss Captain Walter Kutschmann, sometime lover of Coco Chanel, was stationed in Hendaye on the border and organized deportations to Spain. He briefly became *persona non grata* to all combatant sides when on the liberation of France he failed to report for duty on the Eastern Front, heading instead for Spain, and thus anticipating the later more organized escape routes. His operations were very cloak and dagger and certainly opportunistic. Accused by his erstwhile employers of stealing money from the customs office at Hendaye, Kutschmann continued to hang around the borderlands after he fell out with the Nazis, possibly now more in the guise of a smuggler than a policeman. Later he found refuge with Carmelite monks in Madrid, taking on the identity of one monk for his escape to Argentina in 1948.

Another Axis

The fascist ratline to South America was amazing, intriguing and geographically widespread: it constitutes the main thread of this chapter.

The game was all but up for the Third Reich following the Battle of the Bulge in December 1944 in the Belgian Ardennes. Now the call to action was *Ausweichmassnahmen*, Nazi slang for alternative methods of withdrawal – actually meaning the moment to run for it. But where to run to? Into hiding for most, or at least into the confusion of migrations and internments that ensued from the Soviet and Allied agreements at Yalta.

Frederick Forsyth's novel *The Odessa File* (1972) dramatizes an escape line to South America for scheming Nazis that resides in public imagination somewhere between conspiracy theory and 'factional' thriller. The name Odessa has become synonymous with Nazi flight, although there was probably no such organization, and this Black Sea port beside the river Dneister was never the departure point, despite its pre-war and more recent reputation for smuggling. However, Madrid, Berne, Stockholm, Genoa and Rome are central to this lurid tale.

The Argentinian journalist Uki Goñi has written the definitive account of this ambitious people-smuggling operation in his book *The Real Odessa* (2002). He outlines not just the desperation of the fugitives but their sustained hopes. The flight of so many fascists to the one country, Argentina, meant that a loose affiliation of war criminals cohered and, however much in vain, it sustained an illusion that there would be a third Germany-led world war, with the added imperative this time of wiping out communism as well as finishing off the Jewish race. One of the early foot soldiers of the *Bonzenflucht* was Friedrich Rauch, the ss officer who had organized shipments of Nazi gold bullion from Berlin to Bavaria as the Russians and Allies closed in on the capital. This 'evacuated' treasure was intended to finance the Nazi resistance, precipitate another war and establish a Fourth Reich. He himself later fled to Argentina.

Croatian fascists are also central to the story and they too had made some preparations for covert retreat, even before the start of the war. Ante Pavelic was the supreme leader, the *Poglavnik*, and also head of the openly murderous Ustashi, the group in charge of the final solution in Croatia. Remarkably this group was so extreme that even the Nazis urged that it be diluted, and this led to its first contact with Colonel

Perón in Argentina, and early feelers for a potential Ustashi escape route. In 1943, 60 Argentinian passports were purchased and funds were transferred to Argentina. Perón was quite generous with the provision of Argentinian passports to his allies in the Axis countries at this time because he was relying upon Nazi intelligence in South America to choose the ideal moment to precipitate a coup in neighbouring Bolivia. One of Pavelic's lieutenants, the priest Krunoslav Draganovic, was subsequently sent to the Vatican to sound out potential help for smuggling Catholic fascists into the arms of Perón's new Catholic nationalism.

Much of the backing for the 'real Odessa' remains obscure but a sizeable proportion of the loot from the 22 April 1945 raid by SS men on the Berlin Reichsbank HQ, in which gems, securities and currency were stolen, is supposed to have remained with legendary SS commando leader Colonel Otto Skorzeny (he of the raid to rescue Mussolini from mountain captivity in the Abruzzi region in 1943).[1] In 1950 he was living comfortably in Madrid but it was also assumed that he had put much of his share of the loot towards setting up an escape line to South America and the Middle East, organized by his sinister network known as *Die Spinne* (the spider).[2] Four hundred million dollars of bonds later disappeared from the same central bank and they too were smuggled abroad. In 1969, for instance, £27 million of them appeared in New York; ironically, given their fascist origins, probably smuggled there from East Germany to finance covert Soviet operations in the U.S.[3] In 1998 some surfaced in Central America. Others were submitted over the years for redemption around Europe.

Why was Argentina so obliging? The Catholic connection with Croatia makes some sense but the Nazis were atheistic. One answer is German knowhow, in particular jet technicians, which were attractive to Perón, who had ambitions to build a powerful aerospace industry and establish civil-military air dominance in South America. There was a more sinister racial dimension to the affinity with Germany in the eugenic views of Argentinian Immigration Commissioner Santiago Peralta, an anthropologist with anti-Semitic views. His ideas for a racially modelled immigration policy led some way to the setting up of the state-sponsored operation.

However, these honeymoon plans for a potential Germany–Argentina alliance did not simply hinge on this twisted racial hatred: cultural diplomacy between fascist leaning countries and proto-fascist Argentina had something of a history. A measure of the sympathies between Argentina and those parts of Europe that were in thrall to Nazism can be seen through the initiatives of the Belgian fascist Pierre Daye. He first visited Buenos Aires in 1925 and was accorded significant respect for his exploits as soldier, journalist, diplomat, traveller, intellectual, novelist and travel writer. His urbane personality charmed the Europhile sections of Argentinian society. His influence stemmed from meetings with Hitler, Hess, Ribbentrop, Pope Pius XII, Shah Reza Pahlevi of Iran, General Franco and Leopold III of Belgium. In Belgium he had an on–off relationship with the pro–Nazi Rexist party and by 1943 had been appointed Belgian sports minister. Early that year he visited the Vatican because, as a fervent Catholic himself, he was keen to ascertain that the Church's sympathies were with the Nazis and not the communists. As German defeat became more and more certain, he held private conversations with Perón to organize escape routes.

So what got the fascist flight moving after the war? We might begin on the Argentinean side, for, as indicated above, ties had already been made. For instance, Enrique Moss, a career Argentinian diplomat, was married into a family of Swiss bankers, important for a Switzerland-based escape route. During the war he had been attached to the Berlin embassy and had organized part of Evita's tour around Europe in 1947. He now worked on an escape route alongside Herbert Helfrich, a high-ranking Nazi architect and director of public works who escaped through London but then flew back to Switzerland to help with the trafficking of other Nazis to Argentina. Both attracted large sums of money from Argentina to facilitate the escape routes.

Another cog in the machine was Rodolfo Freude, the son of a German-Argentinian industrialist and conduit of German money to Perón, who became head of Perón's Information Bureau and the newly established Central State Intelligence (CIDE). The apparatus was in place for *Ausweichmassnahmen* and was logistically organized by the Delegation for Argentine Immigration in Europe (DAIE), which in addition to its headquarters in Buenos Aires had offices in Rome and Genoa.

Operations sometimes had the bizarre look of a package holiday. Many of the fleeing or enticed technicians and Nazis who fled Denmark and Sweden were booked up by Vianord, a travel agency in Buenos Aires set up, it seems, to deal only with a certain type of 'tourist'. It continued this specialist travel service into the 1950s, long after the hopes of fugitives had shifted focus from Scandinavia to Switzerland, Spain and Italy. The Dutch airline KLM was the preferred carrier for Nazis fleeing to Argentina from Switzerland. It welcomed the business and refused to hand over passenger lists to the Americans who were investigating this comfortable method of escape for wanted war criminals. Others left from Genoa by ocean liner. A select few went to Rome to fly on Perón's new airline FAMA. One such was Hans-Gerd Eyting, a skilled aviation technician who along with other colleagues was airlifted out of Rome on a plane owned by the airline. Emile Dewoitine, a collaborating jet aircraft designer, was the first documented war criminal to make it to Argentina. He travelled first class on the ship *Cabo Buena Esperanza* (The Cape of Good Hope), an auspicious vessel for the early travels of these dark pilgrim fathers.

A Dark Diffusion: the Nordic Route

The clandestine transfer of Nazis to Argentina through Scandinavia bears comparison with the earlier leakage of technologies across the Atlantic as described in Chapter Twelve: both were all about gaining advantage through acquired knowhow.

General Perón wanted to make Argentina the dominant power of South America, and for this he needed a modern air force. Connections with fascism in Europe were based on conservatism, anti-Semitism, militarism and the existence even before the war of outposts of German industry in the River Plate region. The ratline, then, was intended not only to save and hide war criminals but to be a catalyst for Argentina's modernization.

A Nordic escape route was initiated in 1947 by Perón's Information Bureau, which specifically aimed at recruiting aircraft designers and engineers. In some ways it parallels the American Alsos mission to smuggle out scientists from the V2 projects and set them to work on the American nuclear programme at the beginning of the Cold War arms race. Sympathetic Argentinian consuls, like the Germanophile Carlos Piñero in Copenhagen, were installed in Scandinavia primarily to oil the workings of this escape route.

One specific channel was initiated by German businessman Friedrich Schlottmann, owner of a large textile firm in Argentina. It was run by 24-year-old German Argentinian Carlos Schulz and was known as Service Group Denmark (Dienstgruppe Dänemark). Schulz posed as the representative of an evangelical church from the city of La Plata as he arranged transfers from Oslo and Stockholm to South America. He brought with him to Denmark 1,000 landing permits, authenticated as stamps in Red Cross passports.

However the fugitives first had to reach Scandinavia. To this end the SS officer Günther Toepke, who now worked for Danish intelligence, smuggled Nazis from Germany into Denmark and then on to Sweden. A Prussian priest, Georg Grimme, also took Nazis covertly to Denmark, helped financially by Ludwig Freude, a German Argentinian manufacturer and the father of Rodolfo Freude, one of the main architects of Nazi flight from Europe. The smuggling operation from then on was often quite straightforward, relying more on false documentation than circumventing border control; the fugitives sometimes simply boarded commercial flights from Stockholm to Buenos Aires via Geneva. Two of the last to take the Danish route were Ronald Richter, an atomic physicist, and Kurt Tank, director of the Bremen Focke-Wulf factory, who on arrival in Argentina became the director of the jet fighter project.

The Nordic route operated with impunity for a while: arguments were made at the time that these technicians were better off in Argentina than falling into the hands of the Soviets – not an entirely misplaced anxiety. There had been an instance of a shipload of Germans boarding a boat for Argentina only to find themselves arriving in a Soviet port. But it all fell to earth with a crash. Schulz and Piñero were arrested in Stockholm in November 1947 and deported. Toepke was also expelled from Denmark along with Argentinian diplomats. The strategy had some success – a modern air force was developed – but Argentina never came to dominate South America as the United States did North America.

There was, however, a colourful coda to the story. Ludwig Lienhardt, a former German SS officer, arranged for a group of Nazis to sail from Stockholm for Buenos Aires on the *Falken*, an old sail training ship, on 30 December 1947. En route it avoided (after a storm in the Baltic) two Soviet torpedo boats, and seven months later it arrived at the Argentinian capital. Carlos Schulz had been on board but disembarked in London and flew straight on to Madrid to help with the escape route there. The *Falken* was later turned into a floating headquarters for Nazi expatriates and fugitives.

The Swiss Connection

Switzerland's involvement in smuggling fascists ran deeper. The main man behind the Swiss operation was Carlos Fuldner, a German Argentinian former SS captain and agent for Himmler. In 1947 he had escaped to Argentina where he joined Freude's Information Bureau. As with the Nordic operation he was particularly interested in aerospace technicians, although by the end of his covert dealings he had also arranged passage for arch war criminals Adolf Eichmann, Josef Mengele, Erich Priebke, Josef Schwammberger and Gerhard Bohne. But first he had to find an operating base in Europe from which to direct the smuggling operation. Powerful elements in Switzerland proved sympathetic to the cause and he was able to set up headquarters at the Argentinian Emigration Centre at 49 Marktgasse in Berne. Besides Fuldner, the ring was made up of the recently arrived Gualterio Ahrens, an Argentinian colonel of German descent; Perón's Polish agent Czeslaw Smolinksi, who was in the Argentinian president's intelligence circle; and Enrique Moss, who looked after most of the cover documentation for the fugitives.

The anti-Semitic Swiss chief of police, Heinrich Rothmund, collaborated with the Marktgasse organization as he was eager to ship the Nazis along with some of his own Jewish 'problem' to Buenos Aires, while Swiss president Eduard von Steiger turned a blind eye. Steiger, serving as justice minister during the war, had ensured that no Jewish refugees could escape from the nightmare in Germany by entering Switzerland. As the Swiss delegate to the International Refugee Organization (IRO), Rothmund's role was to resettle and support victims of Nazism after the war but he also facilitated the passage of wanted Nazi criminals into his country. Several Swiss made substantial amounts of money through granting temporary residence documents to Germans whose backgrounds went uninvestigated. Sums handed over for just one of these documents reached 200,000 francs. Among the 'refugees' were members of the Schlottmann family whose Argentina-based wealth had funded the Swedish smuggling route. Josef Mengele is said to have made immediate contact with a Schlottmann businessman upon his arrival in Buenos Aires in 1949.

Still, entering Switzerland was often a perilous business, and so the strategic operation drew upon the expertise of specialists in cross-border covert operations. One such operative was Herbert Helfrich, who brought Nazis across the border using Cologne and Aach bei Singen, a halfway house for guided missile technicians, as stopover points within the former Third Reich. The Red Cross was also involved, transporting Germans clandestinely in ambulances across frontiers. These crossings did not always go to plan. Samuel Pomeranz, a Swiss employee of the Marktgasse office and seasoned people smuggler, was arrested at Lake Constance trying to bring in an undocumented German 'technician', Erich Bachem.

It threatened to cause a scandal that would embarrass Rothmund, lead to the closure of the Marktgasse office in 1949 and ruin Pomeranz's smuggling business. In the event Rothmund simply covered up the lack of documentation and reprimanded Pomeranz.

The contradiction in the Swiss emigration policy – aiding passage of both hated Jews and respected Nazis – led to the Argentinians also being forced to play this double game. They particularly wanted technicians but realized that others might come as well, both Jews and war criminals. A cruel twist to this misuse of the IRO's mandate came in the form of its funding: Nazi gold secreted by the SS out of concentration camps which had fallen into the hands of the Allies.

As with the Nordic route, once documentation had been obtained, onward passage was more or less above-board, often taking the form of legitimate overland travel to Genoa and then sea passage to Buenos Aires. Some travelled under their own names; others used aliases on their passports. The Swiss route via Genoa operated until 1950 by which time Fuldner's operation had smuggled some 300 Nazis to Argentina.

The Croatian/Vatican Ratline

If Sweden and Switzerland's involvement in Nazi smuggling is surprising, more shocking still is the complicity of the Vatican. This route came to be known as the *Römischerweg* or 'Roman Way'. Argentina, staunchly Catholic, had strong links with Vatican City, and not long after the war the escape route began to take the shape of a Vatican-Argentinian-Croatian triangle that was still amenable to the plans for flight of the atheistic Nazis.

This holy smuggling triangle was embodied in three priests with distinguished patrons: Perón, of course, but also Pope Pius XII, some of whose lieutenants worked closely with the Croatian efforts in smuggling their wanted men to South America. From Argentina came Cardinal Antonio Caggiano, the newly consecrated bishop of Rosario and leader of the Argentinian chapter of Catholic Action that was to mediate between the Vatican and Perón to set up an escape route. He supplied Argentinian papers, ready for use, to the second figure, Krunoslav Draganovic, a Croatian priest and Vatican representative, in his late forties. Draganovic was ostensibly a representative of the Croatian Red Cross but he was also a Ustasha colonel. His most important client was Ante Pavelic, leader of Croatia. Draganovic, who had been in Rome since 1943, was Pavelic's right-hand man when it came to escape channels as the Croatian regime began to fall apart in 1944. As the representative of a country whose recent national profile, ethnically cleansed, had a distinctive Catholic tinge, he had considerable access to the upper echelons of power in a Vatican regime that feared the submersion of Catholicism in Eastern Europe under a communist tide. He was also the bearer of valuables of dubious origin, including 40 kg of gold smuggled out of Croatia.[4] Draganovic was helped in this more traditional smuggling operation by Stjepan Hefer, one of the first arch Croatian criminals to make it to Argentina, and was sponsored by Croatian archbishop Aloysius Stepinac. The third figure in this geometry of infamy was an Austrian ex-Nazi bishop, Alois Hudal, now based in Rome. Hudal was a prolific organizer and was the figurehead for the brazen involvement of the Vatican in people smuggling. In August 1948 he petitioned Perón for 5,000 visas for Austrian and German ex-soldiers. He worked under the umbrella of the Pontifical Commission of Assistance (PCA), an aid organization whose caring services were all too easily co-opted by undeserving refugees and their agents in the business of trafficking war criminals, perhaps the most notorious of whom was Franz Stangl, Commandant of Treblinka. The pragmatic agents of Hudal's mission were the German Captain Reinhard Kops and his mentor, a charming Austrian-born Italian officer called Franz Ruffinengo, a fixer based in Genoa who often managed to replace last-minute cancellations on South America-bound ships with his own less respectable passengers. Ruffinengo himself made his escape in 1948. Soon after he arrived he put his skills to good use, setting up a travel agency in Buenos Aires. Hudal and Kops considered broadening the smuggling network to include Colombia as a destination for Nazi war criminals but the most common alternative countries for the desperate fugitives were Chile, Paraguay and Bolivia.

In response to a deteriorating situation, the haven of San Girolamo, a Croatian monastery at 132 Via Tomacelli in Rome, became the barely concealed hideout for the fleeing Ustasha war criminals, who with scant regard for the efficacy of international policing would shuttle at will to and from the nearby Vatican City. During this period the monastery was controlled less by pious monks than by gun-toting Ustasha youths. For a while the escape route ran through Spain before Draganovic shifted the focus towards smuggling his people out of Genoa on ships such as the *Andreas Gritti*, *Maria C* and the ocean liner *Tucumán*. Draganovic's younger brother Kresimir, formerly a diplomat in Berlin, benefited from the service, making it to Argentina on a Red Cross passport. Draganovic received help from the International Red Cross but aid also came from other worthy quarters: in circumstances that mimicked the informal Swiss patronage of Nazi people smuggling, the Vatican indirectly sponsored the ratline through the Pontifical Welfare Commission for Refugees.[5]

The smuggling route blossomed in late 1946 when Perón gave out 250 blank landing permits for the use of Croatians. After these had been filled in with fake names and returned to Argentina for rubber stamping, the now validated documents were enough to secure the issue of a passport supplied from Red Cross offices in Genoa or Rome.

Ante Pavelic hid in Rome for a couple of years before making his break for Argentina. He was protected by the Vatican because he stood for Catholicism, and was a figurehead for the so-called 'Krizari' freedom fighters who were battling against communism in the Balkans. It was inconvenient for both the Allies and the Church to bring him to justice and inevitable execution as one of the most heinous of war criminals. He remained unrepentant and for a while even harboured thoughts of a triumphant return to Zagreb. Vatican protection for him was direct and unequivocal. He stayed in various Vatican properties, including such institutional landmarks as the Castel Gandolfo just outside Rome, the Dominican monastery of St Sabina and the Vatican college on via Gioacchino Belli, and was able to use its diplomatic cars. He seems to have had almost complete immunity and travelled relatively freely about the city, meeting with whomever he liked, including Monsignor Montini, the future pope Paul VI.

In October 1948 Pavelic fled for Genoa armed with a Red Cross passport, made out under the name Pal Aranyos, and a first-class ticket on the *Sestriere* bound for Buenos Aires. His wife and two children had taken the same path in May of that year. As Pavelic at times appeared to maintain a standard of living in Buenos Aires far higher than those of his Ustasha legion, it is thought that he had been able to smuggle much of the Croatian treasure out of Europe, leading to much resentment among some of his formerly loyal henchmen, who saw none of it in their new world.

Many fugitives disguised as priests arrived in Buenos Aires, where they fell into the welcoming hands of real clergy. Franciscan brothers organized by Father Blas Stefanic, in Buenos Aires and in the town of José Ingenieros in particular, ran the Argentinian end of the operation.

Thousands were to benefit from this branch of the escape line known as Caritas Croata Argentina. Other Croatians were met by Branko Benzon, formerly Croatian ambassador to Berlin but now unofficial head of the growing Croatian expatriate community in Buenos Aires. He acted as agent for the supply of labour to some of Perón's prestige building projects such as the new airport.

The ring operated until 1951 and in later years became particularly murky. Josef Mengele had escaped in 1949, Adolf Eichmann in 1950. Mengele had followed the most common route taken by Nazis out of Germany – through Austria – arriving in Genoa after several tense border crossings. In 1951 Draganovic personally organized the flight to Bolivia of Klaus Barbie, the 'Butcher of Lyon', on yet another ship out of Genoa. Barbie had been handed over to Draganovic by the Americans, who had benefited from the former's anti-communist cooperation after the war and now wanted to 'lose' him in South America. The American Counter Intelligence Corps (CIC) wanted to brush under the carpet most of its more dubious informants, and so it subcontracted this problem to Draganovic, who smuggled them to South America. It participated in smuggling out certain Nazis who had cooperated in intelligence matters, sometimes into Austria in U.S. army vehicles. Here they were welcomed into Draganovic's operation. Some high-profile beneficiaries of this convenient alliance were particularly loathsome, for instance the eugenics enthusiast Gerhard Bohne and Dr Vjekoslav Vrancic, who had been in charge of the Croatian concentration camps. Others simply abetted this bizarre welfare to the stateless: one of the beneficiaries of the Pontifical Commission of Assistance was the Luftwaffe ace Hans Ulrich Rudel, who enthusiastically insinuated himself into the upper echelons of South American society as a friend of Perón, and later of the archetypal dictator Alberto Stroessner of Paraguay. It enabled him, in turn, to distribute his own largesse to other 'deserving' New Worlders such as Mengele.

Draganovic relied on patronage for the effectiveness of his operation but after Barbie's flight in 1952 the Americans expediently closed off the channel, and with the death of Pope Pius XII in 1958 the Vatican swept clean its tracks.

CONTRASTING THE HEROIC OPERATION COMET in Nazi-occupied France with the flight of fascists with Caritas Croatas takes a leap between Manichean extremes. But the risks and ingenuity involved are comparable.

There were failures on both sides. The tragic ending to Walter Benjamin's flight is perhaps redressed, to some degree, by the denouement of a shipload of Nazis also on the verge of escape. This is the story of a vessel, an ark, departing Genoa with every expectation of escape. From the decks 110 hearty young Nazis taunted with renditions of German war songs the pursuing carabinieri, who stood haplessly on the quay as the liner cast off. However, the ship broke down, re-docked and delivered its Teutonic cargo into the long-ish arm of Allied law.

For the most part, though, the project of semi-overt smuggling of Nazis to Argentina was extremely successful, and although its geopolitical importance did not extend to catalysing a Fourth Reich out of South America, it did preoccupy intelligence agencies around the world for years to come, albeit perhaps not always enough.

The passage to freedom of Allied aircrew and continental intellectuals, among others, was a more palatable story. There were to be new horizons for these lucky passengers but the territories they left behind after the war was over were a complete mess. Despair and poverty hung like smoke over the former Reich. But there was also opportunity for profit emerging in the black markets, another side to smuggling that was taking root across Germany.

FIFTEEN

BLACK MARKETS

Everything at a Good Price

As the Second World War drew to a chequered standstill – standoff is perhaps the more appropriate term – between Soviet East and Allied West, black markets appeared all over the now humbled Axis lands. Severe shortages of virtually every commodity, not least food and medicine, led to desperate demands from multitudes of destituted people. For many others, however, this offered a good chance for profiteering on their supply. The forests of the Ardennes had provided excellent cover for smugglers from the Great War all the way up until the outbreak of the Second World War, and this picked up with a vengeance again when hostilities ceased, particularly near the town of Hondschoote on the French side of the border with Belgium. The German frontier with Belgium was no less porous, and the 70-mile stretch south of Aachen was known as the 'Hole in the West'. More centrally, Berlin, in ruins, was a particularly black spot with one of its main 'irregular' sites known as Satan's Market.

By comparison, the picturesque Bavarian ski resort of Garmisch-Partenkirchen, never the scene of a battle, was relatively unscathed. At first appraisal, it seems a little perplexing that in this deceptively bright spot the black market seeped more pervasively into society than anywhere else in Germany. But in Garmisch, as elsewhere, a bleak future unfolded before all, affecting workers, bourgeoisie and aristocracy alike. A barter economy was the new reality here. It is even more surprising that the heart of the black market, the site of its scheming, wasn't a dark alley or a freezing warehouse (although no doubt there too) but rather a lively and welcoming Bavarian hostelry, the White Horse inn. Its attractive, young, flame-haired hostess Zenta Hausner provided traditional music and good food; it warmed the souls of a diverse clientele, from wretched, defeated souls to officers of the Allied occupation. Some of these, out of desperation or recognizing an opportunity, were or became smugglers and black marketeers.

Then again, perhaps this is an anomaly: we don't get this hedonistic sensation watching Carol Reed (director) and (screenwriter) Graham Greene's comparable scenario in the film *The Third Man* (1949). For all its cinematic stylishness,[1] this story of the smuggling of stolen, diluted penicillin for sale on the black market, by way of the sewers of Allied- and Soviet-occupied Vienna, is very bleak.

It could be that the reason for this juxtaposition of bon viveur beside exploitation in the black market derives from the diversity of its products. Inauthentic penicillin seems a long way from the authentic Old Master paintings that were falling off the back of the Soviet trophy train and finding their way one by one into curiously durable antique shops in among the ruins of occupied Berlin. But regarding devastated post-war Europe, we perhaps shouldn't be surprised that these very different contraband items circulated by similar means and channels.

The point is that the unravelling of the Third Reich, desperate though it mostly was, did not entirely play out under a dark sky. Indeed, 'black' is perhaps too simple a term for the kind of market that emerged here. More generally speaking the term 'black market' has become a little too synonymous with all informal dealing and supply across the board. While some of what was traded in Germany was most definitely proscribed – narcotics or loose radioactive industrial materials, for instance – most of the products were not actually illegal in themselves. Foodstuffs, clothing, liquor and cigarettes – when not stolen – appeared on what should more accurately be described as a 'grey' market (a grey market differs from a black one in that the goods are not imported illegally, although their sale is unauthorized). Similarly the term 'clandestine' – one among many for the kind of alternative economy that black and grey markets might be said to be a part of[2]– does not quite square with the image of complicity, conviviality and openness heard and seen through the doors of the White Horse. Another description of this alternative economy that seems more brazen than hidden is of a 'culture of spoils', which certainly seems to fit well with the activities of the Soviet Trophy Brigades and the unequal bartering of gems for foodstuffs in the immediate aftermath of the end of the war in Germany.[3]

The black-market phenomenon seems to be complex, multiform, confusing and sometimes contradictory. What, then, are the other variant colours of the informal economy between the darkness of the smuggler Harry Lime in *The Third Man*, its grey setting, Vienna, and the red of Zenta Hausner at the White Horse inn? The enduring bonhomie in and around this Bavarian inn raises the question of just how dark the black market always has to be. With this in mind I shall run through a number of examples of other informal markets and attempt to get to grips with what has, perhaps too often and too quickly, been called the black market when often it is something subtly different, and to consider its diversity in its global spread. If we can tease out its nuance it might also nudge us into paying more attention to the broader cultural, rather than simply economic, aspects of the black-market scene.

Beginning with the cosy interior of the inn at Garmisch-Partenkirchen, this chapter will explore the various emergences and entanglements of shadow trading in more recent times. It will address questions around how the informal economy affects our lives, saves us a dollar or two and, more generally, allows the planet to continue to tick over when formal economies fail us. And if we begin to sense that the formal might actually be touching (and sometimes overlapping) the informal, then we will be right back at the question that is at the heart of this book: what is the nature of the relationship between the state and smuggling?

Garmisch Business and the *Weisses Rössl*

Garmisch-Partenkirchen is the picturesque regional capital of the mountainous Bavarian region of Werdenfelser Land. It has always, after Munich, had a certain importance in the region. In 1936 the Winter Olympics were held here. From a smuggling point of view it has the great advantage of lying close to both the Swiss and Austrian borders, particularly the latter, and is a mountain pass or two away from Italy.

The meltdown of the Third Reich at the end of the Second World War had left a pool of nationalities here and the authorities set about a variety of responsive activities, many of them punitive and regulatory but just as many iniquitous and illicit. Rationing of food and consumer items was inevitable and, with a near-worthless currency unable to meet the extortionate prices, intense black and grey markets developed. These for the most part ran as barter economies, if in some part buoyed by American dollars. At its most desperate the family jewels were sold for medicines and bread. Coming from the occupying side, American cigarettes were the primary form of alternative currency, and there was also demand for the soldiers' sugar, coffee, bread and soap and the silk stockings that they could import. If the desperate Garmisch citizenry could obtain these staples in exchange for their gems, art, watches, Leica cameras and binoculars, they might also in turn trade some of them with their rural compatriots for bacon, poultry, flour, eggs and potatoes.

At the more obviously criminal end of the spectrum, the main movers were opportunist American soldiers and the mafia-style providers or pushers (*Scheiber*). As well as German nationals, these pushers included displaced individuals who sometimes formed gangs with their fellow countrymen. Such were the protagonists in one particular case of cross-border narcotics smuggling when an opportunity arose, as so many did, because valuable materials fell into the wrong hands, their keepers having fled. A large stash of cocaine had been abandoned by the German Army Medical Corps not far from Garmisch. It soon hit the black market and large amounts of it were smuggled via Mittenwald to Italy and via Konstanz to France by a number of Polish former POWs from Murnau. Drugs and luxury items frequently traversed the Alps to Italy and in return came textiles and wine, among other scarce commodities.

Certain American Counter Intelligence Corps (CIC) officers of Polish or German origin were also deeply involved. The CIC were sometimes just interested in the profit, but were also often implicated as part of their intelligence work: in another part of Germany, Memmingen, we find the quasi-CIC agent and war criminal Klaus Barbie being given cigarettes, sugar, medicines and petrol by his handlers so that he could support himself selling them on the black market.[4]

Scheiber were not particularly interested in nutritional fare, but rather in more lucrative contraband which tended to fall into three broad categories. First were luxury items released onto the informal market from their bourgeois entrapment: motor cars, diamonds, furs and paintings. Second were materials from the spluttering industrial machine: petrol, coal and chemicals, as well as nuclear materials such as radium, plutonium, uranium and heavy water. And finally there were the narcotics, from aspirins and insulin to opium (especially) and cocaine, as well as penicillin, which was sometimes referred to as 'white gold'. In addition, emanating from the side of corrupt authority, papers, particularly border passes, sloshed around the black market.

Sometimes the trade was inter-regional. A so-called 'potato train' ran between the towns and cities of the Ruhr and rural Saxony. Resilient

Hamburg bourgeoisie took the 'Calory Express' to trade as far afield as Bavaria, which still had a functioning agricultural economy. Dortmunders took the 'Vitamin Train' to Freiburg to pick cherries, while a less healthy but more profitable 'Nicotine Line' carried the tobacco harvests of Pfalz to grey markets almost everywhere across the country.[5]

An international trade emerged in loose dollars. The holding of foreign currency by Germans was banned during the first three years of the occupation, and so dollars were smuggled abroad to escape scrutiny, particularly to Switzerland, often by American service personnel contracted to make the trip by Garmisch civilians. Other compromised currency came in the form of obsolete dollar notes, but one way of reactivating them was to sell them to former Jewish concentration camp inmates who were the only ones allowed to redeem them, and who on arrival in the U.S. would exchange them for current bills of the same value.[6]

The informal headquarters for much of this smuggling and black-market work was the *Weisses Rössl*, the White Horse inn. The inn – really more a kind of late-night bar/restaurant in the centre of town – had its respectable side. It was close to the finest hotel in town, the Partenkirchner Hof, and to the American Military Government Headquarters diagonally across the road. While its frontage addressed established order, the rear of the hostelry backed onto wild Bavaria, constituting a part of the bank of the icy, gurgling rapids of the River Partnach, a tributary of the Danube whose waters eventually spew out into that great expanse of licit and illicit trade, the Black Sea.

The convivial atmosphere of the *Weisses Rössl*, with its fine food and music, provided both a respectable night out and many a shady deal sealed in its snug corners. As stated above, in 1945 the White Horse, named after the comic operetta by Austrian composers Ralph Benatzky and Robert Stolz, was run by the alluring, generous and jovial 35-year-old Zenta Hausner who, with her restaurant manager Charlie, not only facilitated black-market business but was one of its main merchants.

Poker-playing Zenta was smart, feisty and persuasive – not quite a femme fatale but rather a madam of the informal economy who would become known to the Americans as 'Garmisch Nell, Queen of Hearts'. She was supremely opportunistic. In 1944 she had taken over a restaurant in Munich popular with Nazi officials and became the mistress of the Gauleiter (regional party leader) of Bavaria. Now, almost seamlessly, she slipped into her new venture, entertaining, among others, Allied middle-ranking brass. She was facilitated in the first instance by her seduction of one Captain Korner, a German–American officer. Korner gave Zenta her first foothold in Garmisch because he was involved in the granting of food and beverage licences – that is, when he wasn't accepting bribes for the release of prisoners from the internment camp he ran.

Her patronage of the black market, and the inn's prominence as a base as well as a waystation for smuggling, would be an intense but short-lived affair. Just before Christmas in 1947 Hausner was murdered in her apartment above the inn. She had been battered with a blunt instrument and finished off with a kitchen knife. There were many suspects, including jilted lovers, most of whom might also have had the motive of covering their black-marketeering tracks. It could even have been a contract killing: Hausner had mixed with racketeering gangs and with some unscrupulous and corrupt American military administrators who had much to lose should news of their less than noble deeds travel home with them. Conspiracy theorists tend to suspect the latter because the extent of black racketeering that was centred on Garmisch-Partenkirchen, fanning out in smuggling lines over the lakes and mountains, was about to be exposed in the American press and would tar the reputations of many in positions of responsibility.

The White Horse inn, named after a musical comedy, had become the scene of tragedy. One might say that the darker side of the informal economy had overshadowed the light, but the question remains: what lies in between?

The Informal Afterlife of Soviet Trophy Art

Satan's Market doesn't sound much of an in-between, but there were products being traded at the unregulated market in Berlin that were neither at the poles of necessity, such as food and medicine, nor consumable luxuries.

In the early days of the occupation certain antique shops which had emerged under the auspices of the Russians were to be found selling old paintings and precious objets d'art. Each shop seemed to be an individual initiative, such as that at No. 3 Teltower Damm, run by a stateless individual called Graf Kemensky, but they were effectively managed by the Soviet Ministry of Trade. They were off-limits to Americans and should really have been so to private Soviet personnel, because if they frequented them they were more than likely shifting 'official' plunder to the black market.

It was a practice that was to continue in Russia for years afterwards. While most official Trophy Brigade loot was meticulously catalogued and buried in the vaults of Soviet museums, there were still plenty of art and artefacts, usually but not all privately looted, floating around the black markets of Moscow and Leningrad. State-run shops were some of the worst offenders. Prices were low and paintings and other objects could often be picked up for virtually nothing. Sometimes they cost literally nothing: Konstantin Akinsha and Grigorii Kozlov, in *Stolen Treasure*, tell of a collector known as the 'dustbin man', so-called because he occasionally found important if minor Western paintings in rubbish bins. By the 1950s he had acquired works by Rembrandt, Dürer, Cranach, Giordano, Klinger and Schinkel that are now known to have come from Bremen, Dresden and Berlin.[7]

Supply and Circulation Today

In the Soviet Union and elsewhere consumer goods were occasionally stolen from the government, but this kind of channel of supply does not explain the sheer quantity of contraband and fakes that feed markets around the world today, and of course it is extremely rare for precious contraband simply to appear among rubbish. Hence the quantity and the diversity of origin of goods for the black and grey markets is something that requires a little more scrutiny. In particular we must ask: what are the origins and sources of supply of all the cheap goods?

One way that goods become cheap enough to be attractive to smugglers is that they appear for sale at (tax) free markets such as those in the Dutch Antillean islands of Aruba, Curaçao and Bonaire, or at the northern end of the Panama Canal beside the town of Colón. Another form of contraband supply is characterized by its becoming such almost immediately after it comes out of the factory gates. This is the case with much of the product of the small town of Darra Dam Khel in northwest Pakistan, which from 1897 onwards has been entirely devoted to the manufacture of guns. Markets grew around its factories and workshops. The market there is grey because the industry is legal and so too is the sale of guns, but where they go afterwards is another story.

Such manufacturers and wholesalers are feeders for illicit circulation, often because goods are made and delivered so cheaply that traders buy them up and insert them into smuggling circulation elsewhere. But we could go further still in looking for contraband that is made as contraband.

The manufacture of fake and pirated goods is an obvious example of this. But even here they might circulate in various ways, either aimed at actual marketplaces, or alternatively towards vague possibilities of supply that we more usually associate with historical perceptions of the black market. In this latter category we might put gun-running of copied Kalashnikovs or certain fake medicines.

Contrast these with the knock-off fashion accessories from China, Taiwan, Vietnam or South Korea that are supplied to Canal Street in New York and that are sold in more solid, or at least temporarily visible, retail outlets. Some of these fakes are 'real' copies in the sense that they are made in the same territories, same factories even, that are producing the licensed brands, often simply on another shift. South Korea has become known for so-called 'super copies' – high-end luxury goods (such as handbags) – that are pretty much as good as the original and that have to be made in fully equipped factories rather than back-street workshops.

There is plenty of overlap between these illegal and semi-licit points of sale. Take for instance the fake medicine business in northern Mexico. Tijuana, the original health tourist port of call, is awash with this dangerous contraband, which is manufactured in factories nearby but out of cheap Indian chemical ingredients and packaged in Chinese-produced knock-off boxes. This is very definitely a black market, but still these goods appear in shops.

Pirated goods can be responsive to the original in more subtle ways. An historical example is very illuminating here. From the sixteenth century onwards 'hawkers' were the biggest sellers of books in Europe. One might think that they would have posed a dire threat to more regular bookselling, but in reality these licit and illicit channels were intertwined, as Robert Neuwirth points out in his book *Stealth Nation*. He cites several examples of variant Shakespeare editions produced as the informal responded to the formal, and vice versa. For example, street editions might alter endings – *King Lear* would be given a happy ending, or *Macbeth* become a musical – but when these laughably distorted versions took on a kind of normality and the bootleg became the new 'real' edition, it spurred competition, counteractively, into again producing rigorously crafted authentic versions. In another case, when Hans Jakob Christoffel von Grimmelshausen's novel *Der abendeuerliche Simplicissimus* (1668) was pirated and distorted, the copy was considered superior and so became the third sanctioned edition of the book, approved even by the author![8] The informal market, far from being always uncreative and degrading, in this instance has lent a certain validity to the object.

But to go back to the supply today of cheap goods, many of which few of us are totally averse to consuming, the question remains: why are they so available and cheap? What gives the supply chain such efficiency?

The Cost-effectiveness of Contraband Channels

Smuggling and black/grey racketeering are as much a part of globalization as anything else, if not more so because they are able to accelerate supply and because, and this is a key point, they are much more flexible. With the integration of zoned economies comes worldwide product sourcing and long supply chains, but smuggling can speed things up through bypassing bureaucracy. Another advantage of globalization for smuggling is that with increased flows (of licit goods) there simply isn't the capability to check everything.

Supply chains have also become more sophisticated: smuggling for the black market is now strategically astute in developing waystations for goods. For instance, Singapore has become a temporary holding place for animals and plants, Mexico for cocaine and migrant labour (as with Spain), and Moldova, Hungary and the Balkan states for sex slaves. North African countries such as Tunisia and Morocco have become the temporary home and springboard for economic migrants seeking a new life in Europe. It is flexibility and adaptability, though, that make contraband supply so effective and unstoppable.

One aspect of this adaptability is the strange re-routings that could only happen in our more deregulated times. An example is Hong Kong-Shenzhen, which became a special commercial zone in the 1980s. These two cities are divided by the river Sham Chun, crossed by the Lo Wu bridge. There are smuggling tunnels underneath the river. Goods made in mainland China, often in Shenzen itself but not available there, are smuggled 'offshore' to Hong Kong, but then immediately back into Shenzen-Guangzhou (formerly Canton), not to appear in the official shops but rather the illicit markets. Real and knock-off computers and other hardware and software are particularly desirable items. Shenzen also produces much of the world's fake clothing and fashion accessories. Similar systems of re-routing are used in the supply of most of the world's smuggled cigarettes. Cheap cigarettes from British and American tobacco companies are offloaded in regions like Eastern Europe and the free markets in the Caribbean, and then smuggled back to the country of origin or on to places where the official supply trades at a much higher price. It is not a new pattern: during the 1950s Corsican mafiosi smuggled American cigarettes into Marseille from North Africa. Until Spain clamped down on it in the 1990s, Gibraltar was renowned for this form of smuggling, bringing in tobacco in high-speed 'cigarette' boats and moving it on to the mainland.

Highly connected individuals are flexible enough to dip their toe in any pond, avoiding specialization, and are therefore more adaptable to market fluctuations. They are able to source goods quickly and along multiple and diverse channels that are often beyond the reach of centralized or large monolithic organizations tied to binding state contracts. The big players can no longer monopolize or bully the market. In the market of fake goods costs can be kept low as there are no research and development expenses. Distribution has also become cheaper because networks bring together so many willing participants at different stages of the chain.

For these reasons illicit supply can't be defeated, because, being highly decentralized, when squeezed in one place it will simply bulge again somewhere else like a balloon. Choking it altogether is difficult – there are multiple leaders and each part is autonomous and self-sustaining. There are millions if not billions of participants.

System D

Why are there so many participants in informal economies? It is not so much the black market and its possibilities for huge profits that brings in multitudes of participants; it is rather that it is an alternative system of circulation and motivation. In French-speaking Africa and the Caribbean it is known as 'System D' – its very name referring to its adaptability. The 'D' of System D stands for *débrouillards* – motivated, self-reliant people – who participate in an economy of improvisation. It refers not just to individual identity but to a modality of living that, out of necessity, avoids paying taxes and bypasses overbearing regulation and bureaucracy. It tends to be self-governing, self-organizing and even, in certain situations, self-regulating. Through the ingenuity and creativity of its participants, System D solves most of its own problems.

Although it can be studied *in situ* – market stalls, pedlars' tables and pop-up this and that are there to be seen if we look hard enough – one cannot imagine System D without taking into account the mobility of the participants who trade and transport goods internationally. The Nigerian who travels to Guangzhou to source goods or the Colombian free trader who looks for them in the Dutch Antilles is a part of System D, and so too was Arthur Rimbaud in the Horn of Africa. But then so are we when we buy a fake watch or accept software from a friend that is licensed only to the original purchaser. Anybody who takes cash-in-hand jobs and neglects to pay their taxes is a part of System D.

There are some 1.8 billion people working in it,[9] about half the world's workforce, and its turnover has been estimated at $10 trillion per annum. Robert Neuwirth has another name for it, 'Bazaaristan', and if it were a nation-state it would be the world's second biggest economy.[10]

System D is really best characterized as a system of circulation and migration and so it would be easy for us to get lost in the abundance, ubiquity and flow of it all. Indeed, although this chapter began with an account of a black-market *place* – the White Horse inn in Garmisch-Partenkirchen – the sheer volume and variety of supply channels and practices just described should indicate that informal markets are dispersed and not simply nodal. Some market centres have a keen sense of place in relation to supply, such as Maicao in Colombia: among the

'Bonaire' contraband store, Maicao, Colombia.

many contraband stores one finds *Comercial Aruba* and *Comercial Bonaire*, referring to the Dutch Antilles tax-free markets from where the goods come.

Let's turn to the stalls themselves – to the black/grey market as market. What does it look like?

Black, Grey and Blue Markets Around the World

Irregular markets have existed since Renaissance times, if not longer, when informal trading took place in Italy around the gates of walled cities. Even today most large cities around the world have a street or a district known for selling unofficial goods. There is usually great diversity in the stock in what is often called the 'smugglers' market', which sells everything from cameras, mp3 players and pirated DVDs to alcohol, knock-off fashions and more mundane fare like soap and toothpaste. Much of it is contraband smuggled across borders to avoid paying taxes, emerging as black-market goods whether sold at these markets or anywhere else.

The non-*flota* goods landed by pirate-smugglers such as Drake and Hawkins on the north coast of South America would be categorized today as black-market goods. If goods illegally run across a border do appear at a market, they are often mingled in with what one would call grey-market goods – items simply bought for a cheaper price in one place than it is possible to sell them at officially in another country or state, and then brought (legally) across a border. The practice is only illicit in that the goods are not licensed by the manufacturer or official distributor to be marketed or sold in the new country. In both cases the stall that the product appears upon might be regulated and so the physical market itself, before the goods arrive, is not usually illegal as such. There are other commodities that are strictly illegal, and dangerous, that sometimes coalesce around these lively sites, for instance guns, drugs and trafficked women – sex slaves.

The proportion of grey and black varies from place to place. There might be a speciality that predominates, or a particular reason for the emergence of the market. Sometimes there will have been an informal market on a particular site for centuries; in other instances it will have sprung up as an effect of a displacement of usage, for instance a sports stadium or park being abandoned, or else through demand coming out of severe shortage and suffering at the end of a war.

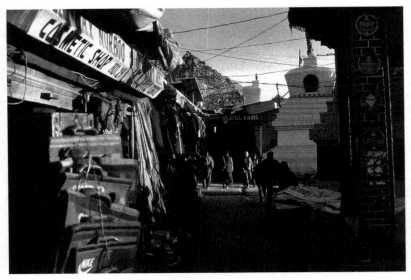

Moti Market, Leh, Ladakh, India.

The architecture and layout of informal markets varies a lot. Some are bounded, often quite claustrophobic, while others spill over onto surrounding streets, or the street itself becomes the market. Occasionally a particular street becomes famed as a grey-market drag, such as Canal Street in New York or Charoen Krung Road in Bangkok. Others appear on out-of-town sites as complexes paralleling official superstore trends, while in a small number of instances the informal market effectively *is* the town.

Bounded markets, purpose-built and officially licensed, aren't usually set up as contraband havens, but the sale of illicit goods will have infiltrated more regulated practices. Ambling through the Moti market (more like a small medina than a market block) of Leh in Ladakh, which borders Tibet, one can't help noticing the abundance of Chinese goods. Much of the household wares – plates, cups, containers and so on – and clothing is contraband, brought into Ladakh in trucks over the arid Chang Tang plateau. It is more difficult to spot the contraband in the Palika Bazaar in the centre of Connaught Square in New Delhi, but it is there, as it is in the National Market in Bangalore.

However, some bounded markets *were* built as grey or black markets. These tend to look more like malls (*galerias* in Latin America) than partitioned stockades. There is a Galeria Pagé in both São Paulo and Ciudad del Este in Paraguay, and both sell black-market goods. In the latter city the plushness of the Lai Lai Centre, which mainly sells computers, is evidence of the money that over the years has been made in smuggling electronic goods, and which has turned the city from a low-rise, unpaved market town into a major regional centre. The San Andrésitos in Colombia, the long-established network of semi-legal markets to be found in all of its major cities, have also taken on the architecture of the mall rather than the traditional bazaar.

Generally, though, it seems impossible to contain the energy and sense of bonanza that animates many smugglers' markets and they spill over into the street. Markets of this type include Silk Alley in Beijing (Xiùshuijiē) and the Karkhano and Barra markets on the edge of Peshawar, the haunt of Pashtun smugglers and black marketeers.

The black/grey market in São Paulo takes place along the Rua 25 de Março, which like Canal Street is lined with stalls and semi-permanent shops, but it differs in that much of the trading actually occurs in the street. In one example the road pattern itself is key: at Oshodi Junction in Lagos the sale of contraband is linked to the time spent in jams on the buses. Sometimes less regulated markets take over entire districts, as is the case at Karol Bagh in Delhi which, like Palika Bazaar, is a regular market infiltrated with grey-market goods. The market at Maicao in southern Guajira, Colombia, near to the Venezuelan border, is another extensive street bazaar.

When the irregular market moves out of town there are other possibilities, mainly to do with land available for sprawl. In Lagos Ikeja Computer Village, an IT retail park, and Alaba International, a wholesale market, have had the paradoxical effect of regularizing the informal economy to some extent. These complexes have outgrown the chaotic informality of the city because they are important as pan-African distribution centres that do much of their (often smuggling) import business with China and other Asian manufacturing countries.

It is not always possible for all of these kinds of markets to follow the out-of-town model, and if they do not they often occupy adaptable corners of the city. There have been a number of instances of transformation of purpose of existing buildings from the formal to the informal. The irregular part of the Tahtakale market in Istanbul for a while occupied a beautiful disused hammam, taking up a full city block at the heart of this district. From 1989 onwards there has existed a market, Cherkizovsky (aka Izmailovo Market), that 'officially' squatted on the grounds of the former Stalinets Stadium in Moscow. It attracted, among others, Tajiks, Uzbeks, Chinese and Southeast Asians.

Cherkizovsky Market, Moscow.

Cherkizovsky, rather like the market presided over by Zenta Hausner, exhibits something other than pure economics. Its business has become entertainment as well as commerce – it also functions as a funfair/theme park. As with most markets there is a dimension of the carnivalesque here. Bizarrely, in this case, it takes place in the grounds of a recreational facility underneath which was built Stalin's bunker in the extensive tunnels striating its foundations – his place to fiddle should Moscow ever burn.

Jarmark Europa in Warsaw was another informal market with prismatic hues. It too was housed in a football arena and was founded in 1989. Stallholders in the Tenth Anniversary Stadium (Stadion Dziesięciolecia – the former national football stadium) were known as *chelnoki*, which translates roughly as 'weaver's shuttle', referring to the itinerant shuttling traders. Trading ceased in 2008 to make way for a new national stadium. A little-known fact about this irregular market is that it had a library for its informal traders.[11]

In other cases a town becomes synonymous with smuggling – this is what has happened to Maicao. But the smuggler town par excellence in Latin America is Ciudad del Este in Paraguay on the border with Brazil, which is given over almost entirely to contraband. The town lies opposite Foz do Iguaçu in Brazil, and both of them bestride the Rio Paraná crossed by the Friendship bridge that was built in 1956. Ciudad del Este is the dynamo of the Paraguayan economy. *Sacoleiros*, bag

Cherkizovsky Market, Moscow.

carriers, come from Brazil for shopping trips, usually on Tuesdays on buses marked *Tourismo* that return the next day. These are special buses operating just two days a week from the bus station in São Paulo. At the bridge on the Brazilian side there are *guada-roupas* (left luggage) that are also social waystations. Officially there is a limit of $300 on exports, but it is easy to obtain undervalued, false receipts beside the bridge. There is some mixing of grey and black goods here. Computers, bulk imported, can easily nowadays cost under $300 each, and so there is no longer any need to smuggle them. But large operators (so-called *laranjas*) who want to re-export in bulk have to smuggle and so act in the time-honoured ways of the black market.[12]

The Informal Touches the Formal

Much of the activity described in this chapter might fall under the heading of opportunistic free trading, individualist profiteering or petty commerce – quite distant from any notion that a formal external force, state or otherwise, is involved in its informality. There is however some speculation and some more concrete evidence of formal or at least more organized entities touching the informal.

Few deny that the Paraguayan state is heavily involved in smuggling, but other links in the region are more tenebrous. According to the U.S. Treasury department, Galeria Pagé in Ciudad del Este is owned by the Ahmad Barakat brothers, both of whom have been arrested in recent times, ostensibly for illicit business practices, but also possibly because they have had connections with the Lebanese Iranian Islamic group Hezbollah.[13] There have been rumours over the years, unproven, about Nazi hideouts in Paraguay, and now the Rio Paraná region is being linked with Islamist extremism.

Another case where official support for black marketeering may be demonstrated, and not simply rumoured, is Arizona Market beside Brcko in Bosnia, near to the Serbian border. This informal market emerged after NATO (mainly American) troops saw the positive side of impromptu trading at a road junction, and how it was getting people talking and trading again after the November 1995 Dayton Peace Accords. It exploded into trading life after the military facilitated its growth in 1996. It is called Arizona because it lies on the U.S. military's dividing corridor 'Route Arizona', and in the early years had the look of a booming Wild West town. The market soon covered the area of six football pitches and had much the same contraband on offer as most of the markets described above. But it had a much darker side: it quickly emerged as a centre for gathering and trafficking women into the sex trade and became the final destination for many of these enslaved women, the majority from the Balkans, Romania, Moldova and Ukraine.

It would be crass to call it a blue market simply for these reasons, but there is another reason for it: the main customers for sex, sold out of so-called 'coffee bars', were the soldiers themselves, including a sizeable number of United Nations peacekeepers who came in from surrounding areas. Renegade peace enforcers even ran some of the trafficking businesses. The military was not only instrumental in setting up the black market here, and one of its major customers, but was also one of its main movers.

I BEGAN THIS CHAPTER by asking just how dark the black market is. After the black and white of fleeing Nazis and escaping aircrew of the preceding chapter, might there be more nuance to illicit flows, and to marketplaces? There is the possibility that what makes up most of the informal economy is simply 'petty' trading – a kind of grey area – that squeezes itself between mafia trafficking (the dark side) and state involvement (the light side in terms of the rhetoric of the 'war on drugs' and 'war on terror'). This grey area in between, paradoxically, could be seen in a more romantic light because the cultural dimension of the informal economy – lively contraband taverns, libraries in football stadia, carnivalesque markets and the thrill for us of wandering around exotic smugglers' markets and getting something on the cheap – is in excess of the pure profit motive.

Another view is that it is the poles that dominate this spectrum: so-called black holes and bright spots, with the relatively unimportant grey areas merely transit points or thresholds between the two. In this argument energy is either pushed out from black holes through desperation and greed or pulled from perceived bright spots as legitimate states are infiltrated and seduced.[14]

Perhaps this is all a little Manichaean, particularly as there are instances of quite happy accommodations between formal economies and their shadow. Exemplary in this regard is a place near to the Tahtakale informal market in Istanbul where there is a street that for centuries, and until quite recently, played the role of an informal currency exchange market. It is a narrow, elongated alley of wooden architecture belying its importance as the site of multi-million-dollar deals, and the barometer by which the Turkish national bank set its official exchange rates. It looked informal and was very atmospheric, even convivial, but does it make sense in a context of such influence to call it informal in an economic sense?

The author of *Stealth Nation*, Robert Neuwirth, questions the whole concept of the term 'informal'. He suggests that the genealogy of the term itself plays out an incompatibility between formal and informal. Neuwirth tells us that the term 'informal economy' was coined by the anthropologist Keith Hart during the early 1970s but that he himself finds in his travels around the variable geographies of System D that participants never think of heir activities as informal.[15] Is it at all helpful, then, to speak of formal and informal economies as if they were entirely separate, not inextricably linked worlds? Certainly there are worlds apart – very black spots and murky channels for gun running and drugs (even involving the 'light side' during and for a time after the Cold War) – that are in general considered pretty irregular. But of equal interest for us should be the grey middle ground because we are never far away from it, and occasionally right in it. Here it is difficult to spot what is merely petty trading or criminal activity, what is individual or collective, because always, beside the carnivalesque, there will be something sordid, and beside the misery there will be the bon viveur.

Generally speaking, with some clear exceptions, there is probably little state involvement in System D. It is largely self-organizing but society must take account of such a huge phenomenon that, as Neuwirth suggests, offers an alternative vision of globalization. In peacetime it seeps into the more regulated world through corruption or, more brightly, through the seductions of living one's life a little on the edge, or in spite of commercial regulation. We nevertheless tend to have a fairly passive relationship with the black and grey markets.

The following three chapters concentrate on contraband in time of war, presenting very different scenarios in which there was very active state involvement in smuggling: contraband wars and quite sinister espionage around the narcotics and arms trades during the Cold War.

SIXTEEN

SOUTH BY SOUTHEAST

Air Opium and the Arteries of Indochina

Among the various accounts of aviation that persuade us that flying is a noble calling, Antoine de Saint-Exupéry's *Wind, Sand and Stars* is perhaps the one that most poetically escapes the gravity of everyday affairs. In one passage recounting the difficulty of organizing a rescue in the Andes in winter, he sets himself apart as an aviator from those on the ground in quite moralizing terms, talking of smugglers as 'bandits who would commit a crime for a five-peso note [and] refused to form a rescue party'.[1] Many of the airmen of this chapter, by contrast, *are* the smugglers.

Regular and irregular air forces, airlines, pilots, pathfinders and their controllers during the twentieth-century wars in Indochina were experts in the low-level arts of airlifting, air-dropping and evacuation – earthly and often very political pursuits. One only has to look at some of the aircraft of the Vietnam conflict to get a feel for this. The iconic aircraft was of course a helicopter, the Huey, but the aeroplanes that played the largest part in U.S. covert warfare in Laos, where much of this smuggling went on, were a variety of ungainly but very effective short takeoff and landing (STOL) craft, in particular the small, single-engined Helio Super Courier and later on the Pilatus Porter. Elsewhere in the region the South Vietnamese and Lao air forces (as well as the French and the American) relied heavily on that brilliant workhorse from the Second World War, the C-47 Dakota. These were some of the classic military aircraft of the era and each smuggled opium at one time or another in addition to carrying war supplies. A not insubstantial number of servicemen in the Vietnamese and Lao air forces used these aircraft, among other tasks, to smuggle opium, heroin and morphine. Quite a few French and Americans turned a blind eye to the sticky crates in among the munitions and nervous passengers they flew into and out of the various war zones.

Most of us know this episode in history as simply the Vietnam War, but it was in fact two wars as far as the West was concerned: the French one between 1946 and 1954 and the American one that ended in the evacuation of Saigon in April 1975. It might alternatively be thought of as a war between the West and communism, with America and China the titans behind it all, but this would be to oversimplify the complicated nature and motivations of the various protagonists of what was actually a series and array of wars of independence, civil wars and, most pertinent for this enquiry, contests to control opium-smuggling trails. They took place across Vietnam, Laos and Cambodia. Some mapping out of this geopolitics might make the stage and timeline for the unfolding of smuggling patterns a little clearer.

The French fought the independence-seeking Viet Minh in Vietnam, with the latter prevailing and splitting the colony in two. Later on, allied South Vietnamese and American forces battled with the Viet Cong (the insurgent army arising in South Vietnam, famous for carrying out the Tet Offensive in 1968) and against the North Vietnamese Army (the NVA, the successor to the Viet Minh, later called the Vietnamese Peoples' Army, the VPA). From 1962 civil war raged in Laos between Royalist forces and the communist Pathet Lao, escalating from a lower-key conflict that began in 1953. The China- and North Vietnam-backed Pathet Lao eventually overran Vientiane, the capital, in 1975. Meanwhile in Cambodia government forces, occasionally backed by the U.S., fought the communist Khmer Rouge, who also triumphed in 1975, taking over Phnom Penh in that year.

These wars were configured not just by opposing ideologies but by territorial invasions, for instance by the Ho Chi Minh Trail, along which the North Vietnamese ran military supplies down across southern Laos (its so-called panhandle) and Cambodia to fight their war in South Vietnam, and through periodic pushes across the Plain of Jars in northern Laos by combined communist armies fighting their way southwards towards Vientiane. The Americans were never officially in many of these places but of course they were everywhere. In the case of the area around the Plain of Jars, which was important as a refining and distribution zone for opium harvests, they were there as supporters and advisors. A key question that I will come to later in this chapter, though, is the extent to which they were there as opium smugglers as well.

The Golden Triangle Region at the time of the Vietnam War.

Regarding smuggling's geopolitics, just as important as the opium trails out of northern Laos were the cultivation and distribution zones of northern Thailand and eastern Burma (the Shan States in particular). Together they make up the infamous 'Golden Triangle'.

One shouldn't leap to conclusions about the presence of Americans in these traditional opium-trafficking regions – for every flight carrying opium there were thousands employed exclusively for the logistics of fighting. But then again, in strategic terms, neither should one under-estimate the desire to control smuggling routes, which also acted as a driver of conflict: this was a powerful motivation smuggled beneath the declared ideology of the war on communism. And if such a broad subtext was at work, it is not surprising that certain influential people high up in the opium trade would make such profitable use of the war machinery at their disposal.

Aerial Smuggling Corridors

The smuggling itinerary was usually a series of relays leading out of the opium-cultivating highlands and down to the market: small aircraft picked up where the mule trails ended and they in turn handed over to large transports. They flew out of the Golden Triangle, which was, as it still is today, a sort of perverse cradle of culture (in this case opium-related culture), and their markets lay down to the south and the southeast: flight paths to Bangkok and Saigon.

The southern route from the Golden Triangle still feeds opium down to Thailand. It was developed initially by Shan State warlords and Lao cultivators (from the Hmong tribes) before it was organized more efficiently by the magpie entity that was the militarily defeated but organizationally intact exiled nationalist Chinese army of Chiang Kai-shek (the Kuomintang, otherwise known as the KMT) that had been pushed out of China's Yunnan province by Mao Zedong. It was facilitated in Thailand through the involvement of the Thai chief of police, General Phao Siyanan, who continued to enrich himself on the trade up until his exile after a coup in 1957. For a while the Kuomintang had support from the CIA, who trained them as a counter-communist force, but they were dropped after early setbacks. This is when they went into the opium business as their main concern, spreading out over the Shan States of Burma in order to colonize and organize the trade more efficiently.

The southeastern route ran through northern Laos across the region dominated by the Plain of Jars and its encircling mountains. Phong Savan was the main transhipment point here. Also significant for heroin refining was a congregation of processing labs around Ban Houei Sai in the northwest, near to the Burmese border. From here it was flown either to Long Tieng in the highlands just to the south of the Plain of Jars or to the capital, Vientiane, situated on a broad plain, before being carried on to Saigon in South Vietnam or air-dropped in the vicinity.

This might seem rather a simple diagram – at its core an off-balance triangle – but the labyrinthine, tenuous and changeable geopolitics of broader Southeast Asia that ran through it during the quarter-century following the Second World War make it very difficult to make sense of. The dense and complex political geometry of the broader theatre of war can scarcely be touched, let alone understood, in just a single chapter. Nevertheless if one were to pull out a couple of threads here and wind them around some of the key events of this three-decade-long war, one might at least tie up a small amount of elusive meaning.

One thread would, of course, be smuggling, and the other, my choice here to convey it, might be the air networks that offered certain wholesale possibilities for the smugglers in a mountainous region over which land transport was difficult. I want, then, to pursue the issue of state involvement in smuggling in Southeast Asia through its aerial dimension – to get above it, so to speak.

Background to the Opium Trade in Southeast Asia

Despite the ending of the European opium trade in China, there remained a powerful legacy of addiction and trafficking in East and Southeast Asia. The Chinese, now growing their own opium, smuggled it to French Indochina as well as to Thailand, although this all ended with Mao Zedong's victory in 1949. Indochina also had its own cultivation, operating under a French monopoly since the inception of the colonies in the 1860s.

However, although there was ever-increasing production in Southeast Asia, for a long time after the Second World War European and American markets were served by poppy fields located elsewhere. The main areas of opium cultivation for supplying Europe and America at this time were not in Southeast Asia at all; rather they were in Iran and Turkey. But after 1955 the former source dried up, although the latter continued to supply until the early 1970s. As the old fields of poppies were eradicated, Golden Triangle opium production grew towards ascendancy, at first to provide for Southeast Asian addicts (at the end of the Second World War there were at least 100,000 in Vietnam alone), then for American GIs in Vietnam, and eventually the world. A key moment in this rise was the arrival in Laos in 1969 of the knowledge (through Hong Kong lab technicians) of how to make high-grade opium.

Throughout this time, even in the period when Iran and Turkey dominated supply to the West, intelligence agencies as well as crime organizations from Western countries were involved in the opium trade in Thailand and across French Indochina. At the end of the Second World War Sicilian-American and Corsican gangsters, as well as the CIA and French intelligence (the Deuxième Bureau), began to manoeuvre for position in the intertwined political-criminal networks of opium/heroin trafficking in the region, against the backdrop of the spread of communism.

It broadened into clandestine warfare as the French in Saigon, exploiting colonial networks around Indochina, moved deeper into the opium business. This wasn't simply a criminal trade, it was a form of colonial warfare. Colonial agents bought up opium harvests, selling them to finance their counter-insurgency operations against the Viet Minh in what was initially called 'Operation X'. It continued during all-out war with the communists and only ended for the French with the debacle at Dien Bien Phu in 1953–4.

The Deuxième Bureau and the CIA did not get on. Following the defeat of the French, there was increasing rivalry between the two intelligence agencies despite each of them being acutely attuned to the possibilities of turning an opium-generated warlord/paramilitary network into an instrument of war against communism. The French Intelligence service, alongside the South Vietnamese government, could never quite disentangle itself from the criminal gangs of the Binh Xuyen (river pirates who also acted as spies and assassins for the politicians) and from the Corsican mafia. Both ran Saigon at street level. The CIA, for their part, although wanting to concentrate much of their efforts up in the mountains of northern Laos, did not want to emulate previous French tactics in these areas. The Americans did not want to be seen to be openly buying up opium harvests, although in other ways they did patronize the business, albeit in a much more covert way than the Lao and Vietnamese military. Such patronage flourished throughout the 1960s until military defeats irreversibly changed this geometry, although not immediately.

The Tet Offensive of 31 January 1968 forced a rethink on the heroin corridor down to Saigon. But then again an epidemic in GI heroin addiction meant that this artery of supply would not be squeezed for long. Besides which, trafficking gained a new channel after the 1970 coup in Cambodia and an invitation by its government for American and South Vietnamese forces to come in and deal with the communists who had infiltrated, with Khmer Rouge support, from the north.

Generally speaking, as most people knew already from mass media coverage, things were not going the Americans' way. The Paris Peace Accords of 1973 meant that once again they were no longer able to have an on-the-ground presence in Laos. This effectively ended their operations there. On 30 April 1975 Saigon fell to the Viet Cong and the North Vietnamese army – the same year that Pathet Lao communists overran Vientiane and the Khmer Rouge surged into Phnom Penh. This was the end of the southeastern opium trail out of the Golden Triangle.

However, it hasn't seen the end of the Golden Triangle, although it has been superseded in recent years by the so-called Golden Crescent of Afghan and Pakistani opium production (with Iran acting as a consumer and conduit to the west). In the 1970s and '80s the opium warlords of this part of Southeast Asia continued to send vast amounts of narcotics down the southern route. During the latter decade an infamous but strangely media-friendly warlord, Khun Sa, outmanoeuvred the Kuomintang, becoming the dominant force in Golden Triangle opium production up until his 'surrender', or should one call it retirement, in 1996.[2]

Over the decades the wars ebbed and flowed and personnel changed, but the one constant, from the 1950s until mass evacuation in 1975, was the pattern of arms in and narcotics out. War supplies were continually being flown in to various armies and counter-insurgency forces with heroin and opium coming out, often on the same aircraft. Arms supply and narcotics smuggling, then, became inextricably bound together.

The Early Years of the Southern Route – Arms In, Opium Out

The southern smuggling route became an air corridor with the entanglement of the CIA with the Kuomintang, facilitated by corrupt Thai police. 'Operation Paper', begun in February 1951, supplied Kuomintang forces in Burma. Having evacuated much of the KMT army to Taiwan after Mao's victory in 1949, the Americans' recently acquired 'can-do' air transport business, Civil Air Transport (CAT), which had a main office in that country, brought some 600 of them back. Two loads would arrive each week, delivering refreshed Kuomintang forces to Mong Hsat in the Shan State region of Burma – the heart of what would become the Golden Triangle opium-cultivation zone.

Bangkok became the gateway for an arms supply line facilitated by General Phao, the brutal Thai chief of police, who arranged the final leg north from Chiang Mai to the border. Through the marriage of an American, Willis Bird, to Phao's sister, there were strong American-Thai interpersonal relationships facilitating this channel. Bird's relative William Bird was an operative for the Office of Policy Coordination (OPC – a somewhat prosaic name for an organization that rivalled and later merged with the CIA) and organized the import of weapons for Operation Paper, bringing them into Bangkok through a front company, Southeast Asian Supply Corporation (SEA), from Okinawa.

In addition impatient American agents sought to speed things up, themselves taking to the air: Civil Air Transport began making direct air supply drops, five or more a week, to the Kuomintang base at Mong Hsat. A little later on, by the time of the re-injection of Kuomintang back into Mong Hsat after their brief sojourn in Taiwan, it had an airstrip, built in part by U.S. engineers, and so now the arms and narcotics exchange could begin in earnest.

A fundamental principle of trade is never to travel empty. Heeding this, CAT occasionally took opium on the return trip to Bangkok. It was, of course, never on the manifest and the American pilots did not seek publicity, although one, Jack Killam, attracted it in 1951 after he was murdered when a deal apparently went sour.

These irregular transportations were a dress rehearsal for some of the more nefarious activities of Air America (CAT's successor). But it was all relatively short-lived; by 1953 the airline was taking Kuomintang back to Taiwan after they had failed to gain a foothold in Yunnan, the Chinese province just over the border from Burma. The Americans dropped their support programme and the Burmese army began to squeeze those remaining, although many clung on in Burma. The Kuomintang were finally driven out of there by the Burmese army in 1961.

However, this was not the end of them. The Kuomintang continued to control the opium-production areas of the Golden Triangle, although like the CIA they now officially operated out of Thailand. They survived a setback with the so-called Opium War of 1967 – a clash with Khun-Sa – and continued to dominate the organization of cultivation until the warlord began to take over.

Serving Saigon – The Southeastern Route

The other route, to the southeast, was of a very different character: almost from the start it was a state-sponsored smuggling channel. Opium and later heroin and morphine followed this itinerary from Laos to Saigon, usually via the transit point of Long Tieng. By the mid-1960s it was the Lao and Vietnamese air forces that provided much of the transport. Air transportation was the only realistic option as the Annamite Mountains formed a barrier between Laos and South Vietnam. Because of the expense involved in running this form of transportation, it was only the elites or larger agencies that could afford to enter the trade, although it wasn't always the state apparatus that provided the aircraft.

For example, between 1958 and 1960 Ngo Dinh Nhu, the brother of Preisdent Ngo Dinh Diem of South Vietnam, was busily reviving the opium trade (after a short period of probity) as a way to pay for his war against communist insurgents. He relied on small Corsican airlines. It was only after securing the services of the First Transport Group of the air force between 1961 and 1962 that this arrangement changed for him. Other official planes carrying intelligence agents to and from Laos would also carry narcotics on the return journey. The air force again sought narco funding for the war between 1965 and 1967.

It wasn't simply a family business and the brothers never had a monopoly. In these latter years, after Nhu and Diem's assassination in 1963, there was a three-way battle for control of the trade between the air force (under the control of Vice President Ky); a grouping that included the army, navy and lower house of parliament; and an alliance between the customs, port authority and Prime Minister Tran Thien Khiem's national police force. It was the air force that got the upper hand.

However, as the southeastern route began to lift off, the importance of the Vietnamese air force in opium and heroin trafficking was a little way into the future. The Corsicans, as in Europe, were the drivers of the French Connection.

Air Opium

'Air Opium' is the name often given to the assortment of small Corsican transport airlines, operating out of Laos between 1955 and 1965, that smuggled opium down to Saigon. Opium was loaded at small airstrips beside provincial towns such as Sam Neua, Phong Saly, Muong Sing, Nam Tha, Sayaboury or Ban Houei Sai to be flown to Vientiane or Phong Savan, and from there to Vietnam. These officially registered air transport companies sometimes contracted freelance pilots operating their own aeroplanes. Among the legendary operators of Air Opium were three experienced and daring pilots: Roger Zoile, René 'Babal' Enjabal and Gérard Labenski.[3]

Roger Zoile's transport business was bankrolled by a Corsican mafia in Bangkok dominated by Paul Louis Levet and specialized in smuggling morphine base. In 1962 he was operating three brand new Beechcraft aeroplanes. René Enjabal was a former French air force officer whose civil airline was known unofficially as the Babal Air Force. Gérard Labenski was renowned as the best pilot among this trio.

Labenski was a resourceful individual – he managed the Snow Leopard inn at Phong Savan on the eastern edge of the Plain of Jars where he ran his main smuggling business. The inn was used to store opium. One can't help being reminded here of Zenta Hausner's White Horse inn, that mixture of splendid cheer and dark business in post-war Garmisch-Partenkirchen, or, in fiction, of Daphne du Maurier's equally ambiguous Jamaica Inn. Once again, now with these Corsican aviators, we are confronted with a brighter side to smuggling, one vulnerable to romanticization; perhaps specifically to the vision of Saint-Exupéry's *Wind, Sand and Stars*, and with it a soupçon of apparent danger. We are hardly talking about Smuggling, Incorporated, here. But we should not be deceived.

Foremost among the Air Opium operatives, or at least the most ruthless, was a charismatic Corsican gangster, Bonaventure 'Rock' Francisci, linked to the pivotal Guerini brothers of Marseille who ran Air Laos Commerciale (based in Vientiane operating a fleet of twin-engined Beechcraft). Although not large, it managed to outmanoeuvre the opposition through a combination of alliance and treachery: it was a cut-throat business. Francisci was able to 'save' Enjabal after he was compromised (probably shopped by Francisci himself) unloading a shipment. Enjabal inadvertently gained revenge when he fell asleep at the controls of one of Francisci's aircraft, drifting off-course into Thailand, where he was briefly imprisoned and the load confiscated. Labenski was also betrayed after landing his opium-laden plane at Xuan Loc, 45 miles north of Saigon. He was jailed for five years, although he made a plea bargain with American anti-narcotics agents. Not quite the ideal romantic or even profitable path that these pioneer airborne smugglers of Southeast Asia might have hoped to follow.

And nor was this smuggling free of state involvement. The Corsicans were quietly authorized to operate in Laos under a permission category called *réquisition militaire* (military charter), usually approved by the top general, Phoumi Nosavan.[4] Francisci had the patronage of Nhu in Vietnam from 1958. Nevertheless, in Vietnam the Corsican air transport companies did not necessarily have the kind of freedom to operate as smugglers that the official air force later enjoyed, and so often had to make air drops of narcotics, either in Cambodia, in the Gulf of Thailand or in rural parts of south Vietnam.

There were setbacks: in December 1960 Phong Savan fell to Captain Kong Le, the parachute regiment leader on the 'neutralist' side in the civil war,[5] and the Corsicans had to redeploy their operations to Wattay airport outside Vientiane. The Snow Leopard was taken over and renamed the Friendship Hotel, now becoming home for Soviet engineers who were servicing Ilyushin transport aircraft that brought in arms and supplies from Hanoi for the Pathet Lao communists as well as the neutralists.

One might argue that these are the hardships that make the legend, but other setbacks proved insurmountable. After General Ouane Rattikone, a former Pathet Lao commander during the 1940s, came to prominence in April 1964 he wrested control of the opium air transport business from the Corsicans, ending their involvement by 1965.

After a colourful decade of freelance opium supply, the state in both Vietnam and Laos, with its much greater resources, operating as large corporations usually do in relation to small-scale individual initiatives, saw an opportunity to intervene and draw the trade to itself.

Vietnamese Air Force Smuggling

Nguyen Cao Ky was a South Vietnamese Air Force man, an Air Vice-Marshal in fact, and between 1965 and 1967 he exercised his power, as prime minister, over the country and the opium trade. Working alongside him was his comrade and friend in the service, General Nguyen Ngoc Loan, who reorganized all the security services. Ky's former command, the First Air Transport Group, became his praetorian guard and their territory, a large part of Tan Son Nhut international airport, was his power base. He even built a palace within its perimeter. He no longer ran the group on a day-to-day basis, but the new commander, Luu Kim Cuong, became chief of smuggling operations. Many of the airport staff were a part of this major opium-trafficking channel, allowing incoming loads to pass through unsearched. Cuong controlled all security. The boom years for this channel were between 1965 and 1968. It benefited from the diminution of the Corsican airlines following their eviction from Laos in 1965 and was only interrupted by the Tet Offensive in 1968.

The air force flew not only opium but contraband gold out of Phnom Penh, making the most of planes that carried in equipment and supplies. Even AC-47 gunships (the fearsome 'Puff the Magic Dragon' – a Dakota mounted with three powerful, pilot-controlled machine guns) sent up to Cambodia to secure this new South Vietnamese/U.S. zone of influence might return to Tan Son Nhut with contraband. It was a quiet mission after their furious utterances on the outward leg. Gold and opium also came out of an airport near Pakse in Laos. Here Ky's sister put together the cargoes, using as a base the luxury hotel that she ran, the Sedone Palace. This family business model also worked for the notoriously corrupt customs director in Saigon, Nguyen Van Loc, himself prime minister for a while in 1967–8, whose niece carried opium while working as an air hostess on Royal Air Lao.[6]

Aircraft were important, even for non-Air Force smuggling operations: after the president, Nguyen Van Thieu, presided over the overthrow of Ky and Loan,[7] the Vietnamese Navy would take craft up the Mekong river as far as Phnom Penh to be fed by another enterprising corps, the South Vietnamese Special Forces. Some of these used their helicopters, transport and light aircraft to supply opium to the Cambodian capital at the head of the river route. But it was never a large-scale operation.

Eventually Tan Son Nhut was cleaned up, but the flow of narcotics simply shifted to the numerous other airbases in the hinterland of Saigon. One particular senior officer in the Air Transport Division, Colonel Phan Phung Tien, forged strong links with Corsican gangsters in the region. The business now fanned out to the world, taking advantage of new airline networks and the continued involvement of the French and Americans. Beside American military complicity that allowed for the provision of heroin to GIs, American mafiosi, around this time losing their Turkish supply lines, looked for new source areas. Ominously in 1968 the Italian American boss Santo Trafficante Jr visited Saigon, meeting up with Corsican criminal figures.

The Corsicans still dominated onward supply, which was often also taken via air networks. Much heroin was processed in Hong Kong and then flown to Chile on commercial flights before being taken to Paraguay in light aircraft. Paraguay was also a hub for drugs flown in from Europe via Argentina. As well as being the favoured destination of choice for fugitive Nazis, these countries made good refuges for fleeing gangsters who might have had opportunistic connections with the Germans during the war in places like Marseille, and some of them, despite their exile, were not yet ready to end their days as active mobsters.[8]

Much closer to the heart of the Golden Triangle, in Laos at the beginning of the 1960s, these business projections and expansions were perhaps somebody else's business. Besides the Vietnamese politicians and military, there were at least two other state entities that we must consider in relation to the maintenance and expansion of the opium business: the 'quiet' Americans, who couldn't help being dragged in, and certain key elements in the Lao military (but not all, as we shall see) who were more than happy to emerge as tall poppies in a competitive industry.

The Lao Military

Rather like Paraguay, Laos was run by men who cared not, at least in the early 1960s, that its main business was illicit. If the South American country gained the label 'Paraguay Incorporated' because of it, then Laos might also be thought of at this time as incorporated, through its leaders, into the opium and heroin business.

A typical Lao military opium mission could be seen as a model for the CIA's own narco entanglement in Nicaragua two decades later in that it was often an arms-for-drugs deal. It might entail a C-47 flying from Vientiane to Ban Houei Sai, where military hardware would be transferred to an Air Force helicopter that would then fly to a rendezvous on the Burmese side of the Mekong river. The packages of opium wouldn't necessarily come back with the helicopters but might instead have been sent ahead by boat to Ban Houei Sai, where the Dakota would be waiting to transport them to Vientiane and thence, by Lao or Vietnamese air supply, to Saigon.

The tallest poppy was undoubtedly General Ouane Rattikone, the head of the armed forces, who had a particular interest in the Air Force because here was the transport logistic for his opium operation. It didn't go all his way at first. Ouane's main problem was a lack of transport aircraft to fulfil his ambitious smuggling plans because most were occupied in fighting both the civil war and the broader regional conflict against communist forces. In the course of putting into action his great opium-smuggling plan Ouane (Lao generally use the first name in formal address) ran up against heroic and unusually principled resistance – in the Lao echelons of power that is – in the form of Brigadier General Thao Ma.

Thao was a fanatical and dedicated airman who as a part of his battle to stem a tide of incursion showed great attention to detail regarding his equipment. For instance, he converted a C-47 into a flying ordnance platform, thus paralleling the development of that other Dakota gunship, the AC-47. He refused a bribe from Ouane and one of his cronies, General Kouprasith Abhay, to lend them two C-47s for their smuggling business. The Brigadier General was committed to leading air strikes on the Ho

North American T-28D Trojan in Southeast Asia, similar to ones flown
by Brigadier General Thao Ma and his rebellious pilots.

Chi Minh Trail and in supporting the CIA's secret army and could not
spare any aircraft, even if he felt so inclined.[9]

Ouane attempted to rid himself of his dedicated warrior by taking
away his transport aircraft division and sending him, with his remaining
T-28 fighter-bomber section, into internal exile at Savannakhet in the
south, near the border with Thailand. Feeling cornered, Thao responded
on 22 October 1966 by taking a flight of ten raiders, bombing his bosses
in Vientiane and then, on failing to precipitate a coup, flying into exile
in Thailand. Ouane thus prevailed.

There was one more event before the general ascended to the pinnacle
of this 1960s Golden Triangle trade. This was the so-called 'Opium
War' of 1967. This time, far from merely seeing off his enemies, he
acted offensively and decisively.

The 1967 Opium War

This battle (not really a war) was little more than a flash in the pan in
the context of fighting in Indochina at the time, not least in Laos, but
it was very significant in terms of a shift in the geopolitics of opium
smuggling.

Trouble had been brewing for a number of weeks after the
Kuomintang got wind of a massive caravan carrying 16 tons of opium,
guarded by 500 armed men, heading towards Laos: this was the young,
ambitious warlord Khun Sa. They sensed a usurper in waiting and

wanted to crush this upstart rival. The caravan made its way down from the Wa States in Burma and soon the Kuomintang were on its tail. Neither of these protagonists showed much respect for territorial sovereignty as they came to the Mekong river from the west; they crossed into Laos near to Moung Muonge and headed south following the course of the river. They converged at the small lumber town of Ban Kwan some 25 miles further on, still on the banks of the Mekong, where Laos, Thailand and Burma meet (near the opium-refining centre of Ban Houei Sai). The Shan States, the heartland of Golden Triangle cultivation, lay off to the west while just over the river, to the south, was Thailand. But this was not a Thai trajectory: it was a contest to control the southeastern smuggling corridor through Laos and down to Saigon.

As the old and new guards of Golden Triangle opium trafficking squared up they expected a winner-takes-all outcome. This is sort of the way it turned out, but not at all as either side had expected. Ouane, associate and business partner in the opium trade to all suppliers, bombed them both. They limped back to Burma – Khun Sa's grand plan set back a decade or so and the Kuomintang bloodied, but at least still in charge of Shan State production.

Ouane now had full control of the southeastern route and the river regained some significance as a frontier. The bombing had signalled an unequivocal statement of intent, although Ouane did at least now try to keep a lower profile in the trade, conscious of how it all looked to the international community. One aspect of this was that he asked the smugglers from the Shan States to unload their caravans on the Burmese side of the Mekong. Despite his reclusion, however, his importance as a state potentate orchestrating the illicit opium trade did not diminish until his retirement in 1971.

The CIA's Airline

In August 1950 General Claire Chennault, the founder and leader of the famous 'Flying Tigers', an irregular air force operating for Chiang Kai-shek against the Japanese during the Second World War and later against the communists in China, sold his airline, Civil Air Transport (CAT – it had emerged out of his demobilized Chinese fighting force), to the CIA for $950,000. It was the beginning of a network of 'proprietary' aviation companies that would do the agency's dirty work for the next 35 to 40 years.[10] CAT later became Air America (at the end of the 1950s), whose unofficial motto 'anything, anywhere, anytime' has taken on a more sinister turn with the widespread belief that this 'anything' had quite often meant opium. Over the years this myth has grown and was stretched out to dry in the Hollywood movie *Air America* (1990), but what truth is there in it?

The story of CAT/Air America has undoubtedly been a colourful one, and rather than answering this question immediately, we should perhaps trace the circumstances of its involvement in a war that for a long time, officially at least, did not exist. Such secrecy, and its deployment in a country, Laos, that clearly did have an opium-smuggling culture, goes some way to explaining the presumption that Air America was a contraband carrier. But then again, 'anything, anywhere' could also imply a tactic of simply not asking any questions. Regardless, given the clandestine, un-acknowledged nature of so much of what Air America was doing in Laos, wasn't it at almost all times acting *like* a smuggling operation? Again, this doesn't prove anything, but let's follow this path anyway.

The Secret War

In the early 1960s Air America wasn't the only CIA proprietary airline involved in clandestine activity. For Project Haylift, initiated in 1961, a company called Vietnam Air Transport (VIAT), listed in Washington under the front name Aviation Investors, smuggled Vietnamese agents back to their native North Vietnam following training in Saigon. Often they would take in tons of arms and equipment as well.

It was the secret war in Laos, though, for which Air America seemed ideally made. The definitive history of this clandestine conflict, which also provides a broader account of the worldwide geopolitics of heroin, is Alfred W. McCoy's *The Politics of Heroin*. The involvement of intelligence agencies, warlords, generals and paramilitary forces in an opium-financed war made for a very good story. However, this book was almost not published because of CIA attempts at censorship during the early 1970s. Nevertheless it was always going to come out eventually and was most definitely in the public interest given that it proved to be a dress rehearsal for what happened later on, more cynically, in Central America with the Reagan administration's support for the Nicaraguan Contras. One might call this development a shift from the illicit to the illegal, from the secretive to the utterly denied. (That story is for the next chapter.)

In 1960 the CIA began supporting a Royal Lao army officer and ethnic Hmong, Vang Pao, to unite Hmong clans in a war against the communists that continued until 1974, although largely in retreat in the final years. The war mainly took place in the mountains around the Plain of Jars, in particular in the northeast in the beautiful part of Laos where the old salt and rice smuggling trails lead down to Dien Bien Phu. The CIA–Hmong alliance was able to take advantage of the chaos that ensued in the country as it slipped into civil war following a coup in 1960. Hmong, also called Meo (sometimes pejoratively so by metropolitan Laotians and Burmese), were at home in these harsh uplands of knife-edge ridges and jungle and moved freely, as they always had, with little respect for borders. It was a guerrilla army, although its skirmishing was often supported by U.S. air strikes.

In the first years of the decade the war went quite well despite the U.S. having to withdraw from the country under the terms of a 1962 U.S.–Soviet peace accord designed to relieve Cold War tensions. In reality their strategy was little dented by this as its operations largely consisted of air supply and clandestine on-the-ground direction, most of which could be conducted from the new CIA base at Udorn in northern Thailand. It ran its most secret missions out of Tahkli airbase in central Thailand. The U2 and later the SR-71 Blackbird reconnaissance planes also flew from here. From Udorn Air America delivered 'humanitarian aid' (the same designation used in Nicaragua two decades later) to their proxy army. They returned most days by helicopter or light aircraft to direct guerrilla operations, often dropping 'hard rice' – arms and munitions.

In fact the CIA had remarkably few agents on the ground, although at least three of them were extraordinarily effective in the early years, as was Vang Pao. The first of these was William Young, whose father, in earlier decades, had been a CIA operative in the Shan States of Burma. William spoke five local languages. In this respect he was another in a long line of Orientalist interloper-enthusiasts in the region, in a lineage that might include the tea smuggler Robert Fortune and the writer and antiquities trafficker André Malraux, but even Young's grandfather had been a missionary there and so he was much more embedded.

Anthony Poshepny – Tony Poe – was a Second World War veteran of the Pacific theatre. In some ways his attitude mirrored that of the agency as a whole in that he tolerated opium harvesting and heroin pro-duction just so long as it wasn't in his face, and he saw its benefits in holding together the secret army whose main cash crop was opium. He was married to a Hmong princess, the daughter of a Yau leader. Some have made comparisons between his intense means of warfare, for instance taking trophy ears, and the cult of personality around Kurtz as portrayed in the film *Apocalypse Now* (1979), Francis Ford Coppola's adaptation of Joseph Conrad's novella *Heart of Darkness*.

The third wasn't actually CIA at all. Edgar 'Pop' Buell came to Indochina as a farmer, Christian and humanitarian volunteer (part of the International Voluntary Service) but soon became involved in the secret war. Among other services, he provided the agricultural skills to help the Hmong produce a better opium crop. However, Buell was not simply an agrarian technician: he trained the Hmong in explosives techniques and organized the dynamiting of six bridges and twelve mountain pass trails.[11] It was he who discovered the almost uninhabited Long Tieng mountain basin, where the CIA established a settlement larger than Laos's second city. Vang Pao moved in and Poe took charge from the agency point of view. Buell, not wanting to be cramped, moved 19 km up the trail to Sam Thong.

The Hmong, primarily fighters, would not have thought of themselves as smugglers although Vang Pao undoubtedly became one, setting up his own heroin lab at Long Tieng in the early 1970s. Supply of opium to market could not have occurred the way it did without Air America help.

Air America

Pilots of this most famous of the CIA-connected airlines would never have, to co-opt Saint-Exupéry's phrase, 'refused to form a rescue party'. Certainly they were mercenary, but as Christopher Robbins tells us in his riveting book *Air America: The Explosive True Story of the CIA's Secret Airline*, they were also extraordinarily courageous in supplying, supporting and occasionally evacuating the Hmong army and their own compatriots fighting in northeastern Laos. They operated under the most extreme and difficult of flying conditions.

The ground for their heroics was prepared by the CIA men and their proxy army. Young recruited a team of Shan and Lahu lieutenants, known as the 'Sixteen Musketeers', who organized and built small bases and their runways, constructing around twenty of them. Meanwhile Buell worked around the periphery of the Plain of Jars organizing relief, operating at first in parallel and then in conjunction with Poe and Vang Pao's guerrilla units. By the end of 1963 the Americans/Hmong had taken all the ridges for their airstrips. It was a claustrophobic inhabitation: the terrain was knotted and creviced allowing for close-quarter presence of opposing sides – the CIA ran an Air America supply base at Hong Non just 12 miles distant from the Pathet Lao headquarters.

Trees were cut down and ridges planed off. They became known as 'Helio' strips after the aircraft that made such rudimentary runways possible in the first place, and the bases of which they were a part were called 'Lima' sites. They were strung together in a line linking up with Long Tieng.

However, it was one thing to build these strips and another to land the Helio Courier and Pilatus Porter aircraft on them, even if they had impressive low-speed landing and stopping capability. They were often extremely hazardous. The one at Phong Saly, considered the worst, had tigers roaming around it at night. It was about 180 m long, but was only straight for 60 m of it. In fact runways were rarely straight: 15- to 20-degree kinks were typical and they often sloped lengthways. Flying in Laos was more dangerous than in Vietnam because there at least the perimeters of the airfields were guarded. It was best to land in the early morning or evening when there were fewer thermals.

The Hmong relied on Air America for sustenance through staples that the fighters no longer had time to grow, particularly rice. The supply and collection operation went some way to uniting the scattered clans, but it also meant that there were empty planes that could carry opium out. The Air America aircraft were certainly in a position to carry the harvests, vital after the communist Pathet Lao rebels took control of the Plain of Jars, pushing air operations up onto the surrounding ridges. Air America had the advantage over the Lao air force in that, after the plain became a more serious battleground in 1964 (the Pathet Lao captured it that year) and 1965, it was only they who could operate the ridge-top air strips in the mountains around the plain that were too small for the national air force's C-47s. There is little doubt that Air America did fly opium from north and east of the Plain of Jars to Long Tieng between 1965 and 1971 and sometimes wholesale. (The 1970 and 1971 opium harvests were flown down to Long Tieng in Air America helicopters.) But were the pilots and crew in on the trade or was it collateral activity?

Often pilots would transport boxes without knowing precisely what was inside them. On the other hand Air America had been known to fly Hmong merchants to villages where they bought up opium harvests.[12]

Of course this might simply suggest that this was part of a tactical plan to keep the Hmong happy and on-side – what the CIA might consider a necessary evil. It doesn't implicate Air America in some kind of smuggling conspiracy. We might leave that accusation for an analysis of American involvement in Central America.

It was certainly never a stated policy to carry opium or heroin. To the contrary, responding to the adage that there is no smoke without fire, the company did eventually try to screen itself from the trade. Following this policy, in 1967 Vang Pao was given funds to purchase two C-47s, one from Air America and the other from Continental Air Services,[13] thereby setting up his own business, Xieng Khouang Air Transport, on which he could transport his opium between Long Tieng and Vientiane. Bizarrely it even had a contract for flying around personnel of the Bureau of Narcotics and Dangerous Drugs (which later became the DEA) and cooperated in anti-drugs operations.

There were probably in reality very few narcotics smugglers per se among the pilots, even if large profits could be had taking opium as far as Taiwan or Hong Kong. In any case conditions for smuggling gradually worsened. In January 1968 the advantage in the secret war swung the way of the Pathet Lao after the fall of Sam Neua in the hills to the northeast of the Plain of Jars and just 27 km (17 miles) from North Vietnam. With it went the CIA's key signals redoubt, Lima Site 85 (LS-85), at Phou Pha Thi, essential for guiding bombing raids on Hanoi and the Red River Delta. Air America now became vital for evacuations. Just as CAT evacuated the Kuomintang to Taiwan after Mao Zedong's triumph in 1949, so now Air America airlifted 9,000 Hmong out of Sam Neua over a period of two weeks.

Another ferocious year of action in the region was 1970. As the ridges around the Plain of Jars were taken, and the plain and its environs became one of the hottest combat spots on earth, Air America gradually shrank as a quasi-military force and it eventually abandoned some 300 airstrips. As Long Tieng was taken and Vientiane threatened, Laos, from an American point of view, was in serious disarray, not least because much of the southern part of the country was now a part of the great sinuous logistical supply territory known as the Ho Chi Minh Trail. Air America pilots, even if they were smugglers in a certain way (although not as Antoine de Saint-Exupéry saw such men), continued their 'rescue missions' until almost the end.[14] Vang Pao was evacuated to Thailand by the CIA and later travelled to the U.S. which, contentiously, abandoned most of its other loyal Hmong to their fate. With the Paris Peace Accord of 1973 Air America handed over many of its aircraft to the Lao government.

The Golden Triangle, needless to say, lost little of its allure; on maps its arrow to the south simply grew a little wider.

PURSUING THE ARTERIAL FLOWS of opium out of the Golden Triangle eventually leads us to heroin injected into American veins on the streets of New York and Los Angeles. This was a substantial side-effect of the wars in Indochina. In 1969 President Richard Nixon made a declaration prioritizing a 'war on drugs'. The war on drugs, as a crusade, later gave way to the 'war on terror', but for a time there was a focus on a combination of the two menaces. This super-alliance of 'narco-terrorism' may just have been a wishful figment of somebody's paranoid imagination, a justification for intensifying the military expenditure during the Cold War for instance, but as a scare tactic it had power nonetheless.

Playing the fear card was made easier by the proximity to America of the threat: South America already had a reputation as another fount of drugs supply. A succession of right-wing coups and military dictatorships appeared to stem any communist tide, but nevertheless places like Colombia were held up as the main enemies in the war on drugs, although Colombia's terrain of mountains and jungles looked extremely daunting – in fact, rather like that of Indochina, where the terrain had proved to be a natural ally for the communists.

However the Cold War needed another theatre of conflict and the pilots of Air America another contract. Central America, the 'backyard' of the United States, awaited them. Narco-terrorism would provide the excuse and some of the old aircraft were recommissioned. Smuggling skills learned in Laos proved very useful in another proxy war that took place, at least in part, still deeper in the shadows.

SEVENTEEN

COLD WAR
CONTRADICTIONS

*Flying into a Storm in
Central America*

On 17 July 1984 the *Washington Times*, a right-wing daily newspaper set up a couple of years before, published a story that put
the spectre of a 'narco-guerrilla' firmly on the agenda of American
foreign policy. The story revolved around photographs apparently
showing Nicaraguan Sandinista revolutionaries at a small airport near
to the capital city Managua helping senior Colombian drug cartel
members load packages of cocaine onto an American aircraft. It was
an undercover sting operation designed specifically to prove the connection between drug smugglers and guerrillas, even terrorists. This
was a new threat, an implied connection between communism and a
'narco' scourge, and the Reagan administration that had leaked the
photos could now justify its support for the Nicaraguan Contras
against the Sandinistas.

The story looked pretty convincing, if a little convenient. For the
American pilot involved, Barry Seal, a veteran of the Vietnamese and
Laotian wars, its effects were not anticipated. The aeroplane was fitted
out with hidden cameras, and the appearance of the pictures effectively
proved to be his death warrant. He was assassinated by gunmen dispatched by the Medellín Cartel in February 1986 in Baton Rouge,
Louisiana, where he was living under nominal state protection.

'Narco-terrorism' is another term, coined originally by President
Fernando Belaúnde Terry of Peru during the early 1980s, to describe a
supposed link between drug cartels and the Shining Path (*Sendero
Luminoso*) Maoist terrorists fighting a revolutionary war in that country,
which continued effectively until its leader, Comrade Gonzalo (Abimael
Guzmán Reynoso), was captured in 1992. Around the same time the
U.S. ambassador to Colombia used the term 'narco-guerrilla' for the first

time, to much the same effect, and for the same reasons only relating to the more northerly country.

Barry Seal, on the other hand, was never so preachy. Besides his work in the secretive theatre of war of Laos, where there had been a discernible trafficking mindset, he had been involved in CIA-backed ventures in Guatemala and Cuba, but more recently had become a smuggler himself. It would be going too far to call him a narco-guerrilla, but he certainly seemed to circulate in that kind of world. If we were to overstep the mark and call him some kind of narco-insurgent or mercenary terrorist, wouldn't we also be suggesting that his dealings with his employers, the CIA, the DEA and even the American government, implicated these organizations in something close to narco-terrorism?

Unthinkable, of course: no one would characterize the Laotian secret war as a narco-insurgency simply because the transportation of opium was the price to be paid for the effectiveness of CIA operations against communism. So why does so much suspicion continue to surround CIA involvement in Central America? What is so different about the CIA in this part of the world? One reason might be because there seem to have been a lot more out-and-out narcotics smugglers hanging around America's backing of the Contras than there ever were in their support for the Hmong army in Southeast Asia.

However, on that day in July 1984, as President Reagan paraded the photographs on national television, the propaganda was working: the Iran-Contra scandal (weapons to Iran in exchange for movement on the release of American hostages in Lebanon, and slush money accrued redirected towards the Contras) was still a couple of years away. There was no real sense of an impending storm: but there probably should have been.

I once flew into Managua airport in a small passenger aircraft after a few days working in the Corn Islands some 50 miles from the mainland, and experienced a dramatic change in the weather. I was sitting right behind the pilots and so could see out of the front windscreen. I was surprised that it weaved around the clouds avoiding trouble rather than going through them like an airliner. Maybe it was simply because of my position almost in the cockpit that I actually noticed this path of avoidance – usually I would only have been able to see to the sides. The clouds looked a bit daunting: certainly they were rain clouds, but they weren't identifiable to me as storm clouds. As we made our final approach to the airport we could see that the far end of the airfield was being ravaged by a fierce ground-hugging storm that was unfurling our way, directly down the runway, like a carpet being rolled out. The pilots consulted with each other but then, with only a moment's hesitation, went in for the landing. We were on the ground for no more than a couple of seconds before it swept over us. On the way into the city the taxi driver had to make his own choices as to whether or not to take on streets flooded up to a metre in depth. We got stuck in the floods.

It seems to me that this could stand as a metaphor for CIA and, to a lesser extent, U.S. government involvement with the Hmong in Laos and then with the Contras in Central America. They got away with some pretty dubious stuff for a long time, even surviving a certain amount of close scrutiny of their activities, dodging a few dark clouds, but sooner or later they would be held accountable for their increasingly outlandish practices.

How could they have manoeuvred themselves into such a precarious position? How is it that now they seemed to operate with such a sense of impunity, as if this were a Cold War melodrama to end all such theatricalities, and as if any kind of tactic were legitimate? If we go back to a term sometimes employed in regard to Central America we can start to get an idea of the periodic simplicity of the U.S. approach to inter-American relations. A lasting designation of what a Central American country might be came from an American writer, O. Henry (William Sydney Porter), in 1904 in his book *Cabbages and Kings*, when he described the fictional country of Anchuria (based on Honduras) as a 'banana republic' (largely because foreign fruit companies ran the place). This term swiftly became common parlance around the world: Joseph Conrad's fictional country of Costaguana in his novel *Nostromo*, published in the same year, gives us another florid stereotype of a bossed but also revolutionary Latin American country. The subsequent history of CIA involvement in coups in places like Guatemala suggests that they too rode on the back of the power and influence of the fruit companies. When presidents and diplomats come up with terms like 'narco-terrorist', 'narco-guerrilla' and more recently 'narco-insurgent',[1] it is easy for us to think simply: banana republic.

Of course this leads to a somewhat entrenched way of thinking – that for instance these are simply narco states whose melodramatic villains are the new foe. We might well buy some of this Manichaean war on drugs/war on terror rhetoric, except that the nagging question doesn't go away: why does the dirt stick regarding accusations of the

CIA relationship with drug smugglers in Central America while it didn't seem to in Southeast Asia?

Well, one answer perhaps comes out of this narco way of thinking. When there is some truth to a stereotype, when countries like Mexico, Honduras, Costa Rica, Panama, Venezuela, Colombia, Peru and Bolivia have all been effectively run at one time or another by drug traffickers or politicians and security chiefs associated with them, the CIA might also have been tempted to participate in this selfsame melodrama. It could be that it made Faustian bargains with many of these perceived narco cultures and characters in order to continue its war on communism. In terms of the broad narrative of this book, it might be that in order to dance with a smuggler one must become a smuggler oneself.

Before examining this proposition we need to map out something of the history of the cocaine smuggling that has so dominated the northern imaginary of the Americas south of the Rio Grande.

The Narco Theatre of the Americas

Many of us have heard something of the Medellín and Cali cartels of Colombia, in particular figures like Pablo Escobar Gavíria and Carlos Lehder Rivas during the 1980s and early 1990s, and that the Cali Cartel by keeping its head down eventually did much better than its rival; both of them, though, in terms of profile and profits, have apparently been superseded by the Mexican cartels who have gone from middlemen to controllers of the industry. But the story goes further back than this, and almost from the beginning Mexico and Central America were involved.

One of the early Colombian suppliers with a Mexican and Central American connection was Santiago Ocampo Zuluaga (part of the early Cali connection). After running his cocaine through the domain of the apparently complicit Panamanian General Omar Torrijos Herrera,[2] he supplied Honduran Juan Ramón Matta Ballesteros before it was 'trampolined' into the United States by the Cuban exile Alberto Sicilia Falcón, who was based in Tijuana. Sicilia was well connected: he knew Mexican president Luis Echeverría Álvarez's wife and enjoyed protection from Miguel Nazar Haro, who ran the intelligence service, the Dirección Federal de Seguridad (DFS). Both Nazar and Sicilia had connections with the CIA. Matta supplied Sicilia during the early 1970s and afterwards fed cocaine to the earliest of the really big Mexican traffickers, Miguel

Ángel Félix Gallardo, leader of the Guadalajara Cartel. Matta himself enjoyed a certain immunity from indictment by the Americans, partly perhaps because he used to supply the Honduras-based Nicaraguan Contras, the Fuerza Democratico de Nicaragua (FDN), until, that is, he outlived his usefulness.

During the 1970s and '80s there was plenty of cocaine capital in politics. There were the so-called 'cocaine coups' in Honduras in 1978 (supported by Matta) and in Bolivia in 1980.[3] In Peru a decade later the military were happy to protect the cocaine trade, as were the security services of President Fujimori's right-hand man, the mysterious Vladimiro Montesinos Torres – who, it has emerged, is a cousin of one of the so-called narco-terrorists, Óscar Ramírez Durand or 'Comrade Feliciano', a Shining Path leader. Manuel Noriega Moreno was almost as Machiavellian, and his connections with the Medellín Cartel are well documented, although his links to the CIA are a little less so. The Nicaraguan dictator Anastasio Somoza Debayle, around whom the Central American theatre of Cold War initially unfolded, had made aeroplanes available to an American marijuana smuggler involved in an Honduran seafood company.

The Mexican cartels are known for their violence, and to a certain extent for their style. Culiacan in Sinaloa state, the city most associated with the growth of the cartels, is the SUV capital of Mexico and it has streets of showy mansions, a narco cinema industry and a thriving ballad culture in the *narco-corrido*. But cocaine-funded opulence is certainly not exclusive to the obvious participants: it is sometimes reflected in those who are supposed to be their opposite – fearsome security chiefs and politicians who look like mild accountants. The administration of President Carlos Salinas de Gortari (1988–94) has long been associated with cocaine corruption, and his older brother, Raúl, was later jailed for charges related to his amassing an unaccountable fortune and hiding it away in Swiss bank accounts. A succession of drug czars, supposedly fighting drug trafficking, have also proved less than squeaky clean.[4]

U.S. drug enforcement officers have often defined themselves in opposition to this perceived sleaze. The Drug Enforcement Agency (DEA) is generally considered pretty dedicated to its task, the heir to Eliot Ness's Untouchables of the American Prohibition era. But the CIA has never enjoyed this reputation and this is partly down to some of its associates.

Let's go back to this spectre/problem of narco-terrorism to see just how improbable it is that the agency would ever appear whiter than white beside Latin America's dark stereotype. In setting up its supply operation to the Contras, American covert agencies – CIA and parts of the military – relied heavily on Cuban exiles, many of whom had links to, or carried out, cocaine smuggling. One might claim that this is no more and no less 'involved' than working with the opium-trading Hmong in Laos. But some of the Cubans had an even more murky past, belonging to some extremely dubious organizations, such as the Cuban Nationalist Movement, which was linked to the right-wing death squads of DINA, the Chilean secret police. One of the fringe platforms for America's Cold War politics was also pretty dodgy: it was the World Anti-Communism League, led ideologically by militarist elements from Argentina's dictatorship and the El Salvadorian extreme right. Some of the CIA allies in the Central American mission had been members of the Comando de Organizaciones Revolucionarias Unidas, effectively a terrorist movement which bombed, kidnapped and assassinated as part of an armed struggle against communism. Were not these CIA affiliate Cubans simply semi-retired terrorists who could now add narcotics smuggling to their CVs?

Nevertheless the CIA appeared to have risen above this villainy; until, that is, its secret war came out into the open with an unexpected event. Some seven and a half months after the assassination of Barry Seal, on 5 October 1986, the Sandinistas shot down a C-123 aircraft owned by Southern Air Transport, the CIA's former air proprietary company. It was the same aeroplane that Seal had flown into Nicaragua and that had been part of the narco-terrorist sting, although this fact indicates little more than that this particular aircraft had had an interesting life. The pilot, William Cooper, and co-pilot, Wallace 'Buzz' Sawyer, died in the crash, but the kicker (the crew-member who kicks the goods out of the back of the aircraft), Eugene Hasenfus, escaped by parachute and was taken into captivity. He was later put on trial by the Sandinistas. It was this that precipitated the Iran-Contra scandal. It also led to Senator John Kerry's report, researched between 1986 and 1989, on the relationship between American agencies and the drug trade, and this is what exposed the detail and extent of the CIA operation in Central America and its entanglement with smuggling. Basically, on impact, it opened up a whole can of worms.

All of the crew had flown for Air America in Laos. They were delivering hard rice again: the Sandinistas discovered on board 70 automatic rifles, 100,000 rounds of ammunition and seven grenade launchers along with an Air America operating manual.

The crash revealed that once again, it seems, the old aviation firm ('anything, anywhere, anytime') had been reincarnated. But what the report demonstrated as well was the complexity of the air operations on which smuggling depended: as Alfred W. McCoy puts it in comparing heroin trails around this time in Afghanistan with these cocaine paths in South and Central America: 'Deciding who controlled what aircraft in the cat's cradle of trans-Caribbean airlanes was far more complex.'[5]

Stretching Out the Cat's Cradle: Operation Condor

One earlier air strategy that seemed on the face of it to be fairly straight-forward was Operation Condor, the campaign of aerial spraying of marijuana crops, as well as some opium, in the mountains of (mainly) Culiacan and Sonora in Mexico in 1975. Mexican pilots were trained for the task by Evergreen International Aviation in a deal arranged by two CIA members, one of whom had flown in Laos. In all some 76 aircraft were supplied by the U.S. Evergreen had just recently taken over Intermountain Aviation, a CIA-run air operation that had acted as a front for some of the CIA proprietary companies in Southeast Asia. Aircraft were serviced and maintained by E-Systems, which had taken over Air Asia (the massive Taiwan-based servicing operation for Air America) and still had three high-ranking CIA men on its board. Despite privatization these were incestuous networks and there continued to be layering of one front, or dummy company, on top of another.

It is possible that the entire operation was a sham. In 1978 the Mexican authorities refused to allow Americans to fly over the eradication zone to verify results. It is probable that either many fields had been sprayed with water or that herbicides were jettisoned outside of the target zone, over the desert. Alternatively the same zones were hit over and over again, sometimes as show but certainly, after the first time, with very little added effect. And if there was damage it did not touch the important players, such as Tijuana-based Sicilia, who bribed the spraying force to focus its efforts onto the fields of his Sinaloan rivals. These competitors were subsequently pushed out of the state down to Guadalajara, although there to regroup and re-align their forces, emerging as much bigger players when they returned to the northern states. This was the beginning of the cartels in Mexico.

Ominously for the story of CIA entanglement in Central America, by the early 1980s airstrips in Honduras and Costa Rica had become key drug transhipment points en route to Mexico and the U.S.

The Aerial Networks of the Cartels and their Associates

The Central American connection was always predominantly an aviation one, although it was initially all about narcos gaining influence in or over scheduled airlines. Take the case of former Honduran president General Oswaldo López Arrellano, who was overthrown in 1975 by one of his subordinates, Humberto Regalado Lara, who was later arrested in 1988 for importing cocaine. López nevertheless retired from politics a wealthy man, becoming head of the national airline Tan-Sahsa, the carrier of Regalado's cocaine to the U.S. No hard feelings, it seems, or at least profit trumps all.

Another smuggler-infiltrated airline operated through Panama: Aerolineas Medellín (actually based in Cali), owned by Hugo Torrijos (Omar's brother) and Ocampo. The Cali Cartel shipped cocaine and cash in the nose cones of Eastern Airlines aircraft between 1984 and 1986, made possible through bribing middle management. One of the most famous members of the more recent cartel, Gilberto Rodríguez Orejuela, owned his own airline.

The cocaine transit business received a great boost after Manuel Noriega entered the trade following the death of Torrijos in a mysterious plane crash in 1981. During his most profitable years as a provider of transit bases for gold, arms and drugs, Noriega was on the CIA payroll, in 1985 alone receiving $200,000.[6]

The American marijuana smuggler Steven Kalish, who came to possess a Panamanian diplomatic passport, was pivotal at the beginning, forging a relationship with the Medellín Cartel after he facilitated the release of some of their number in Panama. Noriega ran a team consisting of at least five mercenary pilots who carried out his bidding during the early years of his sub-state activities. These included Enrique Pretelt, Costa Rican Werner Lotz, César Rodríguez (Noriega's personal pilot), Teofilo Watson and Floyd Carlton. It was a dangerous business even without heat from the DEA: Watson was murdered in May 1985 and Rodríguez the following year. On one occasion a load went missing and the Medellín Cartel went looking for Watson and Carlton, kidnapping the former's wife and children. When Watson was murdered, suspicion fell on a rancher, Carlos Eduardo Zapporolli Zecca, who was in equal proportions a smuggler and supplier of arms to the Contras. The load was probably diverted to fund Contra activities for whom Zapporolli was a key advocate.

Floyd Carlton was perhaps the most entrepreneurial among these smugglers, possibly benefiting from an oblique relationship with the CIA. It seems that Carlton's flights were not checked at Florida airports, on the orders of the U.S. authorities. He was a business associate of Alfredo Caballero, a Cuban Bay of Pigs veteran and now owner of DIACSA, an aeroplane dealership used by the agency. Carlton was finally arrested in 1986 after being informed upon by Caballero who was looking for a lighter sentence on a charge following the downing of one of their aircraft in Florida on 23 September 1985. In January 1987 the Costa Rican authorities sentenced him to nine years in jail.[7]

And then there was Barry Seal, whose smuggling career, as we know, came to an equally untimely end. Adler Barry Seal was a superb pilot who had flown in Vietnam with Special Forces. Later, on turning smuggler and furnished with aircraft bought from Air America and Southern Air Transport, he imported cocaine from Honduras, mainly for the Medellín Cartel, making drops onto the ranch in southeastern U.S. that he ran with his brother Wendell. His headquarters was at Mena in the Ouachita Mountains of western Arkansas.

In May 1983 he ran into trouble with the U.S. authorities and tried to become a DEA informant to avoid a prison sentence, but was rebuffed. It was not long, however, before he succeeded in forging relations with the DEA after appealing directly to Vice President Bush's office. It was the deal with the DEA that led to the sting operation but, crucially, the CIA, who were in any case involved (they provided the cameras, fitting them inside the nose and at the rear of Seal's C-123), seem to have hijacked the import of the story, turning it into a strategy justification. The photos taken on 25 June 1984 became an attempt by the Reagan administration to project the phantom menace of a narco–guerrilla alliance, verging on narco–terrorism, in order to influence public opinion as well as an imminent vote on Congressional aid to the Contras.

It focused on the Medellín Cartel, and came soon after the raid, in 1984, on Tranquilandia, a large cocaine processing lab in the Colombian jungle that had demonstrated just how organized the narcos were. The details of the sting go like this.[8] On 28 May 1984 Seal and his co-pilot Emile Camp flew to Colombia, setting up a deal with the Ochoa brothers.

However, the aircraft that he was using, a Lockheed Lodestar, was damaged in the pick-up operation after he slid off a mud strip in heavy rain. Borrowing another aeroplane, a Titan 404, he set off for home but was forced to land and refuel in Nicaragua as this aircraft had a more limited range. He took off again but was shot at and forced to land. He claimed that on 25 June he flew back in a C-123 ('Fat Lady') in order to retrieve the load from an airstrip, Los Brasiles just outside Managua, that was mainly used by crop dusters, although the Reagan administration claimed that it was a military airbase.

A lot of smoke surrounds the authenticity of these photographs that supposedly showed the connection between Colombian traffickers and Sandinistas, all in shot as the aircraft is being loaded. Did the photos really show all or any of the infamous cartel leaders Pablo Escobar, José Gonzalo Rodríguez Gacha and Jorge Luis Ochoa Vásquez, alongside Sandinista contact Federico Vaughan Loredo, as was claimed at the time? Some have even suggested that the scene might have been staged in the Corn Islands![9]

The DEA, which perhaps simply wanted evidence as part of an ongoing investigation, were undermined by the premature exposure of the photographs. They were leaked officially by General Paul Gorman of the U.S. Southern Command in Panama, but passed to him, according to the DEA, by Lieutenant Colonel Oliver North. On 17 July the *Washington Times* made the story available to the world.

The instrumental role of the CIA and its military men on the ground in a smuggling operation does not seem to have caused too much of a stir in 1984 – perhaps after years of agency work in the Golden Triangle of Southeast Asia, it wasn't much of a surprise that it was now working in the cocaine sector. The downing of the same aeroplane a couple of years later revealed a whole lot more. So what exactly were the clandestine crusaders (Oliver North, Richard Secord, the CIA's Robert Owen and others) and their new proxy army, the Contras, up to in Central America during those years?

The Contras

In 1973 President Richard Nixon created the DEA in order to bring into focus the war on drugs that he had declared in 1969. It was an attempt to even things up, to pit 'narc' (prevention) against narco (smuggler). However, its effect back then had merely been to push out the

French-Latin connection, leaving space for the home-grown cartels. This is an example of the so-called balloon effect – when you pressure one part of a problem, it bulges in another. The difficulty with applying this truism in relation to Latin America from a U.S. point of view is that while the DEA were busy squeezing away at salient drugs issues all over Latin America, the CIA, focusing intently upon a perceived communist threat in Nicaragua, seemed quite happy to leave the cocaine bubble perfectly round, even blowing some of its own air into it. The Somoza-Sandinista-Contra war was, then, the loose knot in the centre of Central America where some of the old hands from Southeast Asia might once again ply their trade.

This new 'problem' for the Americans (a solution for some who were looking for new roles to justify their funding) intensified early on with the overthrow of the old dictator Somoza in July 1979. He fled to Miami and was then given asylum in Paraguay, where he was assassinated in September 1980. The Frente Sandinista de Liberación Nacional (FSLN), the Sandinistas, took over the country although the Contra movement (actually there were two – one based in Honduras and the other in Costa Rica) arose to challenge them.

The Costa Rican operation, the Frente Revolucionario Sandino (FRS, later evolving into the Alianza Revolucionaria Democrática – ARDE – after it allied with other southern Contra factions) was run by estranged Sandinista Edén Pastora Gómez. It initially had the backing of the CIA until support was withdrawn because it refused to subordinate itself to the Honduran Contras. This northern force, the Fuerza Democrática Nicaragüense (FDN), commanded by Enriqué Bermúdez Varela and composed largely of former Somozist National Guardsmen, was the preferred proxy army for the Americans, although they did maintain some interest in the Costa Rican front, at a remove, through the CIA-entangled smuggler Jorge Morales as well as a rancher, John Hull, who allowed his property to be used as a springboard for Contra supply. Hull was an American expat; a pilot, farmer and humanitarian (one is reminded of Edgar Buell in Laos, the aid worker/CIA fixer whose role was an interesting hybrid of agriculturalist and guerrilla) who was living in Costa Rica beside the Nicaraguan border. He liaised with the Contras and also with another force made up of Cuban Americans.

American aid became more organized with the emplacement of the 'Black Eagle' operation, set up in 1982 by the CIA director William Casey, to supply the Contras. Manuel Noriega was still on board the American freedom flight at this time, contributing to the cause, although his donations fell way short of the $10 million that Carlos Lehder claimed the Medellín Cartel paid to the Contras. For their part, the American military and CIA were eager to become involved on the ground.

American Logistics

Many of the American marijuana-smuggling operations in Latin America during the 1970s had counter-cultural rebellion at their roots (although of course this was secondary to making money). As such we might think of them as projecting the same pragmatic-romantic image as the Corsican Air Opium operation in its adventures in Laos between the mid-1950s and mid-1960s. In a similar vein, as in Robert Sabbag's book *Smokescreen*, there are stories like that of Allen Long, the dope smuggler subject of the book, who wrecks his rickety DC-3 on a dirt airstrip in the Guajira Peninsula. Although this precarious alternative path depended upon other less illusioned participants for supply of the goods, its mishaps were considered all part of life's adventure.

By contrast, the CIA air supply campaign, despite operating in a maelstrom, had more autonomy at ground level. It was basically a reasoned, some would say amoral, response to the impoverishment of its campaign chest after Congress cut off funding for the Contras. Its style and mission goals were much more Air America than Air Opium and it had similar ground support to that enjoyed by the former in Southeast Asia. Like the Air America campaign it was perceived as being part of another crucial episode in the Cold War, whereas Air Opium was much more about the opium. However, networks of drug smuggling seem to have been exploited for the cause more in Central America than in Southeast Asia. This meant, logistically, relying upon some extremely dubious suppliers.

The semi-official supplier for the Contras was Air Force General Richard Secord, who had taken early retirement after he was deemed to have become too close to CIA agent turned terrorist Ed Wilson, who was complicit in Colonel Gaddafi's attempts to make or procure nuclear weapons capability. Secord was a veteran of the Southeast Asian conflict, flying numerous combat missions in Vietnam and later on working towards the supply of the secret army in Laos. His involvement might have played out melodramatically during the inquiry into the Iran-Contra scandal in which he was labelled something of a villain, but given his patriotic motivation one certainly wouldn't call him particularly sinister (or even criminal) in the context of the Cold War.

Others were more mercenary. Israeli Mike Harari, ex-Mossad, was a kind of *éminence grise* to Manuel Noriega and between 1982 and 1986 supplied the CIA base at Ilopango with arms destined for the Contras. Jorge Krupnick was another Panama-based arms supplier who provided for Contra needs, mainly between 1982 and 1984 (at the time of the Black Eagle operation).[10] Like Harari, he probably got most of his arms on the black market in Eastern Europe. In a more patriotic (giving them the benefit of the doubt) vein, an American firm called R. M. Equipment, run by James McCoy and Ronald Martin, provided arms and combat supplies that were warehoused en route in the Honduran capital Tegucigalpa.[11]

Another species of supplier was the fundamentalist anti-communist. At the most extreme end of this mission we find the Cuban sometime terrorist group CORU supplying Edén Pastora with a DC-3 and possibly other aircraft as well. Rene Corvo, a Cuban exile, supplied weapons to the Contras via John Hull's ranch in March 1985.[12]

And then there were the smugglers. Michael Palmer, a former marijuana smuggler and occasional Noriega pilot, sold at least one aircraft, a DC-6, to a CIA-run company. Jorge Morales gave a DC-3 to pilot Marcos Aguado, Edén Pastora's air force chief. It was later transferred to the Honduras Contras after the break-up of Pastora's southern force.

Somewhere in between these categories of logistical supply there were those that defy characterization. Pat Foley, who may or may not have been a CIA agent, probably sold arms and planes to Somoza on behalf of the agency and, more certainly, supplied the Contras with three attack aircraft.[13]

Indeed the mercurial role and shape-shifting attributes of the smuggler/agent over the centuries seem to have reached full potential in the Central American conflict.

The Bases

At the centre of the airborne supply operation was Ilopango airbase in El Salvador. It was the hive of the queen bee, the CIA's airbase, and it mainly served the FRS (the Costa Rica-based Contra forces). Félix Rodríguez, who had been in Vietnam with Oliver North and who had been present at the execution of Che Guevara in 1967,[14] was in charge of Contra supply from the base. It had two CIA hangars and operated at least a couple of large transport aircraft, C-123s, one of which was dedicated for CIA and Contra use.[15] North also used it as his field HQ.

There were other airbases. Aguacate, the main FDN camp in Honduras near to the Nicaraguan border, was also the provisional base for an early aerial aid mission. As Christopher Robbins describes in his 2012 update to his 1979 book *Air America,* one of the veterans of the secret war in Laos, Ed Dearborn, tried to shake up this base by providing a helicopter, a Helio Courier and a Cessna. He also refitted a DC-3, which began making air drops.[16]

Honduran airbases at this time were teeming with military personnel, but in Costa Rica they were also a stopping-off point for smugglers. Contra camps allowed narco pilots to refuel. Several Contra supply pilots, such as Gerardo Duran, were also traffickers and they received logistical help on the ground.[17] For instance, Colonel Edwin Viales Rodriguez (a cohort of Zapporolli, the Panama-based smuggler who was accused of the murder of Noriega's pilot Teofilo Watson) tried to bribe a fellow officer in the Costa Rican rural guard to leave a covert Contra airstrip unguarded for two days each week.

The question, as it was with Air America, is to what extent the U.S. was directly involved in this aerial smuggling world. The term that Senator John Kerry used in his report was 'ticket-punching'[18] – the freedom given to contracted air transport operators who were allowed to operate to and from the United States unmolested, even if they were known or suspected cocaine smugglers. It was all because they were deemed to be invaluable links in the supply chain of arms and equipment to the Contras, even if those resources were bought with the proceeds of drug trafficking.

Who were these contractors?

Privatized Air Supply

Financial details of the covert operations in Laos never emerged whereas in Central America, as detailed in Peter Dale Scott and Jonathan Marshall's *Cocaine Politics,* the Kerry Report uncovered precise accounts. There were four companies, effectively privatized proprietaries, acting for the CIA, and they were given exactly $806,401.20 of State Department money for the dispensation of 'humanitarian aid'.[19] Three of these were aviation firms, while the fourth was a frozen seafood business. Each had some connection or other with cocaine smuggling or laundering of profits from it. The report, analysed by Scott and Marshall and others, provided the following accounting.[20]

SETCO was a Honduran airline set up in 1983, or at least used by the CIA from that year on. It was owned by that great cocaine capo Juan Ramón Matta Ballesteros. Barry Seal had links with it and Oliver North was the conduit for the funding ($186,000). It was used to supply the FDN (the Honduras-based Contras), particularly after Adolfo Calero Portocarrero, fresh from managing Coca-Cola's bottling plant in Nicaragua, gained influence in 1983 with the backing of the CIA. His brother Mario, in charge of logistics, turned to SETCO to ferry narcotics and arms.

Vortex was a Miami-based air transport/supply company. It operated two aircraft that had been used by Michael Palmer (he was actually a company vice-president) for smuggling. It also took some $317,000 in aid business.

DIACSA was another Miami-based aeroplane dealership and parts supplier and it received $41,000. It was effectively reverse laundering the aid money – losing it to more murky corners.

The fourth beneficiary was Frigorificos de Puntarenas, a Costa Rica-based seafood company run by Cuban exiles. Its real speciality was money laundering. It re-routed some $262,000 of government money.

There were at least four other air transport companies involved with the private-public initiative of support for the Contras: Servicios Turisticos was owned by Noriega's pilots Steven Kalish and César Rodríguez. Another, Hondu-Carib, was related to SETCO in that by 1985 it had become Mario Calero's carrier of choice after he forsook, or at least prudently moved on from, smuggling cocaine with Matta's airline. It was set up by Frank Moss, who flew for Mario (a part-owner) and grew out of a narcotics smuggling operation running in 1983. His DC-4 was alleged to have dropped packets of drugs onto Barry Seal's farm. The American company R. M. Equipment used Hondu Carib aircraft to deliver their arms and supplies to the Contras. One of these fringe companies had direct links to drug smuggling in Southeast Asia – Summit Aviation, run by Pat Foley, serviced and outfitted planes for the Thai military that were probably involved in protecting the Golden Triangle heroin trade.[21]

The last of these four, Southern Air Transport, effectively stood in for Air America in another sphere, and was its cousin almost throughout the Cold War. It was Florida-based and was the equivalent for South America of Civil Air Transport, and later Air America, in Southeast Asia. When it was set up in 1949 it had the same CIA consultants and controllers as CAT. On (in)formally taking it over in 1960 the CIA acquired various DC-6s for it from Air America. It was eventually sold off at the end of 1973 to Stanley G. Williams, who had been fronting it for the previous thirteen years.

Another figure entangled in this aerial cat's cradle of licit–illicit warfare was a prominent Miami socialite. Jorge Morales, who was Colombian, was a champion powerboat racer. He was also a smuggler. Morales worked with Floyd Carlton and César Rodriguez (Noriega's personal pilot) bringing cocaine through Panama. In other words he was involved at an early stage, geographically, in the relay of drugs that on arrival in the U.S. would generate funds for buying arms for the Contras. If Morales was ever used by the CIA then this would have been about more than just turning a blind eye to cocaine passing through the Contra camps. A blind eye was certainly turned to his comings and goings as he freely used Fort Lauderdale Executive Airport as well as Ilopango en route. His ticket seems to have been well punched. However, he too outlived his usefulness and was arrested in June 1986 after he was caught shipping 80 kg of cocaine in from 'Liberia', a ranch near to John Hull's. Hull was also implicated but managed to walk through it all unscathed. Morales had somehow lost the immunity that had allowed him to continue to travel and smuggle after an earlier indictment in 1984.

The Narco-guerrilla Spectre Revisited

This whole idea of ticket-punching is sublimated onto another level altogether through the extended network of FDN Contra leader Enriqué Bermudez. One of his main activist-supporters operating in the United States was the Nicaraguan Danilo Blandon, who had managed to tap into the booming crack business of African American dealer 'Freeway Rick' Ross in California and the Midwest. This was the market for the Contra-channelled cocaine which would provide funds for the war on being sold in American cities. It is alleged that they had a certain immunity because of their links to the Contras. This would implicate the CIA in cocaine smuggling on the streets of American cities. This story supplements a more general conspiracy theory: that the federal government had been quite happy to allow the circulation of drugs in the poor neighbourhoods of America in order to weaken African American communities as part of a wider social engineering project.

Whatever the extent of ticket-punching, one thing is for sure: its mere existence undermines the credibility of the so-called war on drugs. This chapter began with the event (the CIA/Seal sting) that tried to precipitate a shift in this war from one purely against a communist threat to a fight against a narco-guerrilla and narco-terror. What credibility is there in this motivation?

The CIA attempted to link the Sandinista guerrilla with the *narco-traficantes* of Colombia, perhaps in the hope that, by extension, it might then draw in Cuba, one of the main backers of the Nicaraguan revolution. But even if the sting did show Sandinistas working with drug smugglers, exactly how different was this alliance to the one that the CIA had with its own cocaine smugglers?

Contradictions in the black and white visualization and rhetoric of the war on drugs have since percolated out. It seems that the CIA was quite happy to do business with drugs smugglers until the Iran-Contra scandal surfaced in November 1986 with the capture of Eugene Hasenfus after his Contra supply plane was shot down. It had a clear relationship with Noriega up until this point, even going back to George Bush Sr's time as director of the CIA between 1976 and 1977. The $10 million that the Medellín Cartel is said to have given to the Contras is alleged to have arrived via a frozen shrimp company, Ocean Hunter, that was owned by the CIA-linked supply company Frigorificos de Puntarenas (a key pillar in the aid programme).[22] It even employed known smugglers, some of whom, exiled Cubans in particular, had been involved with terrorist organizations. The Iran-Contra scandal was in part a way of doing business, via Iran, with an Islamic group holding hostages in Beirut, whom the Americans had labelled as terrorists. Is it not possible, then – given this viscous soup, or *ajiaco* to use the Colombian vernacular, of smugglers and terrorists – that the CIA itself, while acting in Central America, became bogged down in a sort of quasi-narco-terrorism?

Maybe this is going a little bit far, but one could make the case that it was at least acting in a narco-guerrilla sort of way.[23] The American Cold War veterans North and Secord were riding into a storm of revelations and scandal, but weren't they, in a sense, in that storm from the beginning?

THERE ARE ALL SORTS of twists in the Central American smuggling-facilitated counter-revolution. A recent one is that much of the weaponry supplied to the region at this time, especially grenades that were never available for purchase in stores in the U.S., later found its way into the hands of narcos in Mexico. This late Cold War conflict is where state and smugglers really came together – one step up from Southeast Asia, although this is not to say that this was a war simply about cocaine. Finding a trail of powder and being able to track the smuggling of a dangerous contraband does not necessarily mean that this was a war over contraband. It doesn't even suggest that this conflict was much about contraband of war. Both of these phenomena will be the focus of the next chapter.

What, then, is contraband of war, and how might it tip a conflict over into becoming a war of contraband? What happens when the subtext becomes the main deal?

EIGHTEEN

CONTRABAND OF WAR

American Business and
African Diamonds

'He that beareth the diamond upon him, it giveth him hardiness and manhood, and
it keepeth the limbs of his body whole. It giveth him victory of his enemies in plea
and in war . . . And it keepeth him from strife and riot.'[1]
John Mandeville

The definition of 'contraband of war' seems to be pretty straight-forward. It is the material smuggled for waging and sustaining war supplied to one side by a neutral nation, thereby, in contravention of international law, disadvantaging the other; it leads to the neutrality of the providing nation being negated.

There is, however, something of a leap of faith required to imagine a truly neutral party around warfare of modern times, or indeed in wartime smuggling. One might argue that because some of the smugglers of the Napoleonic Wars supplied both sides they balanced out their allegiances, but one would certainly not call this neutrality in any universally recognized definition of the term. In most politically turbulent regions it is very difficult to discern who is not involved, particularly regarding ones in which many states border each other. The framing of wars more recently in Iraq and Bosnia, by the United Nations and NATO respectively, clarified who the belligerents were, making it a little more obvious who was not involved, but surely by then the proxy conflicts of the Cold War and the involvement in them of state-sponsored smugglers had already done away with our lingering naivety. Over the years the entanglement in smuggling of revolutionaries, privateers and pirates, as well as great merchant companies and governments, raises the question of whether there has ever been a war without contraband and a state of partial innocence in which smugglers, be they nations or individuals, have held off smuggling for fear of compromising their neutrality.

The heading of this part of the book is 'A Smuggling World', the implication being that smuggling has spread and accelerated so much since the start of the twentieth century that now it is not only at the vanguard of geopolitics, as it was increasingly over the eras of exploration and empire-building, but has become almost ubiquitous. In relation to contemporary geopolitics, bringing together smuggling and warfare is not so much to think about contraband of war, something supplementary to the conflict, but rather *wars of contraband*, in which contraband is central or even a raison d'être for war.

Both of these concepts have differed between the eighteenth and twentieth centuries. There are two particular conflicts during this earlier period that have become closely associated with contraband of war – the American War of Independence and its later Civil War. Regarding wars of contraband, there can be no more intense an example than the intertwined West African conflicts that were all about so-called blood diamonds – the wars in Sierra Leone and Liberia at the end of the twentieth century, spilling over into the twenty-first. One of the key differences is that contraband of war is largely a supply phenomenon – goods in – whereas wars of contraband are all about securing control of export: goods out.

Smuggling Practice Towards the American War of Independence

Why has the United States proved so adept at smuggling as a practice of geopolitics? Why did it seem so natural and easy for the CIA to conduct secret wars in Laos during the 1960s and early 1970s, and in Central America in the 1980s, that bear comparison with the operations of smuggling networks in its deeper past? Perhaps there is something in the history of the development of America itself that makes smuggling run in its blood. This is probably an overstatement, but the argument has recently been made, convincingly, from a social-historical perspective, by the political scientist Peter Andreas in his book *Smuggler Nation: How Illicit Trade Made America* (2013).

Before considering the American wars – of Independence and the Civil War – in which contraband of war played a major part, one might re-engage with the idea of the Caribbean having become a 'sea of contraband' (as suggested in Part One). The culture and practice of contrabanding in a belligerent milieu across the Atlantic and Caribbean region that would feed the American Revolutionary War like a high-energy supplement had its rehearsal during the Seven Years' War (1756–63). This conflict was waged between various European powers, but in the Caribbean largely between Britain and Bourbon France. It was a conflict apparently won by Britain but prolonged because of the steady supply of contraband of war to the Bourbon side as well as, to a lesser extent, to the British. The American colonists were the main smugglers carrying much contraband on 'flags of truce' vessels that were allowed to exchange prisoners, but which were often just a means to pass through blockades in order to trade. Another supply line was from declaredly neutral Spanish, Danish and Dutch Caribbean islands, especially, in the latter case, St Eustatius in the northern Leeward Islands, east of Puerto Rico.

Although the conflict ended in 1763, tensions between the Royal Navy and smuggling fleets did not diminish and illicit trading became a means to build up arms: a sort of phoney contraband of war channel in preparation for a very real tide of contraband supplying the War of Independence.

The restless colonists began to think strategically. These proto-revolutionaries used their business skills learned through illicit trading to set up supply lines with France, Sweden, Holland and Spain. Obtaining munitions through the West Indies was simple and easy: a matter of adding them to the bills of order for the usual contraband goods. Gunpowder, tent cloth, clothing for uniforms, boots and blankets were now sought out in exchange for cod, lumber, flour, tobacco, cocoa, sugar and paper. At the landing end tactics were well thought through. Patriot smugglers like John Hancock would unload Boston-bound cargoes at Cape Cod to avoid attention at their ultimate destination. Similarly New York goods were often landed at Sandy Hook, New Jersey, on the other side of Lower New York Bay.

Independence War

At the beginning of the war Martinique was the hub for contraband flows, but after the French entered the fray on the American side it was far superseded by St Eustatius (sometimes called 'Statia' or, during this period, the 'Golden Rock'), which was a neutral, centrally located free port. For a time Statia became fabulously wealthy. The Dutch, paying lip service to neutrality, imposed a token blockade, but their own merchants kept it well supplied, sometimes after adding the Caribbean onto officially logged Africa runs. In addition to Dutch contraband, into Statia went American tobacco, timber, indigo and horses, while out of it came gunpowder smuggled in tea chests and rice barrels. It was a fabulous boom, but short-lived: when the Netherlands also entered the war in 1781 the British immediately sacked the island.

War supply became more focused as those with greater revolutionary spirit, such as Benjamin Franklin, began to work alongside habitual smugglers for whom profit was king, like the slave trader John Brown. There were other more official illicit traders: Robert Morris, for instance, was head of the 'Secret Committee of Trade', but even he channelled supply through his own company.

Such was the ambiguity between patriotism and profit that it barely makes sense to question motivations. Silas Deane from Connecticut was perhaps the most successful of the contraband of war suppliers and he was certainly more of a Brown than a Franklin. Plunder from privateering, particularly out of New York, was a good source of contraband, as it was later with those other 'patriotic profiteers', the Lafitte brothers.

Bizarrely, as occurred later around the Napoleonic guinea run across the Channel, a certain amount of trading between the combatant enemies continued on the side. For instance, American tobacco reached Britain via St Eustatius and St Thomas, while British goods reached the rebels via Nova Scotia. This was below board, but other trade, although officially banned, continued as if there wasn't a war on at all. Salt seemed to transcend conflict – Washington's armies needed salt for preserving their foodstuffs and obtained it from British Bermuda![2] At a more provincial level, locals provided timber for the British campaign, while silks and satin from the mother country were still in demand by the Americans.

Nevertheless smuggling was vital for the revolution: the Battle of Saratoga, for instance, would not have gone the rebels' way if it hadn't been for contraband armaments. Contraband of war was both a necessity and an opportunity. Just as the political and social motivations for the outbreak of the American War of Independence were as much an anti-tax protest as a will to revolution, so smuggling at this time was a combination of arms build-up *and* intensified profit motivation. They were never mutually exclusive. Hence high-value contraband, not at all necessary for war, was secreted among the arms. Peter Andreas refers to it as 'smuggling within smuggling'.[3]

Civil War Contraband

The American Civil War is sometimes called the first mechanized war; it might also be called the first industrialized war. This is one of the reasons why it went on for as long as it did – there were fortunes to be maintained and huge profits to be made. In terms of the former, the British Industrial Revolution required raw cotton for its mills and so it defied the northern blockade of southern ports in order to secure its supply. The southern Confederacy played a canny game in that it sold cotton bonds abroad redeemable only in the southern American states, beyond the blockade, thereby encouraging foreign merchants to take risks and cross the line. Logically, in terms of profitability, ships coming out carrying cotton would go in carrying contraband of war. The vast profits to be made lay in the maxim 'business is business', but now framed in a war setting. Many in frontline border states such as Maryland and Virginia found that they could make great sums out of an industry-driven war by transporting goods overland, because the north still wanted southern cotton, even if it were smuggled. The north took almost as much cotton as the British.

The blockade by the north was called Operation Anaconda. At first it was a failure and it was only ever a partial success. British Bermuda and Nassau in the Bahamas served as entrepôts, or staging posts, in the supply line. The main smuggling ports, blockaded but never sufficiently constricted, were Charleston and Wilmington, and to a lesser extent Mobile and Galveston. Matamoros was another entry point for contraband of war. Matamoros lies on the Texas–Mexico border at the corner of the Gulf and avoided blockade because Mexico was a neutral state. Just over the Rio Grande was Brownsville in Confederate hands.

The operation failed in that most smuggling runs succeeded. This was partly because the blockade-running vessels were sleek, low-lying and fast: they were barely visible grey ships burning smokeless anthracite coals. There was little risk to life or limb for the British smugglers who were released after capture, although their vessels were always confiscated.

Some half a million bales of cotton got out and an equal number of good rifles came in, along with sufficient gunpowder, bullets and cannon to fight a long war.[4] Cloth for Confederate uniforms kept the Manchester mills at overflow levels of production. Pig iron was another contraband necessary for the south to mechanize its armies and ramp up its war production.

As in the War of Independence, it wasn't just necessary war supplies that came in. A certain flamboyant lifestyle had to be maintained, as reflected in Margaret Mitchell's novel *Gone with the Wind*, in which the hero, Rhett Butler, smuggles in books, champagnes, wines, needles, hairpins, ladies' hats, satin, lace, pâté and bonbons as well as war necessities. Cigars, coffee, corsets and crystal glass were run alongside teapots and toothbrushes, the latter often carried, in that time-honoured fashion, by crew members conducting their own contraband micro-businesses.

Cotton was the main mover in the south-to-north overland trade. Abraham Lincoln tolerated it and other key Unionist protagonists were implicated. Ulysses S. Grant's father Jesse arranged contraband shipments north, while General Benjamin F. Butler became better known for his cotton trading than his military skills. This was not just corruption: there was a rationale that cotton coming to the north ultimately strengthened its manufacturing base, funding greater war efforts. In addition, this kept much cotton from the lucrative European market, thus impoverishing the southern war machine. Salt also figured, particularly as it was paid for either in gold or northern dollars that could then buy arms.

Landborne southbound contraband of war was smuggled back through the border states, often down the Ohio River. Memphis became a key exchange port after it was captured in 1862. Another Unionist-to-Confederate contraband of war, meat, took a very circuitous route: north to Boston and then to Canada before being shipped to Bermuda or Nassau in the Bahamas and on to southern ports, sometimes even going to Liverpool before the Caribbean. Northern gunpowder was known to have travelled by a similar route, via Canada and Cuba, before reaching the Confederate armies.

Eventually the snake strangled the trade, but only after the southern ports surrendered in 1865. After this a war that was sustained on contraband quickly came to an end.

For many this war had been not been about economics, but about the emancipation of slaves. There is another contraband story here. A 'contraband' in Civil War terminology could be a slave who had escaped to fight on the other side. This alternative concept of contraband had another dimension in the escape network called the Underground Railway. The notion of human contraband, like cotton (the commodity watered with the blood, sweat and tears of slaves), runs through the conflict, south to north. The Underground Railroad was a system of escape routes for contraband slaves and was so named because its trails and points of rest and refuge were organized along the lines of a railway network: abolitionist backers were 'stockholders', guides were 'conductors', fugitive slaves were 'cargo' and hiding places were 'stations'.

Regardless of this placing of a contraband at the centre of conflict, contraband being pivotal to the causes, continuation and outcome of wars is actually a distinctively late twentieth- and twenty-first-century phenomenon. This can only happen if a particularly trafficable commodity takes hold of a nation or region's economy. In Sierra Leone this happened at the end of the millennium. Rather than being riddled with contraband of war, this conflict was a *war of contraband* around something inordinately powerful – diamonds.

Africa's Diamond Problem

Just one company, De Beers, has dominated the diamond industry. It was founded by Cecil Rhodes in 1888 and before the Second World War was given new impetus by a German immigrant to Britain, Sir Ernest Oppenheimer, who consolidated the control of supply and dominated the so-called 'Diamond Syndicate', a cartel of producers who fixed prices that bore no relation to the quantities of diamonds coming out of the ground. With such artificially high prices, and since diamonds are small, light and easy to transport, there was soon a great incentive to smuggle them. In many ways diamonds are the perfect currency for organized crime, particularly to finance narcotics and arms trafficking. Although in the first instance they are often illegally mined and smuggled, they are easily 'cleaned' (usually by falsifying the country of origin) compared to the laundering of narco money. Countries have also tended to stockpile diamonds as insurance against inflation and currency devaluation.

In 1957, just a year after the publication of his thriller *Diamonds Are Forever*, Ian Fleming, creator of James Bond, issued a rather less racy book called *The Diamond Smugglers*, a factual account of the counter-smuggling activities between 1954 and 1956 of an organization spun out of the British intelligence agency MI5 called the International Diamond Security Organization (IDSO). The IDSO's activities in tackling this web of smuggling weren't exactly spectacular: its main tactic seemed to be to buy up loose diamonds on the black market in order to put illicit dealers out of business. The book reads more like a report, although it is spiced up a bit by the narration of a former spy. Nevertheless it gives a good overview of the extent of the problem. Fleming maps out the origins, routes and destinations of smuggled diamonds in the 1950s.

The main international export nodes were Johannesburg, Cape Town and Lourenço Marques (now Maputo in Mozambique) in Southern Africa; Dar es Salaam in East Africa; and Dakar and Monrovia in West Africa. The primary destinations, for both licit and illicit gems, were Pelikaanstraat in Antwerp and Hatton Garden in London, and to a lesser extent Paris (particularly those shipped from Dakar). Many illegally exported diamonds also went to Beirut, partly because Lebanese and Syrian dealers have always had a strong presence on the ground in countries of origin and transhipment. Tel Aviv was another market. Cape Town shipped directly to the United States and Buenos Aires, while Lourenço Marques and Dar es Salaam smugglers preferred to head eastwards to Bombay, from where the diamonds would go on to Hong Kong and China.

From Antwerp, the world centre for diamond trading, illicit gems that were often now legitimized might go behind the Iron Curtain, for instance to Leningrad via the Baltic, or Moscow via Zurich or Beirut. Fleming's source also describes other channels, favoured by a mysterious 'Monsieur Diamant', via West Berlin and also on Russian and Polish ships out of Antwerp.[5] Sometimes the journey of an illicit diamond was even more circuitous, for instance resting only for a short while in Antwerp before being taken to Bombay and Surat in India for cutting and polishing and then smuggled back.

The problem of diamond leakage out of the cartel's grasp was pretty widespread and so it seems a little strange that Fleming's agent–narrator, John Blaize (the pseudonym of John Collard), can reach a point at the end of the book where he can home in on Sierra Leone and declare the problem solved. By 1956, with the reorganization of mining and export in what the IDSO identified as its biggest problem area, West Africa, it was felt that the issue of African diamond smuggling was more or less under control. As Fleming's informant put it, there wasn't much more to be done that couldn't be achieved by mine personnel and local police: 'The next few months were spent tidying up loose ends.'[6]

It was a local problem, then. Perhaps the reason why Fleming can talk of loose ends tied up is that the phenomenon of the blood diamond did not yet exist. How, then, did things escalate?

From Local to Global: Stories of Flying, Fishing and Networking

First let's look at the problem as it might have appeared on a small scale in the 1950s. Fleming describes security checks at the Oranjemund mine located on the border between South Africa and Namibia. Smuggling of diamonds initially might well have been containable around the mine. The first line of defence in detecting hidden diamonds leaving the mine compound was the body search and the X-ray machine, but this wasn't sufficiently rigorous. In the mid-1950s very few white men had to go through X-ray machines. There was a racist assumption that only black men would steal from their employers. But anyway X-rays weren't the whole answer because you can only expose workers to a certain amount of gamma rays. After a while security had to resort to dummy X-rays and spot checks. Another tactic was to put a micro amount of radioactive paint on diamonds so Geiger counters could be used. In recent times at Oranjemund, homing pigeons have been used to fly small bags of diamonds out over the wire. There was also a ban imposed on vehicles travelling out of the sector for fear that they would be smuggling diamonds.

Obviously some diamonds were going to get out. Fleming tells the story of an overly trusted English mine engineer who, near to a perimeter-less diamond camp just up the coast from Oranjemund in southern Namibia, hid gems in the sand and then resigned from the company. Later on he hired an aeroplane and pilot and flew up the coast to pick them up. Unfortunately for him they crashed on take-off from the beach when one of the aircraft's wheels struck a rock.[7]

In *The Diamond Smugglers*, a useful map though it is, we don't get a detailed picture of the international networks of illicit diamond smuggling. Fleming tends to swing between small players with their verifiable human stories, resolved in one way or another, and the faceless channels of illicit diamond flows, which remain obscure, their protagonists rarely brought to account. He doesn't really connect these two ends of the scale. When they are connected it tends to be in the realm of the imagination. For instance, in *Diamonds Are Forever* Bond, under cover, smuggles gems inside golf balls as a lure to infiltrate Ernst Stavro Blofeld's diamond smuggling operation, part of a plan to build a huge satellite-borne laser to blackmail world governments. Here there is an elaboration of the power of diamonds, but it is pure fantasy.

Or is it? One might alternatively read the novel as an allegory of Cold War diamond-smuggling. After all there was great demand from the Soviet Union, America and China for industrial diamonds for use in machine tools and in the armaments industry. Move forward a couple of decades and one can't imagine smuggling that isn't, at all levels, part of a mesh of international intrigue. As so often occurs with smuggling, even a contraband that seems relatively small potatoes can be bound up with more obviously glamorous or dangerous commodities.

Take patterns of smuggling around the fringes of wars in southern and northeastern Africa. During the civil war in Angola South African fishermen would take advantage of the conflict to trawl the teeming waters off the coast, sometimes under the protection of government generals. The fish were then smuggled to places like Portugal, which has old trading links with the country. Illegal fishing and smuggling off Angola might not seem the most obvious way to make a fortune, particularly when it takes place just off a diamond coast, but this is to underestimate the diversification of smuggling.[8]

Elsewhere in Africa, in Somaliland (an autonomous region of Somalia), it has emerged relatively recently that traders from the Warsangeli sub-clan have offered fishing rights in return for guns, cement and plastics smuggled in from the Arabian Peninsula. Fish are obviously an important commodity in a wider network of informal trading. They are a part of the broader illicit economy that links the labourer, be they fisherman or miner, through various dealers and international smugglers with the unscrupulous government or international terrorist. Besides the fact that abalone (sea snail) smuggling is big business out of southern Africa, it is what else is carried in the trawlers, and their potential to rendezvous with larger ships at sea, that matters. Along with fish cargoes off the coast of Angola went even more petty contraband such as cigarettes and beer, and it was just as easy to add small quantities of coltan (the mineral used in mobile phones), brought to the coast from Mozambique. Or of course, in the case of Angola, to secrete diamonds among the cartons.

We are now in the realm of blood diamonds – gems that cause, or at least perpetuate and deepen, war and suffering, both around sites of extraction and across zones through which they are smuggled. Eventually they arrive, cleaned, sparkling and translucent, around the neck or on the fingers of unknowing developed world consumers.

Angola's dirty postcolonial war, which was only partly about diamonds, was a hint of what was to come in Sierra Leone. In the case of

Angola, UNITA rebels financed their Maoist (but bizarrely American as well as Chinese-backed) war versus the Soviet and Cuban-supported government of the MPLA by trafficking in blood diamonds. They were mined on the Bié Plateau before coming to Luande and other points on the coast and then smuggled to Portugal and on to Antwerp and London. Alternatively these diamonds followed other trails across the Iron Curtain.

The main countries involved in blood-diamond mining have been Angola, Democratic Republic of Congo, Central African Republic and Sierra Leone. In the last, an exemplary war of contraband raged on a scale that Ian Fleming's agent could not have envisaged.

Sierra Leone – A War of Contraband

The quotation from *The Travels of Sir John Mandeville*, the (probably fictional) odyssey of a fourteenth-century knight that initiates this chapter, speaks of diamonds conferring manhood. There is a terrible irony in this regarding the blood diamond conflicts of Sierra Leone, Congo and Liberia in that it is child soldiers who are so often forced into proving their man-hood. The rest of the quote, referring as it does to keeping 'limbs of his body whole' and saving 'him from strife and riot', is for the most part, and for most of the populations of this region, very far from reality on the ground. Diamond smuggling, mainly a white-collar crime for Fleming, has become an atrocity-stained business throughout Western and Central Africa, and no more so than in Sierra Leone.

Eastern Sierra Leone and western Liberia, in retrospect, have been cursed by being 'diamondiferous'. The towns nearest to the kimberlite diamond fields are Kenema, Yengema, Koidu, Tongo Field and Bo. In 1954, on a reconnaissance in anticipation of setting up the IDSO described in Fleming's book, Sir Percy Sillitoe, formerly head of Britain's spy organization MI5, visited all the main diamond-producing regions in Africa to assess actual and potential smuggling problems for De Beers. His six-week trip took in Freetown and Yengema in Sierra Leone. One region he didn't visit, Kenema, today has a comprehensive illicit econ-omy, and of course a diamond economy in particular. As in Maicao, Colombia, and especially Ciudad del Este in Paraguay, the informal economy is well represented with Lebanese merchants. Diamond-dealing stores are more often than not run by Lebanese businessmen. Their shoddy storefronts belie a multi-million-dollar industry. But although they make a good living, these merchants cannot control the

Sierra Leone, showing the main diamond fields.

issue of loose diamonds. Many of the dealers in places like Yengema have never even been to an actual mine and so they are dependent upon what crosses their tables.

Mines in the bush and jungle are difficult to access. Diamond mining here is very different from the well-organized operations in Southern Africa: there is little perimeter fencing at the mines and this is perhaps why smuggling, logistically, is so easy. The civil war between 1991 and 2002, known the world over for its brutality and particularly the rebel group's practice of amputating civilians' limbs, only made things easier, and blood on diamonds was never considered an obstacle to smuggling. Indeed it soon transpired that diamonds were both the object of the war and fuel for its continuation. Blood diamonds for weapons for child soldiers is one of the most vicious of cycles ever conceived in the name of rebellion.

How did we get to this horrific situation? Let's go back to the 1950s when things looked more hopeful for the official industry. Before this there had always been something of a problem. In Graham Greene's *The Heart of the Matter*, researched in Sierra Leone during his posting there as an intelligence officer during the Second World War, the author has Lebanese smuggling diamonds in the stomachs of parrots. But by Sillitoe and Blaize's time the situation appeared relatively manageable.

Formal diamond mining near Koidu in eastern Sierra Leone, 2013.

Until the 1950s diamond production was monopolized by one company, the Sierra Leone Selection Trust (SLST), owned by De Beers and founded in 1934, but there were some 30,000 illegal miners operating in the early 1950s. The SLST was dissolved in 1955, succeeded by the Diamond Corporation of Sierra Leone (DCSL), and this is the time when Blaize declares that 'there was nothing more for us to do.' But given the number of illegal miners operating at the time of the previous diamond administration, is it at all likely that the problem had gone away for good? In towns things might have been tidied up a bit, but smuggling continued because deals were often made in the jungle; cash was handed over at the edge of the mine in transactions beyond the company's reach.

At the time of independence from the British in 1961, the marginal diamond territories that the British had no will to police continued to be governed at a distance: they remained as largely unregulated zones, particularly as the new national government offered no new infrastructure to back up the rule of law. The Lebanese dealers, geared towards the illicit economy, continued to maintain the informal structure of these shabby towns and to provide equipment for the miners.

As the war raged during the 1990s official exports of diamonds all but ceased as the diamond fields became battlegrounds. But this did not stop the illicit trade, now orchestrated by the RUF (Revolutionary United Front), the brutal rebel army.

Informal diamond mining near Koidu in eastern Sierra Leone, 2013.

The RUF looked to the borders for their markets. They traded small rough diamonds in Guinea – the neighbouring country which curls around northern Sierra Leone like a horseshoe – for rice, fuel and occasionally weapons. They didn't even have to go to the border themselves: Mandingo middlemen often bought diamonds with cash or weapons, selling them on, 'legally', to Belgian and Lebanese dealers. It was easy for them because they were always coming and going across borders. They also laundered diamonds by taking them further, for instance to Gambia, a country that had no diamond mines but still managed to export its 'own diamonds' to Antwerp (the same situation prevailed in Congo-Brazzaville vis-à-vis its diamondiferous neighbour, the Democratic Republic of Congo).[9] Sometimes the rebels themselves crossed over to Conakry, Guinea. On selling the diamonds, Guinean customs were bribed to issue certificates of origin from this peaceful country and they were exported as if they had come, in a more or less ethical way, straight from its own mines. The Diamond High Council of Guinea turned a blind eye.[10]

In July 2000 there was a brief embargo from the outside on all imports from Sierra Leone until strict regulations could be put in place, but it was largely ignored. It was the same pattern as that in Sierra Leone itself whenever the Government Gold and Diamond Office had tried to issue regulations to tax diamond export – it had no relevance. One of the reasons that it was easier, not just more profitable, to smuggle than to follow the rules was that Liberia, to the east, was a smuggling conduit par excellence. Regarding this fluidity of transit, it bears comparison with the relationship today between Colombia and Central America and Mexico regarding cocaine supply. In both cases smuggling has been facilitated by conflict and incredibly porous borders.

Traffickers and Networks – Liberia

Liberia, like Gambia and Congo-Brazzaville, has virtually no diamond production industry, but nevertheless it is listed as the place of origin of millions of carats of stones – actually almost all laundered Sierra Leonean diamonds. In Fleming's time the majority of stones also came to Liberia, whose dollar was pegged to the U.S. dollar, making it a reliable and desirable currency. Monrovia is a magnet for dodgy diamonds. In 2001 a UN resolution banned the import of 'Liberian' diamonds but this was a case of shutting the stable door after the horse had bolted. During the Sierra Leone war the RUF saw the markets in Monrovia as an ideal means for exchanging diamonds for cleaner money or directly for weapons.

Charles Taylor, former president of Liberia, has been convicted in The Hague of involvement in blood-diamond smuggling, and his administration had always been amenable to re-export. As with the fish trail, the small players are tangled up with these figureheads, and there are many dubious characters behind the scenes.

The Old Road in Monrovia is the area for shady deals and, as in places like Kenema and Yengema, there is substantial Middle Eastern involvement. As detailed in Greg Campbell's book *Blood Diamonds* (2004), the cast of characters is broad and besmirched. Ibrahim Bah, a general in the RUF, was one of the main diamond traffickers out of Sierra Leone, as was another RUF commander, General 'Rambo'. In Monrovia the latter had connections with Khalil Khalil, a Lebanese dealer and 'unofficial finance minister'. A Liberian government helicopter would sometimes take Rambo back to his operating base in Buedu (on the so-called 'parrot's beak', a sharp, salient bit of Sierra Leone jutting into Liberia – a 'hell on earth'). There was always a degree of overlap between contraband of war and a war of contraband: diamonds went one way, arms, food, fuel and medicine the other.

Monrovia seems to have harboured all sorts of interests feeding off the blood-diamond trade. Al-Qaeda was said to have bought diamonds (thereby laundering money and acquiring a 'purer' trading commodity) through the Lebanese diamond dealer Aziz Nassour and his cousin Samih Osailly. According to Campbell, in 1999 another network was up and running, organized by an Israeli of Ukrainian origin, Leonid Menin, a friend of Charles Taylor. He ran guns from Ukraine to Gibraltar where an end-user certificate was secured for Burkina Faso, whose government was sympathetic to the RUF. From Ouagadougou, its capital, Menin used an airliner that also occasionally acted as Taylor's private jet to transfer them to Monrovia. Arms were also brought in from Niamey in Niger.

The weapons were driven to the Sierra Leonean border under the cover of timber transportations along roads built by the logging/gunrunning companies owned, as *Blood Diamonds* goes on to reveal, by Dutchman Gus Kouwenhoven and Israeli Simon Rosenblum. Other consignments were just as covert. In 2000 the Tajik-born former KGB agent Victor Bout was using a Liberia-registered Ilyushin Il-76 aircraft to smuggle guns from Eastern Europe to Sierra Leone via Monrovia.[11] This trade was not especially hidden: it was assisted by Taylor's government and relied upon compliant customs. Bout operated out of smaller airports such as Ostend (Belgium), Burgas (Bulgaria) and Pietersburg (South Africa), using front companies. Later on he operated out of Sharjah. He is alleged to have had clients as diverse as Israelis and the Taliban as well as private security firms operating in Iraq after the fall of Saddam Hussein.

In a different context, another conflict in another part of Africa, Victor Bout's operation has been described by politician-writer Moisés Naím as a kind of eBay, or Wal-Mart, of global trading, and hence of geopolitical importance. It was networked, lawless, even part of global diplomacy; a 'supermarket that knows no borders'.[12] Dealers move around the world, changing bases, supply lines, routes, destinations and clients, everywhere supplying contraband for war. Smuggling around Somalia over the last few decades proves that, although there are now wars of contraband, contraband of war continues to be abundant.

Contraband of War in the Horn of Africa

In order to understand the super-fuelled militarization of the Horn of Africa, in particular Somalia, one must go back to the Cold War. During the 1970s Somalia, though ruled by the military, was a committed socialist state supported commercially and militarily by the Soviet Union. Various wars have left the region heavily armed and have opened up weapons-supply routes.

An indirect route for trafficking in arms came via another Soviet client state, the Peoples' Democratic Republic of Yemen (South Yemen), which after its own wars had a surplus of weapons. Later, after war with communist Ethiopia over the Ogaden region (when Russia backed the Ethiopians), Somalia switched allegiance to the United States. This Cold War gaming produced external arms supply lines that have been expanded during Somalia's recent war, particularly with the supply of contrabands of war from Ethiopia and Eritrea. Ethiopia has backed one side, the Transitional Federal Government, while Eritrea supports the Islamists.[13] Bakaara Market in Mogadishu became the biggest arms bazaar until 2006 (when the Islamic Courts Union left the city), when it fragmented into smaller markets around the city.

Arms pour into points north and south. Guns originating in the Arabian Peninsula are channelled into Burao and Hargeisa in Somaliland, while in the south Kismayo is an entry point for arms which are then transported up to Ogaden and its ethnic Somali liberation army. Arthur Rimbaud's efforts at gun-running in the region were minuscule by comparison. It is difficult not to look at Somalia and Somaliland as a kind of trough into which armaments have been thrown over the decades. However, just as diamonds and coltan travel with fish, and the Warsangeli trade fishing rights for arms, so weapons do not always, or even often, travel in isolation.

Gun-running sometimes follows traditional trading routes. During the Middle Ages the Ajuuraan Sultanate in Somalia traded with all of the points immediately east that now supply arms, and all of those even further east that supply other contrabands. Across the Gulf of Aden come Yemeni dhows, either exchanging cargoes at sea or landing at remote ports like Heis, Maidh and Laasqoray (Somaliland); Haradheere and Hobyo in the Mudug region (central Somalia); and, just to the south of here, Ceel Dheer in the Galgaduud region. They bring not just arms, but also electronic goods, plastics, food, cement and fuel. Gujarati-built dhows also follow ancient routes. They come from Mundra (Gujarat), but trade variously between Karachi, Dubai, Sharjah, Salalah, and ports in Southern Iran, before arriving at places like Bosaaso in Puntland, northern Somalia. Almost all carry contraband of one sort or another. This isn't contraband of war, but it does indicate the historical openness of Somalia's borders, making arms trafficking, no matter on what scale, part of a larger historical trading system.

IN THE COMPARISON IN THIS CHAPTER between contraband of war and wars of contraband they appear to be quite different things. While governments are central to contraband of war they tend to be marginalized in wars of contraband. This of course is a somewhat simplistic contrast – wars are much more complex than this, and what is common to both is the interweaving of flows of military and consumer goods, of individuals and networks, the micro and macro.

In certain contemporary theories on mobility and circulation of goods and people, the backdrop to these flows is the preponderance of war. Smuggling isn't all about war but, as so many of the stories in this book have come out of conflict of one sort or another, it must be acknowledged as something of a prevailing theme, particularly during the twentieth century. Indeed, for some, at the heart of contemporary geopolitics is the notion of 'perpetual war'.[14] This takes us a long way from any idea that free trade might lead to more peaceful international relations, as some of the early free-trade thinkers dreamed. For others – Immanuel Kant, David Hume and Adam Smith, no less – smuggling, that dark cousin to free trade, could even produce and perpetuate warfare, and the example of Sierra Leone would seem to substantiate this.

If we are talking about the ubiquity of contraband and its intensification during war, and if warfare, in one place or another, might be perpetual, then surely we are also talking about smuggling in perpetuity. We might really have arrived at a smuggling world.

POSTSCRIPT

Smuggling continues to be implicated in, and respond to, geopolitical events. A cursory survey of contraband flows today reveals that many of the old lines of activity persist. The Mexico–U.S. border remains an unmanageable line and the Yunnan–Burma frontier is porous, as is the Trans-Himalaya border with Tibet. Afghanistan–Pakistan still has more than 200 crossing points used by smugglers. The Golden Triangle maintains its shape, as does the Golden Crescent. The Ilemi Triangle in East Africa is another traditional smuggling area, while the River Plate region in South America goes on peddling illicit wares. Sinai Bedouin, habitual smugglers, continue to transport arms and supplies towards Gaza.

Some borderlands are characterized by intense activity. The Chad Basin in West Africa is one example and so, in a more changeable way, are parts of the former Yugoslavia. Is there state involvement in any of this smuggling? Some, for sure, and this question is rarely even asked these days of the intensive smuggling into Eastern Ukraine, South Ossetia, Abkhazia or right across Transnistria.

The geopolitical map of smuggling is remarkably familiar from decades, even centuries ago. But occasionally political events lead to new smuggling initiatives. The flood of arms smuggled to Mali from a disintegrating Libya in 2011 precipitated an Islamic takeover of Timbuktu that threatened to obliterate its history and culture. In turn thousands of medieval manuscripts that would have been considered blasphemous by jihadists, and were therefore threatened with destruction, were smuggled out of the city, by road and river, to Bamako.

New shapes have emerged. Journalist Damien Cave wrote in the *International Herald Tribune* in 2011 of a 'pistol-shaped arc of flights' towards a remote, forested part of the Caribbean coast of Honduras, northeast of San Pedro Sula.[1] The handle of the gun is the Colombia–Venezuela border, which in large part refers to Guajira. Now that Central America has come to rival Mexico as a transit point for South American cocaine, the flow resembles a great funnel, albeit with gravity reversed. Narco technologies have begun to echo the strategic instruments of the Cold War: submarines for smuggling cocaine were discovered in Ecuador in 2010 and just over the border in southwestern Colombia in 2011.[2]

Old corridors of smuggling are revived or link up to form chains: each of Turkey's contraband-infiltrated borders with Iran, Iraq and Syria are now more than ever viewed in a single context. The Silk Road has been traced over with new flows of contraband, particularly in Central Asia. Smuggling worlds intertwine more than ever.

REFERENCES

Introduction: Romance, Rebellion and Power

1 See for instance, Itty Abraham and Willem van Schendel, eds, *Illicit Flows and Criminal Things* (Bloomington, IN, 2005); Nils Gilman et al., eds, *Deviant Globalization* (New York, 2011); Moisés Naím, *Illicit: How Smugglers, Traffickers and Copycats are Hijacking the Global Economy* (London, 2007); Robert Neuwirth, *Stealth of Nations* (New York, 2011); and Carolyn Nordstrom, *Global Outlaws* (Berkeley, CA, 2007).
2 Smugglers were often called free-traders in eighteenth- and nineteenth-century Britain. Actually smuggling has only ever mimicked free trade because, paradoxically of course, smuggling likes and relies upon protectionists' high duties.
3 Writer and political scientist Ayçe Çelikkol has analysed some of these viewpoints. In her book *Romances of Free Trade: British Literature, Laissez-faire, and the Global Nineteenth Century* (Oxford, 2011), she reads the history of free trade and smuggling through the lenses of nineteenth-century socio-economic narratives and romance literature, and isolates a number of individualist and sometimes alienating traits attributable to smugglers.
4 See in particular chapters 2 and 3 ibid.
5 Ibid., pp. 34–8.
6 See Simon Harvey, 'Smuggling in Theories and Practices of Contemporary Visual Culture', PhD thesis, University of London, 2005.
7 Nathaniel Hawthorne, *The Scarlet Letter* (London, 1986), p. 50.
8 Ibid., p. 45.

ONE: Great Ambitions: Smuggling in the Age of Discovery

1 'Contrabanding' is a term used more often than 'smuggling' regarding illicit trading in the Caribbean during the early modern period. It was usually more about supplementing legal trade, often in regions where law was notional anyway, than about dedicated criminality.
2 Some cocaine also almost certainly goes out in the ships from the

ports, and guns come in, carried in the holds that are mainly full of everyday consumer items.

3 'Strong-arm' trading is the name given to coerced deals, either in goods other than what the colonists were permitted to trade, or against their will. Refusal would probably have been met with violence, thus tipping over into piracy. However behind the backs of local colonial officials, sometimes even led by them, many were quite happy to trade.

4 C. R. Boxer, *The Portuguese Seaborne Empire, 1415–1825* (Manchester, 1991), p. 326.

5 Ibid., p. 327.

6 Ibid.

7 John Keay, *The Spice Route* (London, 2005), p. 187.

8 Kris E. Lane, *Blood and Silver: A History of Piracy in the Caribbean and Central America* (Oxford, 1999), pp. 14–15.

9 Kenneth R. Andrews, *The Spanish Caribbean: Trade and Plunder, 1530–1630* (New Haven, CT, 1978), p. 79.

10 Lane, *Blood and Silver*, pp. 21–2.

11 Andrews, *The Spanish Caribbean*, pp. 127–8.

12 Lane, *Blood and Silver*, p. 35.

13 Ibid., p. 33.

14 Andrews, *The Spanish Caribbean*, p. 114.

15 Ibid., p. 96.

TWO: Monopoly! The Spice Islands and the South China Sea

1 Giles Milton, *Nathaniel's Nutmeg: How One Man's Courage Changed the Course of History* (London, 1999), pp. 32–3.

2 Ibid., pp. 212–14.

3 Jonathan Clements, *Pirate King: Coxinga and the Fall of the Ming Dynasty* (Stroud, Gloucestershire, 2004), p. 14.

4 Ibid., pp. 14–15.

5 Ibid., p. 14.

THREE: Sea of Contraband: The Caribbean and the 'River of Silver'

1 Kenneth R. Andrews, *The Spanish Caribbean: Trade and Plunder, 1530–1630* (New Haven, CT, 1978), pp. 206–7.

2 Ibid., p. 177.

3 James Lang, *Conquest and Commerce: Spain and England in the Americas* (New York, 1975), p. 55.

4 Andrews, *The Spanish Caribbean*, p. 179.

5 See ibid., pp. 185–6.

6 Ibid., p. 195.

7 Quoted in Peter Sloterdijk, *In the World Interior of Capital* (Cambridge, 2013), p. 113.

8 Andrews, *The Spanish Caribbean*, p. 225.

REFERENCES

9 Lang, *Conquest and Commerce*, pp. 56–7.
10 Ibid., p. 56.
11 C. R. Boxer estimate, quoted in Dennis O'Flynn, 'Comparing the Tokagawa Shogunate with Hapsburg Spain: Two Silver-based Empires in a Global Setting', in *The Political Economy of Merchant Empires*, ed. James D. Tracy (Cambridge, 1991).
12 Lance Grahn, *The Political Economy of Smuggling: Regional Informal Economies in Early Bourbon New Granada* (Oxford, 1997), p. 18.
13 See Andrews, *The Spanish Caribbean*, pp. 175–81.
14 Fernand Braudel, *Civilization and Capitalism, 15th–18th century*, vol. III: *The Perspective of the World* (London, 1984), pp. 416–17.
15 Lane, *Blood and Silver*, p. 109.

FOUR: A Smuggling Desert: The Spanish Main Today

1 Gabriel García Márquez, 'Death Constant Beyond Love', in *Collected Stories* (London, 1996), p. 219.
2 Ibid.
3 Hunter S. Thompson, 'A Footloose American in a Smugglers' Den', in *The Great Shark Hunt: Strange Tales from a Strange Time* (London, 1980), p. 366.
4 García Márquez, 'The Incredible and Sad Tale of Innocent Eréndira and her Heartless Grandmother', in *Collected Stories*, pp. 251–2.
5 Ibid., p. 277.
6 García Márquez, 'Blacamán the Good', in *Collected Stories*, p. 237.

FIVE: A Taste for Contraband: Smuggling Blows Across the World

1 Ruth Hill, *Hierarchy, Commerce and Fraud in Bourbon Spanish America* (Nashville, TN, 2005), p. 119.
2 Ibid., p. 127.
3 Ibid., pp. 137–8.
4 See Hill, *Hierarchy, Commerce and Fraud*, chapters 3 and 4.
5 Lance Grahn, *The Political Economy of Smuggling: Regional Informal Economies in Early Bourbon New Granada* (Oxford, 1997), p. 192.
6 Hill, *Hierarchy, Commerce and Fraud*, pp. 115–16.
7 See John Gimlette's travel book about Paraguay, *At the Tomb of the Inflatable Pig* (London, 2003), p. 11.
8 Grahn, *The Political Economy of Smuggling*, p. 38.
9 Ibid., p. 60.
10 Ibid., p. 55.
11 Graham Greene, *Getting to Know the General* (London, 1999), p. 61.
12 Quoted in Adam Leith Gollner, *The Fruit Hunters: A Story of Nature, Adventure, Commerce and Obsession* (New York, 2008), p. 84.
13 Fernand Braudel, *Civilization and Capitalism, 15th–18th century*, vol. III: *The Perspective of the World* (London, 1984), p. 418.

SIX: Revolution and Resistance: Turning Over the Idea of Smuggling

1 See Ayşe Çelikkol, *Romances of Free Trade: British Literature, Laissez-faire, and the Global Nineteenth Century* (Oxford, 2011), pp. 31–2.
2 George Foy, *Contraband* (London, 1998), p. 184.
3 Paul Virilio, *Speed and Politics: An Essay on Dromology* (New York, 1986), p. 42.
4 Ivan Klíma, 'The Smuggler's Story', in *My Golden Trades* (London, 1992), p. 37.
5 Giuseppe Tomasi di Lampedusa, *The Leopard* (London, 2005), p. 117.
6 Richard Platt, *Smuggling in the British Isles: A History* (Stroud, Gloucestershire, 2007), p. 163.
7 James Lang, *Conquest and Commerce: Spain and England in the Americas* (New York, 1975), p. 59.
8 Gabriel García Márquez, 'Blacamán the Good', in *Collected Stories* (London, 1996), p. 237.
9 Foy, *Contraband*, p. 133.
10 Adam Smith, *Wealth of Nations* (Ware, Hertfordshire, 2012), p. 879.
11 Nathaniel Hawthorne, *The Scarlet Letter* (London, 1986), p. 45.
12 Eric Hobsbawm, *Bandits* (London, 2000), footnote, p. 45.
13 Mahi Binebine, *Welcome to Paradise* (London, 2004), pp. 46–7.
14 Avital Ronell, *Crack Wars: Literature, Addiction, Mania* (Lincoln, NE, 1992), p. 51.
15 Winsome Pinnock, *Mules* (London, 1996), Act 2, Scene 10, pp. 45–6.
16 Quoted in Sadie Plant, *Writing on Drugs* (London, 1999), p. 87.

SEVEN: Piratical Patriots: Fickle and Pragmatic Smugglers

1 Quoted in William C. Davis, *The Pirates Laffite: The Treacherous World of the Corsairs of the Gulf* (Orlando, FL, 2005), p. 61.
2 See Hakim Bey, TAZ: *The Temporary Autonomous Zone, Ontological Anarchy, Poetic Terrorism* (New York, 2003).
3 Davis, *The Pirates Laffite*, p. 212.

EIGHT: Business as Usual: Napoleon's English Smugglers

1 Gavin Daly, 'Napoleon and the City of Smugglers, 1810–1814', *Historical Journal*, L/2 (2007), p. 345.
2 Ibid., p. 342.
3 Quoted in Geoffrey Morley, *The Smuggling War: The Government's Fight against Smuggling in the 18th and 19th Centuries* (Stroud, Gloucestershire, 1994), pp. 117–18.
4 See Richard Platt, *Smuggling in the British Isles: A History* (Stroud, Gloucestershire, 2007), pp. 185–7.

5 Ibid., pp. 186–7.
6 See Daly, 'Napoleon and the City of Smugglers', pp. 339–41.

NINE: Smuggling Worlds: From the River Plate to the Red Sea

1 Henry de Monfreid, *Pearls, Arms and Hashish: Pages from the Life of a Red Sea Smuggler* (London, 1930), pp. 105–6.
2 See Charles Nicholl, *Somebody Else: Arthur Rimbaud in Africa, 1880–91* (London, 1998), p. 313.
3 Henry de Monfreid, *Le Radeau de la Méduse* (Paris, 1958), pp. 79–81.
4 Nicholl, *Somebody Else*, p. 4.
5 Quoted ibid., p. 85.
6 Nicholl describes a 'malady' that afflicts seasoned Africa hands, inducing 'silence', 'ennui' and 'lassitude', ibid., p. 113.
7 Hunter S. Thompson, *The Proud Highway: The Fear and Loathing Letters*, vol. I: *1955–67* (London, 1997), p. 338.
8 Quoted in Nicholl, *Somebody Else*, p. 182.
9 Monfreid, *Pearls, Arms and Hashish*, p. 145.

TEN: Shadow Empire: Addicting China to Smuggled Opium

1 Martin Booth, *Opium: A History* (London, 1997), p. 140.
2 Julia Lovell, *The Opium War* (London, 2012), p. 36.
3 W. Travis Hanes and Frank Sanello, *The Opium Wars: The Addiction of One Empire and the Corruption of Another* (London, 2002), p. 40.
4 Ibid., pp. 40–41.
5 Ibid., p. 21.
6 Ibid., p. 42.
7 Amitav Ghosh, *River of Smoke* (London, 2011), p. 427.
8 Hanes and Sanello, *The Opium Wars*, p. 157.
9 Quoted ibid., p. 74.
10 Lovell, *The Opium War*, p. 251.
11 Ibid., p. 250.
12 Quoted in Hanes and Sanello, *The Opium Wars*, p. 189.

ELEVEN: Refreshment and Resistance: Too Much Opium, Too Little Tea

1 See Amar Farooqui, *Smuggling as Subversion: Colonialism, Indian Merchants and the Politics of Opium* (New Delhi, 1998), pp. 115–16.
2 Ibid., p. 112.
3 For more detail on this, and the first of Fortune's tea missions, see Sarah Rose, *For All the Tea in China* (London, 2009).

TWELVE: Industrial Revolutions: Slaves, Cinchona, Rubber
and Technology

1 Fitzcarrald never transported a boat across a mountain, but he did take one apart and portage it across land to another river system.
2 See Joe Jackson, *The Thief at the End of the World: Rubber, Empire and the Obsessions of Henry Wickham* (London, 2008), pp. 189–90.
3 Ibid., p. 193.
4 Robert Neuwirth, *Stealth of Nations: The Global Rise of the Informal Economy* (New York, 2011), p. 61.
5 *The Times*, 24 April 2007, p. 5.

THIRTEEN: Smuggling Cultures: Looted Treasures

1 On 11 February 2011 Yale University and the University of Cuzco (UNSAAC) signed an agreement for the return of the artefacts. On 12 November 2012 the third and final consignment was flown to Peru.
2 Roger Atwood, *Stealing History: Tomb Raiders, Smugglers, and the Looting of the Ancient World* (New York, 2004), pp. 80–85.
3 Ibid., p. 87.
4 Ibid., pp. 46–51.
5 Ibid., pp. 156–7.
6 Sax Rohmer, *Dope* (London, 1919), p. 96.
7 See Roberto Escobar, *Escobar: Drugs, Guns, Money, Power* (London, 2010), pp. 91–4.
8 Reportedly, Botero was unimpressed that his art had become mere currency, adding a certain irony to the relationship when he painted *The Death of Pablo Escobar* (1999).
9 Konstantin Akinsha and Grigorii Kozlov, *Stolen Treasure: The Hunt for the World's Lost Masterpieces* (London, 1995), p. 158.
10 Ibid., pp. 157–8.

FOURTEEN: *Bonzenflucht*: The Third Reich Smuggles Itself
to Argentina

1 See Douglas Botting and Ian Sayer, *Nazi Gold* (Edinburgh, 2003), pp. 47–50.
2 The very existence of *Die Spinne*, and of Skorzeny's involvement in it, is disputed by some, for instance Guy Walters in his book *Hunting Evil* (London, 2010). See chapter 5, 'The Odessa Myth'.
3 Botting and Sayer, *Nazi Gold*, pp. 50–51.
4 Uki Goñi, *The Real Odessa* (London, 2002), p. 209.
5 Draganovic is also said to have had links with the American Counter Intelligence Corps (CIC) who used him when they wanted to 'disappear' their tainted post-war Axis war criminal agents to avoid embarrassing exposés.

FIFTEEN: Black Markets: Everything at a Good Price

1 The film is known for its noir aesthetic, has a famously catchy musical score performed on the zither, and a villain, Harry Lime, played by Orson Welles, who has an enchanting smile and a seductive personality.
2 Other related terms include 'informal', 'unofficial', 'irregular', 'unregulated', 'endogenous', 'second', 'parallel', 'extra-state', 'extra-legal', 'undeclared', 'shadow', 'underground' and 'hidden'.
3 A 'culture of spoils' is a term used for informal trading by Janet Roitman in *Productivity in the Margins: The Reconstitution of State Power in the Chad Basin* (Santa Fe, NM, 2004).
4 See Alexander Cockburn and Jeffrey St Clair, *Whiteout: The CIA, Drugs and the Press* (London, 1999), pp. 167–8.
5 Botting and Sayer, *Nazi Gold*, p. 232.
6 Ibid., pp. 244–5.
7 Konstantin Akinsha and Grigorii Kozlov, *Stolen Treasure: The Hunt for the World's Lost Masterpieces* (London, 1995), pp. 214–15.
8 See Robert Neuwirth, *Stealth of Nations: The Global Rise of the Informal Economy* (New York, 2011), pp. 101–4.
9 Ibid., p. 18.
10 Ibid., pp. 27–8.
11 Minze Tummescheit's documentary film *Jarmark Europa* (2004) tells this story.
12 For a more detailed account of the specific excursion patterns of shuttlers between São Paulo and Ciudad del Este, see Neuwirth's chapter 'Can Anybody Tell Me How to Get to the Bridge?', in Neuwirth, *Stealth Nation*.
13 See 'Treasury Targets Hizballah Fundraising Network in the Triple Frontier of Argentina, Brazil, and Paraguay', www.treasury.gov, 12 June 2006. Also Joshua L. Gleis and Benedetta Berti, *Hezbollah and Hamas: A Comparative Study* (Baltimore, MD, 2012), pp. 71–4.
14 See Moisés Naím, *Illicit: How Smugglers, Traffickers and Copycats are Hijacking the Global Economy* (London, 2007), pp. 263–5.
15 See Neuwirth, *Stealth Nation*, pp. 20–22.

SIXTEEN: South by Southeast: Air Opium and the Arteries of Indochina

1 Antoine de Saint-Exupéry, *Airman's Odyssey: A Trilogy* (Orlando, FL, 1984), p. 29.
2 Khun Sa avoided the violent end of his contemporary in the demonology of the war on drugs, Pablo Escobar of Colombia. He lived out his days in some comfort in Rangoon until his death in 2007.
3 For more detail on the exploits of the pilots and backers of Air

Opium, see Alfred W. McCoy, *The Politics of Heroin: CIA Complicity in the Global Drugs Trade* (Chicago, IL, 2003), pp. 71–4.

4　Ibid., p. 299.

5　'Neutralist' in Laos at this time did not mean non-belligerent, simply openness to coalition.

6　The familial network model of the opium/heroin trade in Vietnam is perhaps comparable with the structure of a smuggler society in Buenos Aires during the seventeenth century (see Chapter Nine).

7　Ky continued to serve as vice president under Thieu, but remained a bitter rival.

8　Auguste Joseph Ricort, the name most associated with the Marseille French connection in Latin America had been one such collaborator. His heyday was between 1968 and 1973.

9　It was not all about transport aeroplanes. T-28 pilots had been known to fly opium around in their planes, and only ceased after an American intervention which secured the Lao air force a Dakota to do the job, thus freeing up the fighter-bomber squadrons to concentrate on the war.

10　So economically successful were these semi-private airlines and air transport companies that their substantial profits would enable not just a few 'black' operations but an entire culture of black ops that would eventually lead to the CIA-drug smuggler alliances around the Nicaraguan Contra counter-insurgency in Central America in the 1980s.

11　McCoy, *The Politics of Heroin*, p. 313.

12　Christopher Robbins, *Air America: The Explosive True Story of the CIA's Secret Airline* (London, 2012), pp. 241–2.

13　This was an offshoot of Continental Airlines, prepared to do much more than merely transport civilians.

14　It was an Air America helicopter that lifted embassy staff from a roof, depicted in that iconic photograph as Saigon fell in 1975, and they were doing the same thing in Phnom Penh.

SEVENTEEN: Cold War Contradictions: Flying into a Storm in Central America

1　In his book *El Narco* (London, 2012) the British journalist Ioan Grillo uses the term 'narco-insurgent' regarding the rise in the twenty-first century of warring, apparently anti-state cartels in northern Mexico. He labels Osiel Cárdenas, head of the Gulf Cartel, as the world's first narco-insurgent (p. 99). It is a symptom of what he sees as a shift from 'wars on drugs' to 'drug wars'; from fighting for profit through drug smuggling to smuggling to finance a fight.

2　Peter Dale Scott and Jonathan Marshall, *Cocaine Politics* (Berkeley, CA, 1998), pp. 82–3.

3　A cocaine coup is one in which the conspirators act, in part at least, to protect and enhance cocaine trafficking.

4 Drug czar José de Jesús Gutiérrez Rebollo was fired in 1997 and imprisoned for taking pay-offs; his successor Mariano Francisco Herran Salvatti (czar between 1997 and 2000) was charged on other corruption charges, but later exonerated after spending three years in prison; Noe Ramirez Mandujano (czar 2006–8) was accused of taking $450,000 of drug money, although he was also cleared later on.

5 Alfred W. McCoy, *The Politics of Heroin: CIA Complicity in the Global Drugs Trade* (Chicago, IL, 2003), p. 89.

6 Scott and Marshall, *Cocaine Politics*, p. 67.

7 Carlton was later a star witness in the trial of Manuel Noriega in 1991.

8 See Alexander Cockburn and Jeffrey St Clair, *Whiteout: The CIA, Drugs and the Press* (London, 1999), pp. 323–5.

9 A 'reliable source' makes this claim to Peter Dale Scott and Jonathan Marshall, as detailed in *Cocaine Politics*, pp. 100–101.

10 See Scott and Marshall, *Cocaine Politics*, p. 105.

11 Oliver North is alleged to have called this transhipment warehouse 'the supermarket'. See Cockburn and St Clair, *Whiteout*, p. 282.

12 See Scott and Marshall, *Cocaine Politics*, p. 119.

13 Ibid., pp. 16–17.

14 Rodríguez is alleged to have worn Guevara's wristwatch for years afterwards.

15 See Christopher Robbins, *Air America: The Explosive True Story of the CIA's Secret Airline* (London, 2012), pp. 332–3.

16 Ibid.

17 CIA operative Luis Posada Carriles arranged for safe houses for pilots involved in flying aid to the Contras. See Cockburn and St Clair, *Whiteout*, pp. 294–5.

18 'Ticket punching' was a policy with a long history, running back to legislation stemming from the 1947 National Security Act. Now, most pertinently, it meant that probable drug courier planes were not checked on arrival in Florida.

19 The 'humanitarian aid' programme was set up under the name Nicaraguan Humanitarian Assistance Organization (NHAO).

20 See Scott and Marshall, *Cocaine Politics*, pp. 10–12.

21 Ibid., pp. 16–17. It was Foley who recommended Vortex to the CIA as a candidate for aid.

22 The source here is Ramon Milian Rodríguez, accountant for the Medellín Cartel, speaking with journalists. See Cockburn and St Clair, *Whiteout*, pp. 308–9.

23 The erstwhile U.S. Ambassador to Colombia, Lewis Tambs, who we might recall coined the term 'narco-guerrilla', was later accused of assisting Oliver North and Secord after he moved to Costa Rica in 1985.

EIGHTEEN: Contraband of War: American Business and African Diamonds

1 Sir John Mandeville, *The Travels of Sir John Mandeville* (London, 1973), p. 39.
2 Peter Andreas, *Smuggler Nation* (New York, 2013), p. 59.
3 Ibid., p. 47.
4 Ibid., pp. 157–8.
5 See Ian Fleming, *The Diamond Smugglers* (New York, 1965), pp. 144–8.
6 Ibid., p. 154.
7 Ibid., pp. 42–8.
8 See Carolyn Nordstrom, *Global Outlaws* (Berkeley, CA, 2007), pp. 105–13.
9 The 2003 Kimberley Process that was supposed to have created transparency in the journey of diamonds between mine and consumer has arguably reduced the visibility of blood diamonds still further. Whereas in the past one might have been able to follow the entire journey of blood diamonds, now, once past the Kimberley procedure, there are no more checks. After mixing with legitimate diamonds they effectively become legit themselves.
10 Greg Campbell, *Blood Diamonds* (New York, 2012), pp. 40–42.
11 Ibid., pp. 64–9.
12 Moisés Naím, *Illicit: How Smugglers, Traffickers and Copycats are Hijacking the Global Economy* (London, 2007), p. 57.
13 In 2006 a consignment labelled with the mark of Kazakhstan, but possibly arranged by Victor Bout at the behest of the Eritreans, was detected arriving at Mogadishu airport. It might actually have originated in Libya or Yemen. The customer was the Islamic Courts Union (ICU – forerunner of al-Shabaab and Hizbul Islam, the fundamentalist armies of the region).
14 See for instance this theory put forward regarding piracy in Chapter 16, 'Toward Perpetual War', of Daniel Heller-Roazen's book *The Enemy of All: Piracy and the Law of Nations* (New York, 2009).

Postscript

1 Damien Cave, *International Herald Tribune*, 25 March 2011.
2 Nico Hines, *The Times*, 5 July 2010, p. 32, and Joel Taylor, *Metro* (London), 6 February 2011, p. 25.

SELECT BIBLIOGRAPHY

Abraham, Itty, and Willem van Schendel, eds, *Illicit Flows and Criminal Things: States, Borders, and the Other Side of Globalization* (Bloomington, IN, 2005)

Akinsha, Konstantin, and Grigorii Kozlov, *Stolen Treasure: The Hunt for the World's Lost Masterpieces* (London, 1995)

Alwi, Des, and Willard A. Hana, *Turbulent Times Past in Ternate and Tidore* (Banda Neira, 1990)

Andreas, Peter, *Smuggler Nation: How Illicit Trade Made America* (New York, 2013)

Andrews, Kenneth R., *The Spanish Caribbean: Trade and Plunder, 1530–1630* (New Haven, CT, 1978)

Atwood, Roger, *Stealing History: Tomb Raiders, Smugglers, and the Looting of the Ancient World* (New York, 2004)

Barrera Monroy, Eduardo, *Mestizaje, Comercio y Resistencia: La Guajira durante la Segunda mitad del Siglo VXIII* (Bogotá, 2000)

Bey, Hakim, *T.A.Z.: The Temporary Autonomous Zone, Ontological Anarchy, Poetic Terrorism* (New York, 2003)

Booth, Martin, *Opium: A History* (London, 1997)

Botting, Douglas, and Ian Sayer, *Nazi Gold: The Sensational Story of the World's Greatest Robbery – and the Greatest Criminal Cover-up* (Edinburgh, 1998)

Boxer, C. R., *The Portuguese Seaborne Empire, 1415–1825* (Manchester, 1991)

Braudel, Fernand, *The Mediterranean, and the Mediterranean World in the Age of Philip II* (London, 1992)

—, *The Perspective of the World: Civilization and Capitalism, 15th–18th century*, vol. III (London, 1984)

Calvino, Italo, *Invisible Cities* (London, 1997)

Campbell, Greg, *Blood Diamonds: Tracing the Deadly Path of the World's Most Precious Stones* (New York, 2012)

Çelikkol, Ayşe, *Romances of Free Trade: British Literature, Laissez-faire, and the Global Nineteenth Century* (Oxford, 2011)

Cervantes Angulo, José, *La noche de las luciérnagas* (Bogotá, 1980)
Clements, Jonathan, *Pirate King: Coxinga and the Fall of the Ming Dynasty* (Stroud, Gloucestershire, 2004)
Cockburn, Alexander, and Jeffrey St Clair, *Whiteout: The CIA, Drugs and the Press* (London, 1999)
Daly, Gavin, 'Napoleon and the City of Smugglers, 1810–1814', *Historical Journal*, L/2 (2007), pp. 333–52
Darnton, Robert, *The Forbidden Bestsellers* (London, 1996)
—, *The Kiss of Lamourette* (London, 1990)
—, *The Literary Underground of the Old Regime* (Cambridge, MA, 1982)
Davis, William C., *The Pirates Laffite: The Treacherous World of the Corsairs of the Gulf* (Orlando, FL, 2005)
Donkin, R. A., *Between East and West: The Moluccas and the Traffic in Spices up to the Arrival of Europeans* (Philadelphia, PA, 2003)
Edberg, Mark Cameron, *El Narcotraficante: Narcocorridos and the Construction of Cultural Persona on the U.S.–Mexican Border* (Austin, TX, 2004)
Escobar, Roberto, *Escobar: Drugs, Guns, Money, Power* (London, 2010)
Farooqui, Amar, *Smuggling as Subversion: Colonialism, Indian Merchants and the Politics of Opium* (New Delhi, 1998)
Farjeon, J. Jefferson, *The Compleat Smuggler* (London, 1938)
Fleming, Ian, *The Diamond Smugglers* (New York, 1965)
Forbes, Duncan, *Rimbaud in Ethiopia* (Hythe, Kent, 1979)
García Márquez, Gabriel, *The Story of a Shipwrecked Sailor*, trans. Richard Hogan (London, 1996)
Gilman, Nils, et al., eds, *Deviant Globalization: Black Market Economy in the 21st Century* (New York, 2011)
Gimlette, John, *At the Tomb of the Inflatable Pig: A Riotous Journey into the Heart of Paraguay* (London, 2003)
Gollner, Adam Leith, *The Fruit Hunters: A Story of Nature, Adventure, Commerce and Obsession* (New York, 2008)
Goñi, Uki, *The Real Odessa: How Perón Brought the Nazi War Criminals to Argentina* (London, 2002)
Grahn, Lance, *The Political Economy of Smuggling: Regional Informal Economies in Early Bourbon New Granada* (Oxford, 1997)
Greene, Graham, *Getting to Know the General* (London, 1999)
—, *The Captain and the Enemy* (London, 1999)
Grillo, Ioan, *El Narco: The Bloody Rise of Mexican Drug Cartels* (London, 2011)
Hanes, W. Travis, and Frank Sanello, *The Opium Wars: The Addiction of One Empire and the Corruption of Another* (London, 2002)
Harvey, Simon, 'Smuggling in Theories and Practices of Contemporary Visual Culture', PhD thesis, University of London, 2005
Hawthorne, Nathaniel, *The Scarlet Letter* [1850] (London, 1986)
Heller-Roazen, Daniel, *The Enemy of All: Piracy and the Law of Nations* (New York, 2009)

Hill, Ruth, *Hierarchy, Commerce and Fraud in Bourbon Spanish America* (Nashville, TN, 2005)

Hobsbawm, Eric, *Bandits* (London, 2000)

Jackson, Joe, *The Thief at the End of the World: Rubber, Empire and the Obsessions of Henry Wickham* (London, 2008)

Jobson de Andrade Arruda, José, 'Colonies as Mercantile Investments: The Luso-Brazilian Empire, 1500–1808', in *The Political Economy of Merchant Empires*, ed. James D. Tracy (Cambridge, 1991)

Karras, Alan L., *Smuggling: Contraband and Corruption in World History* (Lanham, MD, 2010)

Keay, John, *The Spice Route* (London, 2005)

Kelly, Robert J., Jess Maghan and Joseph D. Serio, *Illicit Trafficking: A Reference Handbook* (Santa Barbara, CA, 2005)

Lampedusa, Giuseppe Tomasi di, *The Leopard* (London, 2005)

Lane, Kris E., *Blood and Silver: A History of Piracy in the Caribbean and Central America* (Oxford, 1999)

Lang, James, *Conquest and Commerce: Spain and England in the Americas* (New York, 1975)

Langewiesche, William, *The Atomic Bazaar* (London, 2007)

Linaje, Veitia, *The Spanish Rule of Trade to the West Indies Containing an Account of the Casa de Contratacion, or India House* (New York, 1977)

Lovell, Julia, *The Opium War* (London, 2012)

Lumpe, Lora, ed., *Running Guns: The Black Market in Small Arms* (London, 2000)

Ly-Tio-Fane, Madeleine, *Mauritius and the Spice Trade: The Odyssey of Pierre Poivre* (Port Louis, 1958)

McCoy, Alfred W., *The Politics of Heroin: CIA Complicity in the Global Drug Trade* (Chicago, IL, 2003)

Madsen, Axel, *Silk Roads: The Asian Adventures of Clara and André Malraux* (New York, 1989)

Mandeville, Sir John, *The Travels of Sir John Mandeville*, commentary by Norman Denny and Josephine Filmer-Sankey (London, 1973)

Milton, Giles, *Nathaniel's Nutmeg: How One Man's Courage Changed the Course of History* (London, 1999)

Monfreid, Henry de, *Hashish: A Smuggler's Tale* (London, 1994)

—, *Le Radeau de la Méduse* (Paris, 1958)

—, *Pearls, Arms and Hashish: Pages from the Life of a Red Sea Smuggler* (London, 1930)

Morley, Geoffrey, *The Smuggling War: The Government's Fight against Smuggling in the 18th and 19th Centuries* (Stroud, Gloucestershire, 1994)

Moxham, Roy, *The Great Hedge of India* (London, 2001)

—, *Tea: The Extraordinary Story of the World's Favourite Drink* (London, 2009)

Naím, Moisés, *Illicit: How Smugglers, Traffickers and Copycats are Hijacking the Global Economy* (London, 2007)

Neuwirth, Robert, *Stealth of Nations: The Global Rise of the Informal Economy* (New York, 2011)

Nicholl, Charles, *Somebody Else: Arthur Rimbaud in Africa, 1880–91* (London, 1998)

Nordstrom, Carolyn, *Global Outlaws: Crime, Money and Power in the Contemporary World* (Berkeley, CA, 2007)

O'Flynn, Dennis, 'Comparing the Tokagawa Shogunate with Hapsburg Spain: Two Silver-based Empires in a Global Setting', in *The Political Economy of Merchant Empires*, ed. James D. Tracy (Cambridge, 1991)

Observatoire Géopolitique des Drogues, *The Geopolitics of Drugs* (Boston, 1996)

Pérotin-Dumon, Anne, 'The Pirate and the Emperor: Power and the Law on the Seas, 1450-1850', in *The Political Economy of Merchant Empires*, ed. James D. Tracy (Cambridge, 1991)

Perusset, Macarena, *Contrabando y Sociedad en el Río de la Plata Colonial* (Buenos Aires, 2006)

Plant, Sadie, *Writing on Drugs* (London, 1999)

Platt, Richard, *Smuggling in the British Isles: A History* (Stroud, Gloucestershire, 2007)

Prakash, Om, *The Dutch East India Company and the Economy of Bengal, 1630–1720* (Princeton, NJ, 1985)

Preston, Diana and Michael Preston, *A Pirate of Exquisite Mind: The Life of William Dampier, Explorer, Naturalist and Buccaneer* (London, 2005)

Quinn, Tom, *Smugglers' Tales* (Newton Abbot, 1999)

Rensselaer, W. Lee III, *Smuggling Armageddon: The Nuclear Black Market in the Former Soviet Union and Europe* (London, 1998)

Robbins, Christopher, *Air America: The Explosive True Story of the CIA's Secret Airline* (London, 2012)

Roitman, Janet, 'Productivity in the Margins: The Reconstitution of State Power in the Chad Basin', in *Anthropology in the Margins of the State*, ed. Veena Das and Deborah Poole (Santa Fe, NM, 2004)

Roldán Vera, Eugenia, *The British Book Trade and Spanish American Independence: Education and Knowledge Transmission in Transcontinental Perspective* (London, 2003)

Ronell, Avital, *Crack Wars: Literature, Addiction, Mania* (Lincoln, NE, 1992)

Rose, Sarah, *For All the Tea in China* (London, 2009)

Sabbag, Robert, *Smokescreen: A True Adventure* (Edinburgh, 2002)

Sainte-Exupéry, Antoine de, *Airman's Odyssey: A Trilogy* (Orlando, FL, 1984)

Scott, Peter Dale, and Jonathan Marshall, *Cocaine Politics: Drugs, Armies, and the CIA in Central America* (Berkeley, CA, 1998)

Sloterdijk, Peter, 'Theory of the Pirate: The White Terror', in Peter Sloterdijk, *In the World Interior of Capital: Towards a Philosophical Thoery of Globalization* (Cambridge, 2013)

Smith, Adam, *Wealth of Nations* [1776] (Ware, 2012)
Streatfield, Dominic, *Cocaine* (London, 2001)
Strong, Simon, *Whitewash: Pablo Escobar and the Cocaine Wars* (London, 1996)
Thachuk, Kimberley L., *Transnational Threats: Smuggling and Trafficking in Arms, Drugs, and Human Life* (Westport, CT, 2007)
Thompson, Hunter S., 'A Footloose American in a Smugglers' Den', in Hunter S. Thompson, *The Great Shark Hunt: Strange Tales from a Strange Time* (London, 1980)
—, *The Proud Highway: The Fear and Loathing Letters*, vol. I: *1955–67* (London, 1997)
Tracy, James D., ed., *The Political Economy of Merchant Empires: State Power and World Trade 1350–1750* (Cambridge, 1991)
—, *The Rise of Merchant Empires: Long Distance Trade in the Early Modern World 1350–1750* (Cambridge, 1990)
Virilio, Paul, *Speed and Politics: An Essay on Dromology* (New York, 1986)
Wald, Elijah, *Narcocorrido: A Journey into the Music of Drugs, Guns and Guerrillas* (New York, 2002)
Walters, Guy, *Hunting Evil* (London, 2010)
Waugh, Mary, *Smuggling in Devon and Cornwall, 1700–1850* (Newbury, 1999)
Williams, Neville, *Contraband Cargoes: Seven Centuries of Smuggling* (London, 1959)

Smuggling Fiction

Alcott, Louisa May, 'My Contraband', in *Louisa May Alcott: Short Stories* (New York, 1996)
Baricco, Alessandro, *Silk* (London, 1998)
Binebine, Mahi, *Welcome to Paradise* (London, 2004)
Du Maurier, Daphne, *Jamaica Inn* [1936] (London, 2003)
Foy, George, *Contraband* (London, 1998)
García Márquez, Gabriel, 'Blacamán the Good, Vendor of Miracles', in *Collected Stories*, trans. Gregory Rabassa and J. S. Bernstein (London, 1996)
—, 'Death Constant Beyond Love', in *Collected Stories* (1996)
—, 'The Incredible and Sad Tale of Innocent Eréndira and her Heartless Grandmother', in *Collected Stories* (1996)
Ghosh, Amitav, *River of Smoke* (London, 2012)
Greene, Graham, *Travels with my Aunt*, in *Author's Choice: Four Novels by Graham Greene* (London, 1985)
Kipling, Rudyard, 'A Smuggler's Song', in *Rudyard Kipling: Selected Poems*, ed. Peter Keating (London, 1993)
Klíma, Ivan, 'The Smuggler's Story', in Ivan Klíma, *My Golden Trades* (London, 1992)
Pinnock, Winsome, *Mules* (London, 1996)

Rohmer, Sax, *Dope* (London, 2007)
Serpa, Enrique, *Contrabando* (Havana, 1975)

ACKNOWLEDGEMENTS

There are a number of people towards whom I would like to extend specific thanks for hearing me out, or, just as likely, drawing ideas out of me over the years of working on this book. The idea for the project came out of a trip around the Guajira Peninsula in Colombia with my friend Mark Duffy, a great travelling companion. It became an academic research project, and along that path I owe immense gratitude to Irit Rogoff at Goldsmiths, University of London. There I also met Peter Mörtenböck, whose work on informal markets coincided with some of my experiences, and has greatly enriched my knowledge of them. Ergin Çavusoglu, whose work as an artist has touched on aspects of smuggling, has and continues to be a generous respondent to my labours. Recently I have also drawn on the sound advice of historian Katharina Rowold. At Reaktion Books I would like to thank Michael Leaman, Martha Jay, David Rose and Harry Gilonis. Finally, I owe utmost thanks to my father, Maurice Harvey, a former pilot and military historian, not only for teaching me the difference between a plane and an aeroplane, but for reading through and shaping this book in its latter stages.

PHOTO ACKNOWLEDGEMENTS

The author and publishers wish to express their thanks to the below sources of illustrative material and/or permission to reproduce it. (Some locations of artworks are also given below.)

Maps drawn by the author: pp. 28, 46, 59, 71, 157, 167, 243, 291; photos author: pp. 79, 232, 234; from the author's film *Contraband Desert* (2005), reproduced by kind permission: pp. 74, 75; British Museum, London: p. 156; photos © The Trustees of the British Museum: pp. 33, 156; photo Thierry Caro: p. 93 – this file is licensed under the Creative Commons Attribution-Share Alike 4.0 International, 3.0 Unported, 2.5 Generic, 2.0 Generic and 1.0 Generic license – readers are free to share (to copy, distribute and transmit the work) or to remix (to adapt the work) under the following conditions – you must attribute the work in the manner specified by the author or licensor (but not in any way that suggests that they endorse you or your use of the work); photo Gallica/Bibliothèque Nationale de France: p. 108; photos Library of Congress Prints and Photographs Division, Washington, DC: pp. 36, 185; photos Peter Mörtenböck and Helge Mooshammer: pp. 236, 237; photo Rijksmuseum Amsterdam: p. 44; Tate, London: p. 131; photo USAF/National Museum of the U.S. Air Force, Ohio: p. 254; photos Fabian von Poser/imageBROKER/Rex Features: pp. 292, 293; from Wellcome Images (a website operated by Wellcome Trust, a global charitable foundation based in the United Kingdom): p. 154 – this file is licensed under the Creative Commons Attribution 4.0 International license – readers are free to share (to copy, distribute and transmit the work) or to remix (to adapt the work) under the following conditions – you must attribute the work in the manner specified by the author or licensor (but not in any way that suggests that they endorse you or your use of the work).

INDEX